The Great Masters
of European Art

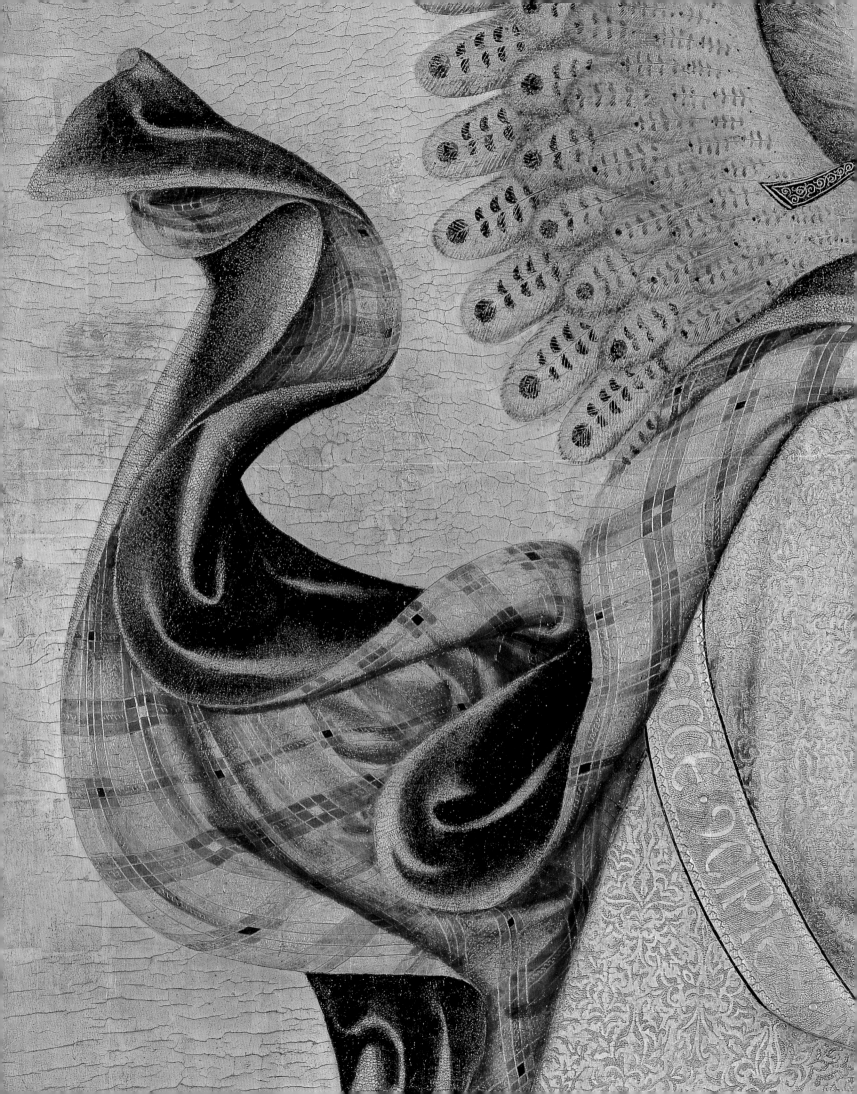

The Great Masters of European Art

Introduction by *Giorgio Bonsanti*

Texts by
Stefano G. Casu, Elena Franchi and Andrea Franci

BARNES & NOBLE

NEW YORK

Graphic design: Matilde Contri
Translation: Huw Evans

Photographs: Archivio Fotografico SCALA Group
except pp. 58, 59, 74, 75, 82, 83, 117b, 118-19, 139, 153, 164-5, 166, 167, 266-7, 268a, 276-7,
278-9, 306-7, 308 (National Gallery, London); pp. 90-1 (Royal Collection of Her Majesty Queen
Elizabeth II); pp. 96, 97 (Curia Patriarcale di Venezia; permission for reproduction granted by
the Ufficio Beni Culturali del Patriarcato di Venezia, Venice); pp. 133, 140, 141, 150b, 151
(Bayerische Staatsgemäldesammlungen, Alte Pinakothek, Munich); p. 138 (Stiftsbibliothek
St. Florian); pp. 154-5, 156-7 (Archivio Fotografico dei Musei Vaticani, Vatican); pp. 170-1,
173b, 174-5 (Kunsthistorisches Museum, Vienna); p. 212 (Cleveland Museum of Art, Gift of the
Hanna Fund, 1951.454); p. 241 (by kind permission of the Trustees of the Wallace Collection,
London); pp. 247c, 248-9, 251 (Rijksmuseum, Amsterdam); pp. 252-3, 254 (Royal Cabinet of
Paintings, Mauritshuis, The Hague); pp. 264-5, 268b (by kind permission of the Marquess of
Tavistock and the Trustees of the Bedford Estates); p. 301 (Staatliche Kunstsammlungen,
Dresden); pp. 302-3 (Bildarchiv Preussischer Kulturbesitz, Berlin/Hamburger Kunsthalle);
pp. 304-5 (Tate Gallery, London); pp. 340-1 (Courtauld Institute Gallery, Somerset House,
London); pp. 384-5 (Digital image © 2003 The Museum of Modern Art, New York / SCALA,
Florence); pp. 388, 389, 390-1 (Art Institute of Chicago, Chicago)

The images in the SCALA ARCHIVES that reproduce cultural assets owned by the Italian State are
published by kind permission of the Ministry for the Cultural Heritage and Activities

ISBN-13: 978-0-7607-8069-5
ISBN-10: 0-7607-8069-2

Printed and bound in China
3 5 7 9 10 8 6 4 2

Introduction

A work of art contains a whole range of meanings. Looking at it, we can focus on the subject represented, or on the historical conditions that led to its creation. These in turn comprise the circumstances of its commission and realization, and the kind of public for which it was intended. And then, of course, there are its specifically artistic values: the quality of the conception or the formulation (whether, that is, the work of art repeats already familiar iconographies without much variation, or takes a much more innovative approach), the refinement and perfection of the execution. In addition, great works of art have yet another value: that of recognizably and effectively documenting the society in which they were created, or the historical context that they set out to represent in a more or less explicit manner. They do so in a different way from a work of history, but one that is at least as revealing, and often much more so. Let us assume, for example, that I intend to pay a visit to Lübeck. I can prepare for my visit by studying a guidebook to the city, just as I can read a history of the events in its past, or a work of sociology or economics that tells me about it from these points of view. But I can also prepare myself by reading Thomas Mann's novel *Buddenbrooks*, and will probably gain a better and deeper understanding of the city in its essence than through any of the other means I have referred to.

In the same way, a great painting, one of those that we very often already see as part of our own, individual culture, can assume the value of an emblem of its time. Even if my understanding of the artist is not particularly deep, careful observation of his or her work can tell me a great deal. The greatest artists, the ones we regard as having made a fundamental contribution to the history of art and to that of civilization in general, are able to fully convey the sense of their experience, their understanding of the society and the historical circumstances in which they live, in a single work. Naturally, my appreciation of their creations will be more complete and satisfying if I am able to place them in context: if I can compare them with paintings by the same artist or by other artists of the day, and if I have some knowledge of the art that preceded him, i.e. that he was exposed to at the moment of embarking on his career, and of what came afterward, on which he may have left his own mark.

So it is that a book like the one you are holding functions not only as an aid to aesthetic appreciation, but also as a distillation of a certain period or a certain situation in the history of civilization. Turning these pages and looking at the reproductions of the paintings, and reading the information provided on the lives of the artists and the individual pictures, also means gaining an insight into the great periods in Western culture, from the close of the Middle Ages to the beginning of the contemporary era. The painting of the fourteenth century commenced with the last great exponent of the Byzantine tradition, the Sienese Duccio di Buoninsegna; after him this tradition died out in the West, while it has survived down to the present day in the Slavic countries. In parallel, the Florentine artist Giotto launched the revolution that discovered, through a new relationship with reality and a revival of classical antiquity, the possibility of representing an outside world that was not symbolic but credible and tangible, and of illustrating the actions of human beings as recognizable examples of conduct.

Giotto's new style of painting was to spread throughout Europe. Through journeys made by artists, far more frequent and significant than we tend to imagine today, the new figurative currents were exported to other countries, giving rise in turn to local schools. Thus the work of the Sienese Simone Martini, active in the last years of his life at Avignon in the South of France, where the papal court had gone into exile, provided the inspiration for the great Gothic art of the Northern European courts, whose manifestations in the late fourteenth-century and first half of the fifteenth we call International Gothic or Late Gothic. A century after Giotto's, a new revolution of realism took place, different in its characteristics but almost simultaneous in time, in Florence and the Low Countries. Masaccio on the one hand and Jan van Eyck on the other were responsible for a profound reappraisal of the functions and means of pictorial art. The changes they introduced allowed it to interpret the new society of the mercantile cities, which experienced extraordinary growth from the beginning of the fifteenth century onward. The great painters of the generations that followed immediately afterward, such as Fra Angelico, Piero della Francesca, Botticelli, Andrea Mantegna and Giovanni Bellini in Italy, and Roger van der Weyden and Hans Memling (German by birth) in the Low Countries, took the premises of the painting of Masaccio and van Eyck and developed them into great and complex systems of art, consistent with the political forms of the European courts of the time as they were described by contemporary historians like Nicolò Machiavelli and Francesco Guicciardini, and centuries afterward by Jacob Burckhardt. In Italy, at the end of the fifteenth century and the beginning of the sixteenth, Leonardo da Vinci, the young Raphael, Giorgione and Titian went beyond the spatial conception of the early Renaissance, founded on exact perspective derived from geometrical rules, and explored the optical possibilities offered by the changes in tone and color produced by the atmosphere. In Germany the extraordinary phenomenon of Albrecht Dürer emerged, overcoming a cultural lag of many decades at a bound and bringing the region into line with other more artistically developed areas. And it must also be borne in mind that even in a historical reconstruction which examines artistic phenomena in terms of networks of relationships and connections that reflect mutual influences, there will always be room for anomalous and essentially isolated figures like Hieronymus Bosch or, later on, the brilliant but little known Mathias Grünewald.

Even an artist like Michelangelo, who liked to describe himself primarily as a sculptor but was, as we all know, a very great painter and architect as well, can in a certain sense also be defined as an outsider. This may seem a strange claim to make about an artist who has been venerated and copied like few others. But in reality his art was so personal in character that we can say he had endless imitators, but no true follower. However, the Italian painting of the sixteenth century had a powerful influence on El Greco, born on the island of Crete but trained in Venice, and Pieter Bruegel, who undoubtedly made a journey to Italy, documented by his paintings even if we have no historical evidence for it in the written records. At the end of the sixteenth century, the Bolognese Annibale Carracci looked back to the great history painting of Raphael. The Lombard artist Caravaggio, who moved to Rome early in his career, drew on the reality of daily life with a despairing force that had never been seen before. And very soon the Fleming Rubens derived from his youthful visit to Italy the inspiration for the magnificent baroque painting that made him the most popular artist in Europe. The French painters Poussin and Lorrain, both active in Rome, came under the spell of Carracci's classicism. Caravaggio's realism, which immediately became a Europe-wide phenomenon, provided the more or less direct inspiration for the art of painters like Frans Hals and Georges de La Tour. And there can be no doubt that without some knowledge of Caravaggism, though it is hard to pin down the exact channel, we would not have had the art of two of the greatest painters of all time, the Dutchmen Rembrandt and Jan Vermeer. Although very different in character, each has left an extraordinarily fascinating body of work. Another country was home to a magnificent school of painting in the seventeenth century: Spain, with the religious art of Zurbarán (more mystical in its spirit) and of Murillo (more approachable and down to earth), and with the more complex phenomenon, as it comprised both these elements, of Velázquez. The richness of motifs in the eighteenth century, the age of the Enlightenment but also of the French Revolution, is reflected in different ways in the rational painting of Canaletto and the scenographic work of Tiepolo (two Venetians who worked extensively abroad, from England to Germany and Spain). The great English school of realism, alternating between criticism of the society of the day and accommodation to it, is represented by Hogarth and Gainsborough. In France, the rococo found expression in the pictures of Watteau and the depiction of daily life in those of Chardin. Spain saw the emergence of a particularly complex figure in Francisco de Goya, who had started out as a rococo painter influenced by the work that Tiepolo created during his stay in Madrid, only to end his days, well into the nineteenth century, producing pictures of tragic realism. The painting of transition between the eighteenth and nineteenth century, in its variants of Romanticism and Classicism, is represented by Caspar David Friedrich and Jacques-Louis David. French purism is epitomized by Ingres, while the very different approaches of the French and English schools of landscape painting are exemplified by Corot and Turner: where the former was fond of gentle and tranquil atmospheres, the latter invented a style in which the forms dissolved into the color. French Romanticism found its fullest expression in the painting of Delacroix and Géricault. The great Gustave Courbet built on their work, soon creating an intensely realistic style, perfectly in keeping with the nineteenth-century French novel and embodying in exemplary fashion the new role of the artist as an interpreter of social realities. And immediately afterward, the early work of Manet and Monet was to spark a revolution that led progressively to the definitive supersession of the traditional forms that had characterized painting up until that time. They introduced a new concept of art, seen not as representation of reality but as an expression of thoughts, ideas and moods. The French painters of the second half of the nineteenth century and the early part of the twentieth century, whether their work was characterized by a more constructive sense of form, like Cézanne and Degas, or chose to focus on visual impressions, like Toulouse-Lautrec, Gauguin and Renoir, along with the Dutch painter van Gogh, are extremely popular today, as the public recognizes in them an art that is capable of translating emotions into a visual form. Cézanne on the one hand, with his discovery of the geometric laws inherent in things, and Seurat on the other, with his breakdown of form into points, recalling the theories about the atom as the smallest possible subdivision of matter, paved the way for the art of the twentieth century: the century that has just come to an end, with its breakneck pace of scientific discovery and social change. Its cataclysms, its extremes of wealth and poverty, have embraced the whole world, demonstrating that, by now, whatever happens, wherever it happens, affects one and all.

So this is the profile that we are presenting in this book. It's aim is to stir readers' admiration, to make them dream and, at the same time, think. It will present some of the highest peaks of achievement in the painting of the European tradition from the end of the thirteenth century to the beginning of the twentieth century, while pointing out that they rise out of an extremely complex landscape. This book (to return to an aspect mentioned at the beginning) also sets out to show that between the great artists, even if they never met or came into direct contact, there has always been an open dialogue. Certainly, looking back from today's vantage point, a number of episodes over the course of these centuries appear particularly significant. Such as the time when Dürer, as he relates in moving fashion in his letters, met the aging patriarch Giovanni Bellini in Venice and was received with open arms. He also tells, in the *Sketchbook of the Journey to the Netherlands*, of having seen Michelangelo's marble statue of the Madonna in a church in Bruges where it can still be found today. And he wrote in his own hand, on a drawing by Raphael now in the Louvre, that he had received it as a gift from the great Italian painter, in exchange for some engravings. A few historical circumstances, with hindsight, are revealed to be particularly stimulating: in the nineteenth century there were years in which someone walking around Paris could have met several of the great painters we have mentioned on the same day; just as in Florence, in the early years of the sixteenth century, it would have been possible to run into Leonardo, Michelangelo and Raphael in the same street. I don't know if situations of this kind are conceivable today; to tell the truth, I believe not. Art has taken other roads, and today signifies something very different from what it has been for centuries and centuries. But the works of the great masters of the past remain to speak to our minds, to our senses and, let us admit it, to our hearts.

Giorgio Bonsanti

Contents

14TH CENTURY

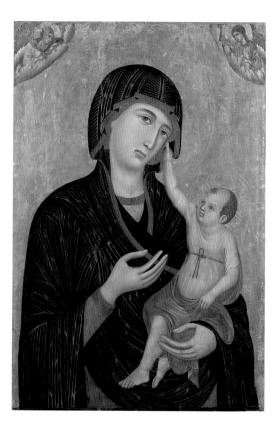

Duccio di Buoninsegna

We have very little information on the life of the Sienese painter Duccio di Buoninsegna, and it tells us nothing about the years of his training. Some scholars even maintain that he was a pupil of Cimabue, and that between the end of the eighth and the beginning of the ninth decade of the 13th century he accompanied the Florentine artist to Assisi. Giotto too may have had an influence on the development of Duccio's painting, but in any case he expressed himself with an original style that made him the founder of the Sienese school.

The earliest reference to him in the archives is a payment made by the Commune of Siena in 1278 for the painting of twelve cases for documents. This was followed the next year by a request for the "painting of books" from the same municipal authorities, which should probably be understood as the decoration of wooden covers for the registers of the Biccherna, the city's tax office. Shortly afterward, in 1280, a fine was levied on the painter. It would not be the only one that the Commune would impose on him, for a variety of offenses: one of the most grave was his refusal to take part in the War of Maremma in 1302. In the absence of documents relating to the date of his birth, these records indicate that Duccio had already completed his apprenticeship as a painter and reached the age of majority in 1278, and provide interesting clues about his personality.

One of the oldest works to have come down to us is the *Crevole Madonna*, datable to around 1280. The earliest document concerning a work still in existence, however, is the commission, in 1285, for the Madonna painted for the confraternity of the Holy Virgin Mary, or Compagnia dei Laudesi, at the Florentine church of Santa Maria Novella, now known as the *Madonna Rucellai* and in the Uffizi. It is a highly interesting document that illustrates the relations between artists and clients at the time, showing for example how the extensive use of gold was not an autonomous choice on the part of the painter but the response to a precise request by the client. Several characteristics of the work, such as the rippling of the golden border of the Virgin's mantle, which unfolds in graceful curves, demonstrate that Duccio's art was still torn between the Byzantine heritage, which led him to emphasize the gleaming colors in the Oriental manner, and the influences of Gothic art, discernible in the taste for elegance that was to become a constant of Sienese art over the following decades.

Between 1287 and 1288 the artist worked on the great stained-glass window dedicated to the Virgin for Siena Cathedral, which has recently been restored, and toward the end of the century painted the *Madonna of the Franciscans* (Pinacoteca Nazionale, Siena). The small panel displays an already mature style, and depicts the Virgin sheltering the faithful kneeling at her side with her cloak. This iconography, today known as the "Madonna of Mercy," was new to Italian painting, and would find its most celebrated expression in the picture by Piero della Francesca now in the Pinacoteca of Sansepolcro. In 1302 Duccio painted one of his most important works, unfortunately lost, a panel representing the *Maestà* for the chapel of the Nove in the Palazzo Pubblico of Siena. What has survived is the splendid *Maestà* for the cathedral, executed between 1308 and 1311. The last mention of the painter in the documents dates from 1318, and this suggests that he had died by 1319.

Madonna and Child with Two Angels (Crevole Madonna)
tempera and gold on panel, 89x60 cm
Museo dell'Opera del Duomo, Siena

The *Crevole Madonna*, together with the similar panel in Buonconvento Museum, is considered to be a work from the beginning of the painter's career, dating from around 1280. It takes its name from the church of Santa Cecilia a Crevole in the environs of Siena, where it was located for a period, but its small size and the intimate character of the composition suggest that it was originally painted for private use.

In it we find a wonderful blend of elements of Byzantine derivation, reminders of Cimabue and innovations that can be ascribed to Duccio himself. From the Byzantine tradition of painting come the stylized form of the hands and nose and the gilded lines in the Virgin's cloak, a method known as damascening and also used by Cimabue. The latter, on the other hand, was responsible for the innovation of the Child's transparent clothing, taken up by Duccio with a more modern technique to produce results of great refinement. Another element of Byzantine origin is the pose of the Child, delicately lifting his hand to caress his Mother's face: this is the type of Madonna known as *eleousa* or *glykophilousa*, a model of composition that was to become a typical feature of Sienese painting – perhaps as consequence of the spread of Franciscan piety – and find its most sensitive interpreters in Duccio and then

the Lorenzetti brothers. It was in Siena, just a few years earlier (1266-68), that Nicola Pisano had carved an *Adoration of the Magi* in bas-relief on the cathedral pulpit in which the oldest of the kings not only kneels but kisses the foot of the Infant Jesus, thereby eliminating the physical distance from the son of God that had always been maintained hitherto.

Note the presence of the angels in the upper corners of the panel, curiously set inside portions of a circular nimbus, something that belongs to neither the Florentine nor the Byzantine tradition of painting, but to that of the French miniature.

Maestà

tempera and gold on panel,
370x450 cm (front), 211x426 cm (back)
Museo dell'Opera del Duomo, Siena

The *Maestà*, painted for the high altar of Siena Cathedral, is the only work of Duccio's to bear his signature, and we have documentary evidence that it was executed between 1308 and 1311. Painted on both sides, the work originally had a complex structure, which included a predella with figured compartments, a crowning section with cusps and pinnacles and a lavish frame in the Gothic style. The front depicted a complex Marian theme, dominated at the center by the *Madonna and Child Enthroned with Angels and Saints* (including the four patron saints of Siena, Ansanus, Sabinus, Crescentius and Victor, kneeling in the foreground) and ten Apostles set inside small arches. The predella depicted *Scenes from the Life of the Virgin* and *Scenes from the Childhood of Christ*, alternating with figures of Prophets. On the cusps were scenes representing the *Last Days of Mary's Life*. The upper part has not survived, but may have been painted with the *Assumption* and the *Coronation of Mary*.

The back presented an equally complex Christological cycle, with a sequence of fourteen panels depicting twenty-six *Scenes from the Passion of Christ* at the center, arranged in two rows. The compartments of the predella were

devoted to *Miracles and Episodes from the Public Life of Christ*, while the six cusps on top represented *Scenes of Christ's Last Days on Earth*. The majority of the elements that made it up are now in the Museo dell'Opera del Duomo di Siena, while others are scattered amongst museums in Europe and America, and a few have been lost.

The terms of the contract drawn up in 1308 throw light on the execution of the commission. It contains precise clauses imposing restrictions on Duccio: he was to devote himself full time to the panel, without taking on other commissions until it was completed, and do the painting himself. The document assumes a tone that suggests a lack of faith in the painter's reliability: he was asked, "for greater prudence," to place his hands on the Gospel and swear to complete the work without deception.

The panel was finished in 1311 and then carried from the painter's workshop to the cathedral in a solemn, religious and civil ceremony. Churchmen and representatives of the city's government took part in the procession, which was held on June 9, 1311. The people invoked the Virgin Mary, to whom the cathedral was consecrated, asking her to defend the city against misfortunes, its known enemies and traitors. The atmosphere is still conjured up today by the inscription on the dais of the throne, which encapsulates the painting's civil and religious importance and Duccio's awareness that he had created a genuine masterpiece: "MATER S(AN)C(T)A DEI – SIS CAUSA SENIS REQUIEI – SIS DUCIO LIFE – TE QUIA PINXIT ITA ("O Holy Mother of God – be a cause of peace for Siena – be life for Duccio – who has

painted you thus"). The significance of such a work for the city is underlined by the fact that in 1302 Duccio had already painted a *Maestà* for the lay setting of the chapel of the Nove in the Palazzo Pubblico of Siena, and that a few years later Simone Martini was to depict the subject again in a large fresco in the same building.
The painting also illustrates the range of artistic models on which Duccio drew. Among other things, it has been pointed out that some figures reflect the style of the statues carved by Giovanni Pisano for

the facade of Siena Cathedral, works whose exceptional attitudes and expressions reveal the psychology of the personages represented.

Scenes from the Passion:
The Marys at the Tomb
tempera and gold on panel,
c. 51x53.5 cm
Museo dell'Opera del Duomo, Siena

The rear part of the *Maestà* houses an
extensive cycle of *Scenes from the
Passion*, the first of its kind. We cannot
be certain exactly how Duccio had
arranged the scenes, and, consequently, in
what order the episodes should be read.
Obviously the scene of the *Crucifixion*
was placed at the center; it is presumed
that the panel with the *Marys at the Tomb*

preceded the *Descent into Limbo*.
According to Ludovico Zorzi, the
iconography is based not on the
customary text of the Gospels, but on
writings connected with the miracle plays
that were extremely popular in Italy at the
end of the 14th century. In particular, he
claims that the representation is the
pictorial transposition of the climax of a
scene turning on the question that the
angel put to the women on their way to
Christ's tomb: *Quem quaeritis*? (Luke 24:
5-6) and the dialogue that follows, which
differs from the text of the Gospels.
"*Quem quaeritis in sepulchro, o*

Christicolae [Whom are you seeking in
the sepulcher...]," was the angel's
question. "*Iesum Nazarenum
crocifixum, o coelicolae* [Jesus of
Nazareth crucified, o heavenly being],"
responded the mourning women. "*Non
est hic, surrexit sicut praedixerat. Ite,
nuntiate quia surrexit de sepulchro* [He
is not here, but risen as he had predicted.
Go and tell that he is risen from the
sepulcher]." – "*Alleluja*" – was the reply
of the messenger from heaven. (A.F.)

Giotto

"Cimabue thought to hold the field in painting, and now Giotto hath the cry, so that the other's fame is growing dim." The lines from Dante's *Divine Comedy* (Purgatory, canto XI, 94-6) make the fame the painter had already attained in his lifetime clearer than any other document, and have turned him into a symbol of the celebrated figure able to surpass the person who excelled before him. Dante believed that Giotto would shortly suffer the same fate as Cimabue, and wrote two triplets later (100-2): "Worldly renown is naught but a breath of wind, which now comes hence and now comes thence, and changes name because it changes quarter." Yet Giotto's fame has persisted to this day, giving the lie to Dante's prediction.

According to the most recent studies, he was probably born in Florence in 1267, whereas his birthplace had previously been thought to be Vicchio in the Mugello region, and nowadays most scholars believe he received his training from Cimabue himself. The works with which the young painter established his reputation, dating from between the end of the ninth and the beginning of the last decade of the 13th century, are the *Crucifix* in the Florentine church of Santa Maria Novella, the *Madonna of San Giorgio alla Costa* (Museo Diocesano di Santo Stefano, Florence), the *Madonna of Borgo San Lorenzo* (in the parish church of San Lorenzo) and the frescoes with *Scenes from the Story of Isaac* in the Upper Church of Assisi. These last are highly controversial and even ascribed by some to Arnolfo di Cambio, but already capable of offering a representation of the human figure solidly located in space. Hence they mark a fundamental shift in the history of Italian art.

The frescoes with *Scenes from the Legend of Francis* in the Upper Church of Assisi were painted over the course of the nineties. These too are of much debated attribution, assigned for the most part to painters of the Roman school, although the question is rendered more complicated by the likelihood of Giotto's presence in Rome in those years.

In any case the cycle constitutes a watershed in the history of Italian art owing to its revolutionary innovations in the three-dimensional representation of space and naturalistic rendering of the figures and settings. A number of scenes are celebrated, such as the one depicting Francis renouncing his worldly goods, in which the saint's breast is painted with a naturalism reminiscent of the sculptures of the Greco-Roman tradition.

After the *Scenes from the Legend of Francis* Giotto painted the frescoes in the Arena Chapel at Padua for Enrico Scrovegni, between 1303 and 1305. Here the seal is set on the figurative renewal commenced at Assisi, in images that display an even more marked naturalism and present an increasingly realistic narration. Later, between 1307 and 1308, Giotto returned to Assisi, where he decorated the chapel of the Magdalen in the Lower Church with the help of assistants. Subsequently (second and third decade of the century), he painted the chapels of the Bardi and Peruzzi families, among the most important bankers in Europe, in the Florentine church of Santa Croce. He also worked for Pope Boniface VIII and for the Angevins in Naples, although only a few fragments have survived, as well as the Visconti in Milan, but nothing remains of what he realized for them. Giotto died in Florence in 1337.

Crucifix
tempera on panel, 578x406 cm
Santa Maria Novella, Florence

The painting, along with other works like the *Madonna* from the church of San Giorgio alla Costa and the frescoes in the Upper Church of Assisi, constitutes one of the most important testimonies to the painter's early activity and is believed to have been executed around 1290. Although in some parts, such as the transparent cloth that covers Christ, it is possible to recognize the legacy of Cimabue, the work constitutes a fundamental step in the move away from the Byzantine tradition and toward a greater naturalism. The art historian Giovanni Previtali, who has made a thorough comparison between this painting and the *Crucifix* by Cimabue in the Museo di Santa Croce in Florence (see picture below), has pointed out how the changes made by Giotto are the sign of a different way of looking at Christ, who is represented as a real man on the cross and not a symbol of the Passion. While the right hip of Cimabue's Christ is shifted to the right with a forced movement that suggests the idea of contortion, Giotto's Savior has a much firmer and more natural posture. The thorax of Giotto's Christ is given a solid appearance by means of chiaroscuro, the light on the breast contrasting sharply with the shade

GIOTTO

on the flanks and creating an impression of volume, whereas the contrast of light in Cimabue's Christ picks out the ribs and other parts of the body but does not help to construct a realistic physical structure. The trend toward naturalism is also revealed by the details: while in Cimabue's figure the palm of the hand, although nailed to the cross, is completely relaxed and the thumb turned upward, in Giotto's the thumb and the tips of the fingers are, more realistically, bent downward. It is also interesting to note how the cross is set on a natural mountain, Golgotha, at whose base is placed the skull of Adam. This was an innovation in painting but had already appeared in sculpture, as the wooden statue carved by Giovanni Pisano for Siena Cathedral testifies.

Presentation of Jesus in the Temple
fresco, 200x185 cm
Scrovegni Chapel, Padua

The frescoes were commissioned by Enrico Scrovegni, the son of Reginaldo, a notorious usurer whom Dante mentioned in the *Divine Comedy* (Inferno, XVII, 64-75). This was not the only chapel that Giotto decorated for rich clients. He painted frescoes for the bankers Bardi and Peruzzi in their family chapels in the Florentine church of Santa Croce. One of the reasons that prompted these people to decorate the chapels intended for the burial of members of their own family was the idea that the redemption of the soul could be attained through donations. It is

significant that the formula used in wills for these donations, made to pay for the decoration of places of worship or the celebration of Masses, was "for the redemption of souls." Nor should we forget the importance of social status for the wealthier members of the rising classes: owning a mortuary chapel and having it decorated by a celebrated artist certainly conferred great prestige. Painted between 1303 and 1305, the frescoes were mentioned in the writings of the contemporary chronicler Riccobaldo Ferrarese (*Compilatio Chronologica*, 1312-13) and the poet Francesco da Barberino (*Documenti d'Amore*, 1313) just a few years after their completion. Still in a good state of preservation, the recently restored paintings are one of Giotto's finest achievements, in which he shows himself not just to be a master of composition, as he had already demonstrated at Assisi, but also an excellent colorist.
The scene represented here is based on a passage in the Gospel according to Luke (2: 21-38). On the left St. Joseph is holding the turtledoves or pigeons to be offered in sacrifice. Jesus is in the arms of Simeon, who has been told by the Holy Spirit that he will see Christ before he dies: the elderly priest of the temple recognizes him as the Savior and communicates this to his mother. On the right is the prophetess Anna, who also recognizes the Child as the bringer of Redemption. The inscription on the scroll she holds alludes to the Child's destiny (with the abbreviations filled in):

Quoniam in isto erit redemptio seculi ("For in him will be the redemption of the world").
One of the most interesting analyses of the work was carried out by John Ruskin, who pointed out the attention Giotto pays to the emotional side of the story and the way that the Child is wriggling in Simeon's arms in an effort to return to his mother, who is stretching out her arms to take him. The priest is holding Christ with his hands covered, an already established iconographic feature that is in keeping with liturgical precepts underlining the sacredness of the gesture of anyone coming into direct contact with Christ. Giotto's ability to tell a story, much superior to that of his predecessors, was also mentioned by Leon Battista Alberti in his *De Pictura* (1435).

GIOTTO

Raising of Lazarus
fresco
chapel of the Magdalen, Lower Church, Assisi

The man who commissioned the decoration of this chapel, dating from between 1307 and 1308, was the Franciscan Teobaldo Pontano, bishop of Assisi from 1296 to 1329, and he is portrayed twice in the frescoes on its walls: in the Franciscan habit at the feet of Mary Magdalene and kneeling in prayer next to St. Rufinus.

The composition of the scenes closely recalls that of the Scrovegni frescoes in Padua, although here the handling is surer and the coloring finer, and can undoubtedly be attributed to Giotto and his workshop. Nevertheless, the extent of the master's contribution is still the subject of debate. According to some critics the hand of a collaborator is clearly discernible, and Giorgio Bonsanti claims, for example, that the anonymous artist who has been given the conventional name of "Giotto's Relative" played a significant role in the execution of these paintings.

The scene with the *Raising of Lazarus*, which reproduces the composition in Padua with few variations, is based on the verses of the Gospel of St. John (11: 1-46), which tell how Christ brought back to life Lazarus of Bethany, dead and buried for four days. The dramatic nature of the scene – depicted with accents of notable realism in the figures covering their faces to ward off the stink of death – is underlined by the words pronounced by Christ: "*Foras veni Lazare*" ("Lazarus, come forth"). It is perhaps worth pointing out that the use of such captions was extremely rare in the painting of the time, except in scenes depicting the *Annunciation of the Virgin*. (A.F.)

Simone Martini

Reliable information on the youth and early maturity of Simone Martini is very scarce. He was born in Siena, or perhaps San Gimignano, in 1284, according to Vasari, who says that he died at the age of sixty in 1344. The *Maestà* in the Palazzo Pubblico of Siena is dated 1315, and so he must have already been a well-established painter by this time. This is confirmed by the granting of an annuity to the artist by Robert of Anjou, the king of Naples, in 1317: the document, which designates Simone *miles*, or knight, tells us a great deal about his rise in society and his success at the court of Naples. For the Anjou, in or before 1317, Simone executed the principal work of his career, the decoration of the chapel of San Martino in the Lower Church of San Francesco at Assisi. The encounter with Giotto's paintings in Assisi was to prove decisive for his artistic evolution. His Sienese training, based on the teachings of Duccio and open to Gothic influences from across the Alps, was reinvigorated by the powerful monumentality and realism of Giotto: Simone, who according to Vasari "had a talent with nature and loved to portray from life, and in this he was considered the best master of his day." In the 1320s and 1330s Simone Martini was at the head of a large workshop (one of his closest collaborators was his brother-in-law Lippo Memmi) and obtained prestigious public commissions in Siena, including the celebrated *Guidoriccio da Fogliano* (although the attribution is controversial). In 1336 he went to the Papal Curia in Avignon. Here he met Petrarch, becoming his close friend and painting for him a portrait of his beloved Laura, now lost but much praised by the poet, and the frontispiece of a Virgilian codex, now in the Biblioteca Ambrosiana in Milan. The stay in Avignon helped to take Martini's painting in a Gothic and courtly direction, which to some extent foreshadowed the International Gothic style that was to dominate European art in the years spanning the end of the 14th century and the first few decades of the 15th.

Saint Louis of Toulouse Crowning His Brother Robert of Anjou
tempera on panel, 200x138 cm; predella 56x38 cm (each scene)
Gallerie Nazionali di Capodimonte, Naples

The work, dated to 1317, constitutes a genuine political manifesto of the House of Anjou. On the death of Charles II, the king of Sicily, in 1296, his son Louis had renounced the crown of Naples in favor of his brother Robert, and had taken vows, entering the Franciscan order. The succession had caused a great deal of controversy and Robert had been accused of usurping the throne, even though the pope, to whom the question had been submitted, had recognized his right to rule. So the canonization of Louis in 1317 was welcomed by the king as an invaluable opportunity to strengthen his own position and confirm the legitimacy of his reign. The work that was immediately commissioned from Simone Martini, almost as an act of propaganda, translates Robert of Anjou's political conception into visual terms: the saint, seated on a throne, receives the heavenly crown from angels. The pluvial, miter and crosier recall his episcopal rank, the habit his membership of the order of St. Francis. On his breast, however, is set a large brooch with the Anjou crest, underlining the fact that he belongs to the royal family of Naples. With one hand Louis places the crown on the head of his kneeling brother: thus we are seeing a double coronation, of the bishop saint by God, and of Robert by the saint. So the king derives his authority from a legitimate succession, through the renunciation of Louis, and is in a way included, again through his brother, in a celestial investiture. The principal episodes in the saint's life are depicted in the predella: his acceptance of the appointment as bishop of Toulouse in exchange for the possibility of entering the Franciscan order, the repetition of his vows in public, Louis serving the poor at table, his funeral and a miracle worked after his death.

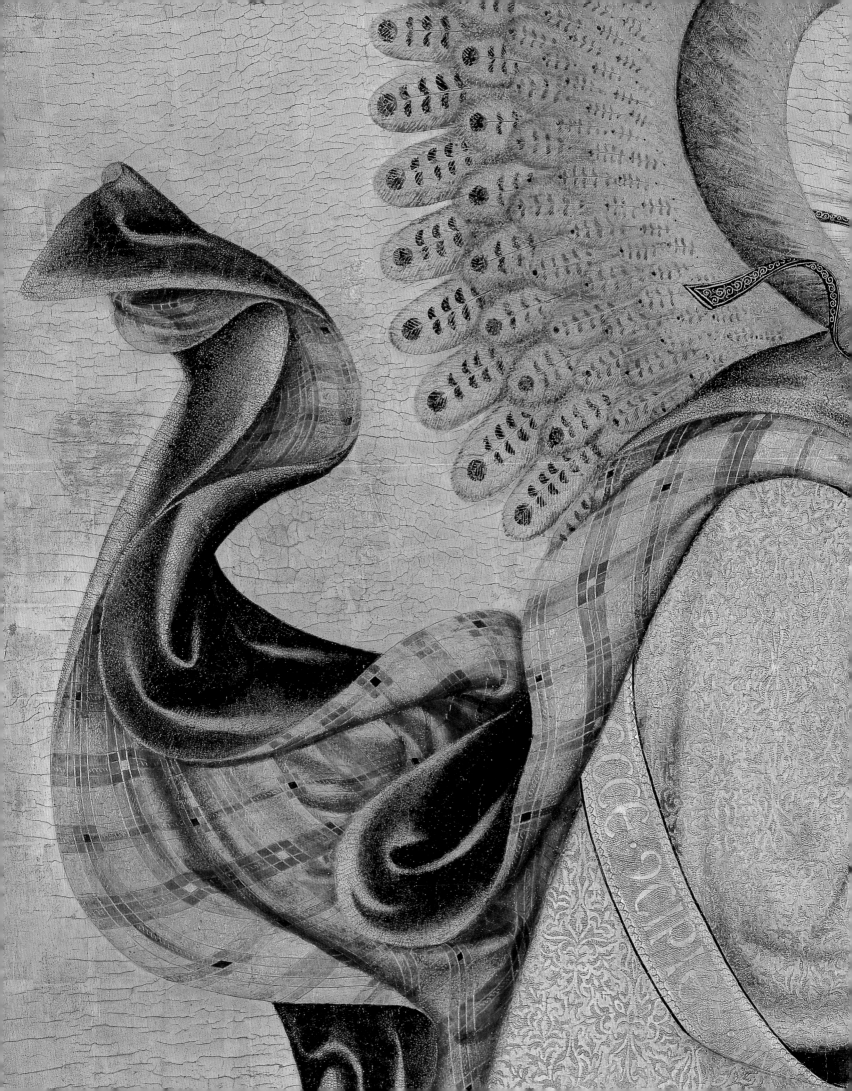

Annunciation

tempera on panel, 265x305 cm
Galleria degli Uffizi, Florence

The work is signed by Simone Martini and Lippo Memmi and dated 1333. It had been executed for Siena Cathedral, to be placed on the altar of St. Ansanus, one of the city's four patron saints, who is represented on the left wing of the triptych. The female saint on the right has been variously identified, but is probably Maxima, Ansanus's godmother. According to one of the most influential theologians of the late Middle Ages, St. Bonaventure, the Annunciation can be divided into three phases: the first is the greeting by the angel, the second, represented by Simone, is the one in which the angel, already kneeling, makes the annunciation proper and the third consists in Mary's consent and the Incarnation. The words just pronounced by the angel, *AVE GRATIA PLENA DOMINVS TECVM*, are written in relief on the gold ground, and have by now reached the Virgin's ear; the ones that she is about to utter are embroidered on her stole. The olive branch in the angel's left hand, while the other hand indicates the dove of the Holy Spirit, is at

once a sign of peace and, as a fruit-bearing plant, a symbol of Mary who, in the writings of St. Bonaventure and others, is identified with the "branch of the root of Jesse" of which Isaiah spoke. We do not know the extent of the contribution made by his brother-in-law Lippo Memmi, who signed the work jointly with Simone: it was probably limited to the execution of St. Maxima, perhaps to the master's design, the gilding and the decoration of the frame (although the one we see today dates from the 19th century). The central panel should in any case be considered entirely the work of Simone. Indeed, it is one of his greatest masterpieces, and marks an important stage in his artistic development, as he moved away from the spatial research of the preceding years and toward a painting of courtly flavor, linear in style and centering on the extreme elegance of the drawing and the splendor of the precious materials. And yet, even in this Gothic phase, which would reach its climax during the years he spent in Avignon, Simone never abandoned a line that could be described as naturalistic and, in open contradiction with the overall composition of the work, atmospheric: note the angel's

cloak, still fluttering from the flight that has just ended, with the marked chiaroscuro that makes it stand out from the gold ground, or the wings separated by a shadow, or again the lilies with their calyxes depicted in perspective.

Frontispiece of Virgil

parchment, 29.5x20 cm
Biblioteca Ambrosiana, Milan

The codex, containing the works of Virgil (the *Aeneid*, *Eclogues* and *Georgics*), the commentaries of Servius and texts by other Latin authors, belonged to Francesco Petrarca, known to the English-speaking world as Petrarch, who had been given it by his father. Stolen in 1326, it had been recovered in 1338: to celebrate the return of such a treasured volume, Petrarch had a title page in parchment added and entrusted its decoration to Simone, who in 1336 had executed a portrait of Laura. This too may have been a miniature or, more likely, a drawing, and was much valued by the poet. The work was probably executed by 1341, and shows Servius raising a curtain, behind which Virgil is seated at the foot of

a little tree with a volume open on his lap and a pen in his hand. Next to the commentator stands a soldier, while in the foreground a farmer is pruning a vine and a shepherd milking sheep: all three figures are looking toward the poet. The inscriptions on two scrolls held by winged hands indicate the subject of the work: Servius explains the meaning of Virgil's writings so that it is clear to leaders, shepherds and farmers (*ut pateant ducibus pastoribus atque colonis*). But the three figures represent, in addition to Servius's public, Virgil's three works, in terms very similar to the celebrated epitaph that the poet is traditionally held to have composed for himself: "*Mantua me genuit Calabri rapuere, tenet nunc / Parthenope: cecini pascua, rura, duces*" ("Mantua gave me my birth, Calabria snatched me away / Naples keeps me today: I sang pastures and farmlands and rulers of earth"). The same lines are echoed in the inscription set in the lower margin of the sheet, which constitutes a signature of the painting and was certainly composed by Petrarch: "*Mantua Virgilium qui talia carmina finxit / Sena tulit Symonem digito qui talia pinxit*" ("Mantua gave Virgil who wrote these poems, Siena Simone who painted these things by his own hand"). An extremely interesting equation is made in the Latin couplet between a poet (indeed the greatest of Latin poets) and a painter, drawing on Horace's phrase "*ut pictura poesis*," "as is painting so is poetry," which was to become so popular in the Renaissance. What we have here is a fully Humanistic work of art, not just because of Petrarch's involvement in its commissioning and conception but also because of the stylistic choices made by Simone, who adopts an "elevated" language, the figurative equivalent of the classical poetry contained in the codex. (S.G.C.)

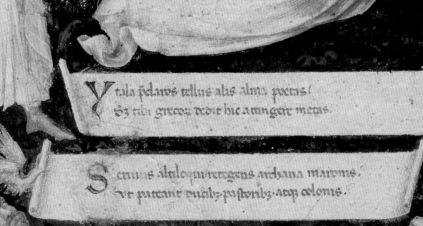

Ytala helaros tellus alis alma poetis!
Sz tibi gircos redie hic a tangere metas.

Scruans alaloqui regens archana maiorus.
Ve pateant ducibz pastoribz atqz colonis.

PIETRO LORENZETTI

Pietro Lorenzetti

Mystery shrouds the life of Pietro, for whom we have no reliable biographical information, but who, like his brother Ambrogio, was active in the first half of the 14th century and must have then succumbed to the outbreak of the Black Death in 1348.

His figurative style is influenced by his origins in the geographical region dominated by the painting of Duccio di Buoninsegna, but the experience he gained in other Tuscan cities and in Umbria, especially at the basilica in Assisi, where he was able to see numerous frescoes by Giotto and his school, brought him into contact with the innovative style of the great Florentine master. The artist seems to have been more faithful to tradition than his brother, and his painting shows a great attention to detail and to the harmony and elegance of the whole, united with a remarkable sensitivity in the representation of emotions.

One of Pietro's earliest works is the mock *Triptych* in fresco in the Orsini Chapel of the Lower Church of Assisi, datable to between 1310 and 1315, which may well be based on a painting by the Master of St. Nicholas in the chapel opposite. Again in the Lower Church the artist painted the *Madonna and Child between Saint John the Baptist and Saint Francis*, a work of great elegance and sensitivity whose figures show the clear influence of Giotto's models. However, his earliest dated work is the *Polyptych* in the parish church of Santa Maria in Arezzo, commissioned in 1320 by Bishop Guido Tarlati. The panel, of great expressive force and chromatic richness, presents stylistic affinities with the frescoes depicting *Scenes of the Passion* in the Lower Church of Assisi, a cycle of controversial date that is assigned by some to roughly the same period because of this similarity.

Among the artist's most fascinating paintings, the *Polyptych of the Madonna del Carmine*, a work of 1329 much of which is now in the Pinacoteca Nazionale of Siena, represents the ancient history of the Carmelites, linked to the example set by Elijah, and their more recent history, that of a mendicant order formed around the 12th century by a group of crusaders who had begun to lead a monastic life on Mount Carmel in Galilee.

In 1335, in collaboration with his brother, he painted the frescoes – regrettably lost during the 18th century – on the facade of Santa Maria della Scala in Siena, and again with Ambrogio carried out, from 1336 onward, the decoration of the cloister and chapterhouse of the Sienese monastery of San Francesco. All that remains of Pietro's work here are the scenes of the *Crucifixion* and the *Resurrection of Christ*. The works of his last years include the *Polyptych of the Blessed Humilitas* and a *Maestà*, both in the Uffizi, and the celebrated *Nativity of the Virgin* (1342, Museo dell'Opera del Duomo, Siena).

Nativity of the Virgin
tempera on panel, 188x183 cm
Museo dell'Opera del Duomo, Siena

This is one of Pietro Lorenzetti's best known works – commissioned in 1335 for the altar of San Savino in Siena Cathedral, but not completed until 1342 – in which the painter drew on the texts of the apocryphal Gospels, since the episode does not appear in the Bible.

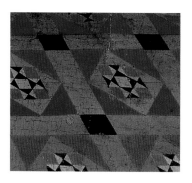

The scene is set in two different rooms, constructed in such a way as to fit the division of the frame into three sections. In the room on the left, filling one compartment of the polyptych, we see Joachim, Mary's father, waiting anxiously. In the background, a lunette and a window open onto the outside, offering a glimpse of just a few details of a Gothic building opposite. The compartments in the middle and on the right house the main scene, set in a room roofed with two cross vaults. Anne is lying on the bed after giving birth to the Virgin, who is being washed by two serving women. The episode is described with feeling and precision: one of the women is pouring warm water into a basin while the other holds the baby and tests the temperature of the water with her hand. A similar scene had already been depicted in a panel of the pulpit carved by Giovanni Pisano by 1301 in the church of Sant'Andrea at Pistoia, representing the *Nativity of Christ*, but according to the critic Enzo Carli this is not Pietro's only debt to sculpture. In fact, the figure of St. Anne recalls the Virgin sculpted by Arnolfo di Cambio for the façade of Florence Cathedral.

The scene, constructed with studied perspective, is striking for the care that has been taken over the interiors: note the meticulous representation of each tile, each piece of furniture, the cloth covering the bed, the drape that serves as a screen and the ceiling with a double cross vault frescoed with a starry sky.

PIETRO LORENZETTI

Blessed Humilitas: The Blessed Humilitas Talking to Her Husband
tempera on panel, 128x57 (central),
45x32 cm (each panel)
Galleria degli Uffizi, Florence

The painting had been commissioned from Lorenzetti by the conventual church of San Giovanni Evangelista in Florence, to adorn the altar erected over the remains of the woman who had once been abbess of that nunnery. Following the destruction of the church (1529), the work was moved to the monastery of San Michele a San Salvi. Subsequently dismembered and then reassembled in the 19th century on the basis of a drawing made in the previous century, it lacks one of the cusps, several elements of the predella and two panels in the bottom row, now in Berlin.

Like similar works, it has an image of the protagonist at the center, standing and full length, surrounded by smaller panels with scenes from her life that give the painter an opportunity to show off his great narrative skill. The Blessed Humilitas is depicted in a nun's habit, covered by the modest flock cape that she was accustomed to wear in her lifetime,

holding a book and a palm; at her feet, perhaps, the Blessed Margherita who succeeded her as head of the convent. The panels representing scenes from Humilitas's life and her miracles are arranged in three rows and place the emphasis on the figures, and in particular the protagonist, at the expense of the highly simplified settings, in such a way that every one of her acts assumes a paradigmatic value.

The story of Rosanesa, the secular name of the Blessed Humilitas (who, according to tradition, was born in 1226 and died in 1310), starts with her leaving her husband Ugolotto to embrace the religious life, and is illustrated by the married couple seated in the middle of a room open at the front. The woman explains her decision to her husband, moving one hand like a preacher and

holding a book, probably the Bible, in the other. In the background is set a bed, symbol of the married life that she is about to give up. Her husband, still wedded to the values of earthly life and looking more disappointed than contrite, clutches his gloves in an allusion to their prosperous lifestyle: in fact, both come from wealthy families and Rosanesa is actually of noble origin. After an initial refusal, Ugolotto is persuaded to follow her and like her will take vows and become a monk. (A.F.)

Ambrogio Lorenzetti

D ocumentary references to Ambrogio Lorenzetti are scanty, and cover the period of time from 1319 to 1344. The earliest dated work of the Sienese painter, a *Madonna and Child* (1319, Museo Diocesano, San Casciano) comes from Vico L'Abate. This was in Florentine territory, although on the periphery, and the picture reveals Ambrogio's familiarity with the principal Florentine artists of the day, not just painters like Giotto but also sculptors like Arnolfo. At the time Ambrogio may have been living in Florence, where his presence is documented up until 1321. He returned there after a gap of a few years in Siena, and between 1328 and 1330 his name figures in the registers of the *Arte dei Medici e Speziali*, the Guild of Physicians and Apothecaries that also looked after the interests of painters. In Florence he painted a polyptych for the church of San Procolo (1332), now in the Uffizi, where there are also several panels with *Scenes from the Life of Saint Nicholas* from the same church. In these paintings, characterized by a lively narration, Ambrogio shows that he is able to handle space in the manner developed by Giotto. In 1335 he executed the frescoes, now lost, on the facade of the Spedale di Santa Maria della Scala in Siena, in collaboration with his brother Pietro. It was probably in the same period that he worked on the *Maestà* in the Palazzo Comunale of Massa Marittima, a painting with a complex composition rich in symbolic references.

In 1336 he and his brother started on the wall paintings with *Scenes from the Life of Saint Francis* in the monastery of San Francesco. Much of the cycle, which earned enthusiastic praise from Ghiberti, has been lost and only two scenes by Ambrogio survive today. But the work with which his name is indissolubly linked is the decoration of the Sala della Pace in Siena's Palazzo Pubblico, whose execution is documented by payments made between 1338 and 1339: the cycle has an ethical and political message and constitutes an invaluable source of artistic, historical and iconographic information, as well as reflecting a new interest in representation of the landscape. At some time between 1334 and 1340 he painted the frescoes in the Montesiepi Chapel near the Cistercian church of San Galgano, and two years later the *Presentation in the Temple* for the altar of San Crescenzio in Siena Cathedral, now in the Uffizi. This was followed by an *Annunciation* (Pinacoteca Nazionale, Siena) in which the handling of space is highly advanced, and a painting (*Cosmography*) for the Palazzo Pubblico in Siena that unfortunately no longer exists. The last documents relating to Ambrogio's life are a few testamentary dispositions in his own handwriting, drawn up (June 9, 1348) just prior to his death in the terrible epidemic of the Black Death.

Suckling Madonna (*Madonna del Latte*)
tempera on panel, 90x48 cm
Museo Diocesano, Siena

The inscription on the Virgin's halo, "*Ave Maria Gratia plena Dominus tecum bene…*," is incomplete, but it is easy to complete it with "*benedicta tu in mulieribus…*," inasmuch as these are the words in the Gospel that the announcing angel addresses to Mary (Luke 1: 28). The picture, probably painted around 1340, offers a representation of the ancient theme of the Virgin suckling the child, but with new accents, and is a superb example of the sensitivity with

which Ambrogio approaches the mother-son relationship. The naturalness of the attitudes of the two figures is striking, as is the freedom of movement granted to the Child, who sucks greedily at his mother's breast with one foot braced against her arm. The Virgin, whose tender expression is subtly veined with sadness, clasps the Child affectionately, in a maternal gesture underlined by the position of her arm. Curiously, she is not located at the center of the panel but shifted to the left from the viewpoint of the observer, so that her shoulder seems to lean against the edge of the frame. This emphasizes the centrality of the figure of the Son, true protagonist of the painting.

AMBROGIO LORENZETTI

Effects of Good Government in the City and in the Country

fresco, length *c.* 14 m
Palazzo Pubblico, Siena

The frescoes in the Sala della Pace in the Palazzo Pubblico of Siena, executed between 1338 and 1339, are a masterpiece of 14th-century painting and a very rich source of historical documentation. Their location is extremely significant: the room was used for meetings of the Government of the Nine, which ruled the city from 1287 to 1335, and the wall paintings, which have an openly political character and display an extraordinary visual and conceptual richness, were intended to reflect its political and administrative choices. The cycle of paintings is inspired by the Aristotelian idea of good, and in a complex and sophisticated allegory represents the moral principles that should guide the behavior of rulers: Justice is inspired by divine wisdom and guaranteed by civil Concord, and the Common Good is to be pursued by subordinating the interest of the individual to that of the community. The frescoes show the consequences of choosing to respect or ignore the rules of Justice and cover three walls of the room; on the wall opposite the entrance, the *Allegory* and *Effects of Bad Government* catch the visitor's attention with images of death, violence and destruction, while on the other two walls extend, serene and majestic, the *Allegory of Good Government* and the *Effects of Good Government in the City and in the Country*. The scenes that illustrate the positive effects of a just administration present the reassuring image of an active and peaceful life: in the city, filled with noble palaces and towers, old buildings are being renovated and new ones constructed; in the streets and squares all the people are engaged in their own activities; commerce thrives, children are being taught their lessons. A group of nine girls, larger in size than the other figures represented, dance harmoniously hand in hand, in what is probably a symbolic reference to the Magistracy of the Nine that held power in the city of Siena. Above the gate of the city a winged figure (*Securitas*) holds in one hand a hanged man and in the other a scroll bearing the inscription: "*senza paura ognuom franco camini / e lavorando semini ciascuno / mentre che tal comuno / manterrà questa donna in signoria, / chel alevata arei ogni balia*" ("without fear every free man walks / each sowing seed / while the commune / will maintain this woman's sway / who has stripped the evil of all power." The short text, inviting the honest to work and fear nothing, while the Comune will deal with the dishonest, effectively sums up the programmatic intent of the painting. The prosperity guaranteed by good government extends beyond the city walls and into the countryside; farmers are at work amidst the gently rolling hills, covered with well-tended fields and woods, and merchants are transporting their goods by mule along the roads. This may not have been Ambrogio's first work in the City Hall. Up until 1336 the post of the city's official painter had been held by Simone Martini, but in that year he moved to Avignon, leaving the position vacant. According to the Sienese chronicler Agnolo di Tura del Grasso, Ambrogio painted some frescoes with *Scenes from Roman History* on the walls of the Palazzo Pubblico in 1337, and later a *Maestà with the Four Cardinal Virtues*, unfortunately now in a very poor state of preservation. (A.F.)

SECVRITAS

SENZA PAVRA OGNVOM FRANCO CAMINI
E LAVORANDO SEMINI CIASCVNO
MENTRE CHE TAL COMVNO
MANTERRA QVESTA DONNA I SIGNORIA
CHEL ALEVATA AREI OGNI BALIA

15TH CENTURY

Masaccio

ommaso di ser Giovanni Cassai, called Masaccio, was born in San Giovanni Valdarno in 1401. Moving to Florence, he was already working as a painter in his own right in 1422, when he signed the *San Giovenale Triptych*, the earliest of his works known to us. While still very young he came into contact with the leading artists in Florence, in particular Donatello and Brunelleschi. The latter was greatly impressed by his talent and played a decisive role in his development, instructing him in the use of mathematical perspective. This is clearly demonstrated by the fresco of the *Trinity* in Santa Maria Novella, where the architectural view appears to be the work of Brunelleschi himself. Masaccio was also deeply influenced by Donatello's sculpture and, above all, Giotto's painting, which he studied and understood thoroughly. In 1424 he began to collaborate with the older Masolino, and together they painted the frescoes in the Brancacci Chapel in Florence: rightly considered one of the greatest glories of Italian painting, they marked the definitive passage from late-Gothic art to Renaissance painting. In all probability work started on the decoration, commissioned by Felice Brancacci, in 1424 or in the first few months of 1425: we are not sure whether a collaboration between the two painters was planned right from the start or the task was originally entrusted to Masolino alone, who then asked Masaccio to join him on the scaffolding in order to finish the job before his departure for Hungary in September 1425. We do know that between 1425 and 1427 only Masaccio worked on the paintings, before leaving for Rome, where Masolino had been active for some time. Thus he left the cycle incomplete: it would only be finished in the 1480s, by Filippino Lippi.

Masaccio died in Rome at the age of just twenty-seven, in 1428. He brought about a revolution in Italian art, with a painting that focused wholly on the definition of solid figures, located firmly in a space structured in perspective, and an unprecedented dramatic tension in the representation of emotions and expressions.

Madonna and Child with Saint Anne
tempera on panel, 175x103 cm
Galleria degli Uffizi, Florence

The panel, which comes from the Florentine church of Sant'Ambrogio but whose original location is unknown, was painted by Masaccio and Masolino. The distinction between the work of the two artists, first proposed with precision by the art historian Roberto Longhi, assigns the Madonna and Child and the angel holding the drape on the right to Masaccio and the rest of the painting to Masolino, except perhaps the angel at the top of the composition. The name given to the panel in Italian, *Sant'Anna Metterza*,

refers to the iconography, in which St. Anne is placed behind (and therefore *messa terza*, or "put third") the group of the Virgin and her son. It is not clear whether it is a collaborative effort, painted some time around the decoration of the Brancacci Chapel (or perhaps even executed for the altar of the chapel itself), or a picture left incomplete by Masaccio and finished by Masolino. Certainly it is an exceptional document that allows us to gauge exactly the distance, in terms of style, between the two painters. Note, for example, the confident handling of the perspective of the Child's hand resting on his mother's, in contrast to Masolino's attempt at foreshortening St. Anne's hands. Even though the older artist

strengthens his chiaroscuro, as if seeking a three-dimensional effect similar to that of his young colleague, he cannot compete with the classical solidity of Masaccio's figures. Here the painter, probably around twenty-three at the time, draws on a work of art from antiquity, a marble Roman copy of a Greek original representing a putto, now in the Uffizi: the beautiful nude of the Child is an antiquarian and classical citation, concealed in a sacred context, that brings Masaccio's art into line with the Humanistic and archeological culture that fascinated Brunelleschi and Donatello in those years.

Saint Paul
tempera on panel, 51x30 cm
Museo Nazionale di San Matteo, Pisa

The work, originally part of the large
polyptych executed in 1426 for the chapel
of San Giuliano in the Carmelite church in
Pisa to a commission from Ser Giuliano
di Colino, was described *in situ* by
Giorgio Vasari in both the 1551 and the
1568 edition of his *Lives*. Later it was
dismembered, and the other panels are
now dispersed between London
(*Madonna and Child*, National Gallery),
Naples (*Crucifixion*, Gallerie Nazionali di
Capodimonte), Berlin (parts of the
predella and small figures of saints,
Gemäldegalerie) and Malibu (*Saint
Andrew*, Paul Getty Museum). The *Saint
Paul* in Pisa was in the upper row of the
polyptych, probably immediately to the
left of the *Crucifixion*. To unify the work
Masaccio uses a strong source of light
located on the left that casts deep
shadows, setting the figures in a three-
dimensional space. The attitude of *Saint
Paul*, with his highly sculptural drapery,
recalls contemporary works by Donatello,
especially the statues of *Jeremiah* and
Habakkuk: in particular the idea of the
figure's rotary motion, with the head
turned to the right, in contraposition to
the bust, is derived from the great
Florentine sculptor, as is the gesture of
the hand holding the sword. Taking on
board the most advanced of Donatello's
experiments, Masaccio, at the age of just
twenty-five, displayed a realism and a
sense of drama that were without
precedent in painting, marking a decisive
turning point in the figurative culture of
the Italian Renaissance.

MASACCIO

The Holy Trinity

fresco, 667x317 cm
Santa Maria Novella, Florence

The fresco is one of the last works executed by Masaccio before his journey to Rome in 1428. The iconography of the *Trinity*, with the Father holding Christ's cross and the dove of the Holy Spirit in the center, is anything but unusual: what is striking is the location of the group inside a Renaissance work of architecture represented in perfect perspective. It is a mortuary chapel, and God the Father is standing on the tomb located immediately behind the cross. At the side, next to the columns, stand the mourners, i.e. Mary and St. John the Evangelist, while in the foreground are the donors (who have not been identified with certainty). At the bottom is set a skeleton on a sarcophagus with the inscription: IO FV G[i]A QVEL CHE VOI SETE / AND QVEL CHE SON VOI A[n]CO SARETE ("I was what you are / and what I am you too will be"). This portion of the fresco must have been situated underneath the altar that was set in front of it: so it was not a simple *memento mori*, but a theologically more pertinent reference to the death and resurrection of Christ, repeated at every celebration of Communion on the altar, above which loomed the representation of the Trinity. Giorgio Vasari, describing the work, commented that it is "made to recede so skillfully that the surface looks as if it is indented." In fact the foreshortening must have been a sort of cultural "shock" for his contemporaries, and constitutes one of the first systematic applications, verging on the virtuoso, of the principles of the mathematical perspective devised by Filippo Brunelleschi: indeed it has been suggested that the illusory space was designed and perhaps even drawn in outline by the great architect. In reality it is quite possible that Masaccio, while following the suggestions of his older friend, was capable of carrying out an exercise in perspective of this kind independently, and that he had the depth of understanding of classical architecture that is presupposed by the representation of the coffered tunnel vault, modeled on the Pantheon. (S.G.C.)

Fra Angelico

"He was a 'Prophet' of the sacred image: he knew how to reach the pinnacles of art by drawing inspiration from the mysteries of faith. In him art becomes prayer." With these words, on February 18, 1984, Pope John Paul II proclaimed Fra Angelico the patron of artists, after raising him to the glory of the altars in 1982.

Giovanni di Pietro was born in the Mugello, near Florence, probably just a few years before the start of the 15th century. Although we know little of the training he received as a painter, it must have been connected with the monastery of Santa Maria degli Angeli, an important center for the illumination of manuscripts. He is mentioned for the first time in 1423, under the name of Fra Giovanni at the monastery of San Domenico in Fiesole, and therefore a follower of the reform introduced by the Blessed Giovanni Dominici. For some time the Mendicant Order of Preachers founded by St. Dominic had no longer been observing the vow of poverty: at Santa Maria Novella young men from the noblest and wealthiest families in Florence lived a comfortable life, wanting for nothing, that was very far from the spirit of the early days. Following the reform championed by St. Catherine of Siena, the monasteries of the Observance, where strict adherence to the Rule was required, were set up alongside the unreformed ones, known as Conventual. Fra Giovanni Dominici supported the reform and founded the monastery at Fiesole. "Look, and consider the beauty of colors, the sweetness of taste, the melody of various sounds [...] forms, figures [...] and all the arts. And so the soul captivated by beauty [...] feels an all-consuming desire to see what it does not see, and loves nonetheless": for Fra Dominici, preaching, the principal duty of Dominicans, could also find a powerful vehicle in painting. His words referred to the use of the image as an aid to individual prayer and to the conception of the eyes as a door through which Christ could enter the soul.

This was the cultural climate in which Fra Giovanni received his first major commissions, earning a good income for the monastery and demonstrating the artist's willingness to adopt the new language of Masaccio. He attracted the attention of the Gaddi family, for whom he painted the *Annunciation* now in the Prado and the *Coronation of the Virgin* in the Louvre, and then, in the 1430s, of the Strozzi, the great patrons for whom he executed the *Deposition*. He painted the *Linaiuoli Altarpiece* for the meeting room of the Guild of Linen Merchants and the *sacre conversazioni* of the *Annalena Altarpiece* and of the one in San Marco he executed for the Medici, pictures in which the Virgin and the saints interact in a single space and are not isolated in the different compartments of a polyptych.

In the meantime, Cosimo had returned from exile in 1434 and the Medici family was starting on its long climb to dominance over Florentine life. Two years later, the Dominicans of Fiesole installed themselves in the church of San Marco. From that day until his death, in 1464, Cosimo was to make regular payments toward the sustenance of the friars, providing the novices with grain and wine and supplying oil, wood, medicine, clothing, books, stuffing for beds and wax for candles. The rebuilding of the monastery was entrusted to the architect Michelozzo. San Marco became a symbol of Medici power, the fruit of political calculation and spiritual aspiration: the construction of great works in honor of God was a mark of gratitude for the bestowal of good fortune. Between 1439 and 1445 Fra Angelico set about frescoing the new rooms of the monastery, with the help of his collaborators, creating his most intimate paintings in the cells of the friars.

At the end of 1445, the artist went to Rome to work for Pope Eugenius IV. He was to return there in 1447 at the summons of Nicholas V, for whom he frescoed a chapel dedicated to St. Steven and St. Lawrence in a courtly and monumental style that was in keeping with the pope's Humanistic interests. Prior at Fiesole from 1450 to 1452, Angelico was called to Rome again, where he died on February 18, 1455, and was buried in the church of Santa Maria sopra Minerva. For the whole of his life he had adhered to the principle: "Who does Christ's business, should always be with Christ."

Coronation of the Virgin
tempera on panel, 240x211 cm
Louvre, Paris

The low point of view, the perspective of the floor tiles and the steps of polychrome marble render the work painted in *c.* 1430 for the altar of San Domenico in

Fiesole even more majestic: the Gothic baldachin is set in a measurable, three-dimensional space, inspired by the innovations of Masaccio. The Virgin is

kneeling in an attitude of humility, while Christ places on her head the crown of pure gold of which the Psalms speak. The figures are accompanied by numerous inscriptions on the borders of the cloaks or on the haloes, referring to the liturgy: the exaltation of Christ as Lamb of God refers to the Apocalypse, while the words relating to the Virgin are the ones that were recited in the evening. The halo of the Archangel Gabriel repeats the salute addressed to the Virgin, the introduction to any religious function dedicated to Mary. The figures are characterized by an inscription or an attribute, while the presence of many saints bearing the names of members of the Gaddi family in the foreground provides support for the hypothesis that they were the clients. The only saint facing the observer is Thomas Aquinas. The pages of his open book are inscribed with quotations from the Bible and a summary of his dialogue with Christ on the Cross: "Thomas, you have written well of me. What reward will you have?" "Lord, nothing but yourself." It is the *Te Deum* that marks the beginning of the liturgical year, the highest hymn of praise composed to glorify Christ and his Church.

The Last Judgment
tempera on panel, 105x210 cm
Museo di San Marco, Florence

Painted for the Camaldolensian church of Santa Maria degli Angeli in *c.* 1432-35, it probably served as the back of the seat used by the priest at high mass. Some art historians trace its commission to the election of the monk Ambrogio Traversari as abbot general of the Camaldolensian Order in 1431, with reference to the significance of this role in Western monasticism: the abbot represented Christ, the master, lawgiver and judge, but he too would be subject, one day, to judgment. The traditional iconography has been renewed by the unitary spatial setting, in which the striking perspective of the open tombs lends drama to the scene. Christ the Judge has given his verdict, one hand turned upward and one downward in the traditional gestures of salvation and damnation. The Madonna and St. John the Baptist intercede on behalf of humanity, while saints and apostles mingle with figures from the Old Testament: at the edges, St. Dominic with the star, lily and book and St. Benedict stand out on the left; St. Francis with the stigmata and St. Romuald dressed in white and with a hermit's staff on the right. Benedict and Romuald were the founders

FRA ANGELICO

of the Camaldolensians. The torments of the damned are contrasted by the dance of the elect, among whom we can make out the pope and the emperor, the sources of abbatial power.

Annunciation
tempera on panel, 175x180 cm
Museo Diocesano, Cortona

Annunciation
fresco,190x164 cm
Monastery of San Marco, Florence

In the 15th century there was a close connection between the sermons given by preachers and the pictures painted by artists. Preachings on the Annunciation spoke of the various states of mind with which the Virgin had received the angel's announcement. Fra Angelico's *Annunciations* reproduce the state of *humiliatione*, the moment in which Mary humbly accepts the will of God. He

presents the same subject, however, in different ways for different purposes: the altarpiece in Cortona (*c.* 1435) is intended for public devotion, the fresco in Florence (1439-45) for the private meditation of a friar. In Cortona, the Virgin receives the angel in a porticoed Renaissance villa in which the perspective of the columns links together all the protagonists of the mystery of the redemption: Adam and Eve expelled from the Garden of Eden and Mary. God the Father is present in the medallion above the central column, while the Holy Spirit is represented by the flying dove. The *Annunciation* in San Marco, on the other hand, is located in a monk's cell. The *Constitutiones* of the Dominican Order stipulated that cells could house images of Christ Crucified, the Madonna or the founder of the order, and the monastery of San Marco had Fra Angelico paint an incredible cycle of pictures in which each cell had its own fresco, suited to the role of its occupant. In fact the community provided lodgings for novices, clerics and

lay brothers, who took care of the monastery's material needs. In particular, the frescoes in the friars' cells were intended to stimulate meditation as a preparation for their study of the sacred texts and preaching. The presence of a witness, either St. Dominic or St. Peter Martyr, in the painted scenes, was supposed to indicate the attitude the observer should take to the event portrayed, in accordance with the teachings of a popular treatise on prayer that proposed nine different approaches to it. In the *Annunciation*, St. Peter Martyr is meditating on the meeting between Mary and the angel in order to be worthy of explaining it, the fifth mode of prayer. The scene is set in an austere portico that recalls the architecture of the monastery itself. But Mary's dress is incomplete, lacking the layer of blue that used to be painted over the traditional preparation in red earth: this expedient, combined with the position of her head, lower than the angel's, conveys a message of humility. In fact even colors had a meaning. Gold and the blue pigment made from powdered lapis lazuli were the most costly, and therefore reserved for particular scenes and personages. Because of her location, the Madonna in cell 3 could not be given her precious mantle. (E.F.)

Van Eyck

J an van Eyck was born around 1390 in the region of Limburg, perhaps at Maastricht. With his elder brother Hubert, also a painter, he shared several commissions, including the celebrated *Ghent Altarpiece*. The earliest work attributed to him is the *Book of Hours* in Turin, also the fruit of collaboration with his brother and executed around 1417. However, the earliest reliable records of his artistic activity date from 1422-24, when he was at the court of John of Bavaria, count of Holland, in The Hague. On the count's death in 1425, Jan joined Hubert in Flanders, first at Bruges and then at Lille, where he entered the service of Philip III, duke of Burgundy. In 1426 his brother died. The following year he met the painter Robert Campin at Tournai, where he had been sent on a mission by the duke. Between 1428 and 1429 he went to Portugal and Spain, as part of the diplomatic mission that was supposed to bring Princess Isabella, daughter of King John I, back to Flanders to marry the duke. During his stay in the Iberian peninsula he painted several pictures, including the *Stigmata of Saint Francis*, now in the Johnson Collection in Philadelphia.

In 1430 Jan settled in Bruges: his reputation was well established and the duke, in order not to lose his services ("for we shall not find another so excellent in art and in science," as Philip of Burgundy himself wrote), raised his annuity from 100 to 360 livres. Jan van Eyck died in Bruges on July 9, 1441. His contribution to the evolution of Renaissance painting in Flanders, and more generally in Europe, was of fundamental importance, comparable only to the role that Masaccio played in Italy over more or less the same years. His interest in optics and light effects, his development of a painstaking and sometimes virtuoso naturalism and his use of perspective (based on different principles from Brunelleschi's) to create a realistic space are the features that characterize his work and that marked the passage, in Northern Europe, from late Gothic to fully Renaissance art.

Ghent Altarpiece (Adoration of the Lamb)
oil on panel, 350x223 cm (closed),
350x461 cm (open)
St. Bavo, Ghent

The huge polyptych with folding wings is still in its original location, the Joos Vijd Chapel of the cathedral of St. Bavo in Ghent. An inscription that runs along the bottom of the frame of the outer panels tells us that the work was begun by Hubertus van Eyck and finished on May 16, 1432, by his brother Johannes. The polyptych was badly damaged in a fire in 1822, and some parts have been repainted. It is made up of twelve panels, divided into twenty compartments; the eight panels that form the shutters are painted on both sides. On the outside of the shutters (visible when they are

closed) are depicted, in the bottom row, the donors Joos Vijd and his wife Isabelle Borluut, kneeling in front of statues of St. John the Baptist and St. John the Evangelist. The middle row houses the *Annunciation*, and the arched sections at the top, the *Prophets Zechariah and Micah* and the *Erythraean* and *Cumaean Sibyls*. When the shutters are open the work reveals, in the bottom row, the *Adoration of the Mystic Lamb*, divided into five compartments, and in the upper row, *Adam* and *Eve* at the ends, *God Enthroned* in the middle, with the *Virgin* on his right and *Saint John the Baptist* on his left, flanked by angels singing and playing musical instruments. The whole iconography of the polyptych turns around the representation of the *Adoration of the Lamb*: at the center of a meadow, on an altar surrounded by worshiping angels bearing the symbols of the Passion, stands the Lamb, spilling his blood into a chalice; above, in the sky, the radiant dove of the Holy Spirit. In the foreground we see the fountain of life, symbol of the Redemption as an inscription on the octagonal basin makes clear. On the left, in the foreground, are the patriarchs and, further back, the sainted bishops; on the right the martyrs, including Livinus, patron saint of Ghent, and, in the background, the blessed virgins. The compartments at the sides represent the "upright judges" on the right and the knights of Christ on the left: both groups are making their way toward the altar of the Lamb.

Various hypotheses have been made about the genesis of the work. What does seem clear, however, is that Jan brought together two or three pictures that had been executed separately: Hubert painted

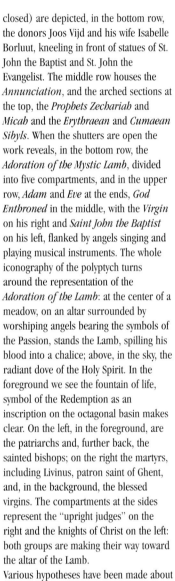

J A N   V A N   E Y C K

part of the *Adoration of the Lamb*, then the figures in the upper row on the inside were added and, finally, at the client's request, the wings. The figure of God may have been commenced by Hubert as a Christ Enthroned (the motif of the pelicans in the brocade is an allusion to the Messiah's sacrifice), and only later been transformed by Jan into an image of

the Father. While the naturalism of the figure's face and hands stirs debate over the extent of Jan's intervention, we can be certain that he was responsible for the virtuoso study of the light and the perspective, clearly visible in details like the crown set at the foot of the throne. The figures of Adam and Eve are entirely his own work. The two nudes, and in particular Adam, reveal a striking capacity for naturalistic representation of the human body, with the light picking out minutiae like the down on the skin. At the same time, the painstaking representation of detail, typical of Flemish painting, does not override the vision of the whole and the illusory character of the figures, which occupy a space rendered in perspective, defined solely by the chiaroscuro and the few shadows cast (Eve's breast, Adam's arm and head). Here Van Eyck, in one of the finest examples of his painting, attempts to create an illusion of life partly through the movement of the male figure, with the right leg stepping forward, a detail only introduced at a later stage, and the foot projecting into the observer's space.

The Madonna of Chancellor Rolin
oil on panel, 66x62 cm
Louvre, Paris

The altarpiece was commissioned by Nicolas Rolin, chancellor of Burgundy and Brabant since 1422, and until 1880 was hung in the sacristy of Autun Cathedral, to which it had probably been donated by the chancellor himself or by his son Jean, who was bishop of Autun. The picture is thought to have been painted around 1435, although some scholars favor an earlier date, and represents the Virgin crowned by an angel and holding on her lap the Child, who is blessing the donor. In the background three arches face onto a terrace with a crenelated wall, beyond which extends a vast landscape with a city on a river. This has been identified with various places, but should probably be seen as an ideal city, although some elements were undoubtedly taken from drawings of real monuments, like the tower of Utrecht Cathedral, visible immediately to the left of Jesus's head.

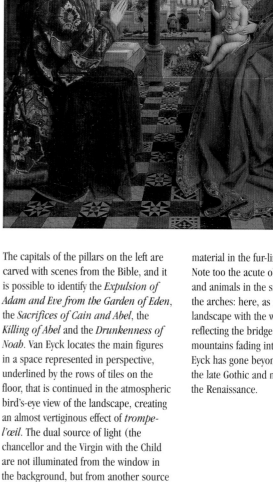

The capitals of the pillars on the left are carved with scenes from the Bible, and it is possible to identify the *Expulsion of Adam and Eve from the Garden of Eden*, the *Sacrifices of Cain and Abel*, the *Killing of Abel* and the *Drunkenness of Noah*. Van Eyck locates the main figures in a space represented in perspective, underlined by the rows of tiles on the floor, that is continued in the atmospheric bird's-eye view of the landscape, creating an almost vertiginous effect of *trompe-l'œil*. The dual source of light (the chancellor and the Virgin with the Child are not illuminated from the window in the background, but from another source that is not visible, located outside the picture) accentuates the spatial effect of the composition and emphasizes the monumentality and solidity of the figures. In the likeness of Rolin the painter displays the full extent of his skill as a portraitist, with the lifelike depiction of the wrinkles, the beard that is just beginning to sprout and the veins and skin of the hands. He also shows a striking ability to convey the texture of

material in the fur-lined brocade robe. Note too the acute observation of plants and animals in the small garden beyond the arches: here, as in the beautiful landscape with the waters of the river reflecting the bridge and the boats and the mountains fading into the distance, van Eyck has gone beyond the naturalism of the late Gothic and moved on to that of the Renaissance.

JAN VAN EYCK

The Arnolfini Marriage Piece
(*The Betrothal of the Arnolfini*)
oil on panel, 82.2x60 cm
National Gallery, London

Considered one of van Eyck's greatest masterpieces, it is signed and dated 1434. Giovanni Arnolfini was a wealthy merchant from Lucca who in 1420 had settled in Bruges, where he had been knighted by Duke Philip the Good and married Giovanna Cenami, also from Lucca. The two are depicted standing, in their bedchamber. In the foreground appears a small dog, symbol of marital fidelity, while on the rear wall a convex mirror, its frame decorated with scenes of the Passion, reflects an image of the room in which we can see, as well as the husband and wife, two male figures, one of them probably the painter himself. It is not certain that Arnolfini's wife is pregnant, as has often been claimed. According to the most accredited interpretation, the work may in fact represent the wedding ceremony, despite the absence of a priest (in this case the two figures would be the witnesses).

From a stylistic viewpoint the painting marks a new level of maturity in van Eyck's work. The window in perspective that lets sunlight into the room, with the still life of fruit on the piece of furniture just under the sill, is one of the most advanced studies of light of the early 15th century and was to serve as a model for painting in Flanders, and elsewhere, until at least the time of Vermeer. Another remarkable feature is the lamp, an extremely difficult exercise in the representation of perspective and light. The very idea of the mirror on the back wall, which presents the image of the room in reverse, distorted by the curvature, constitutes a compositional innovation of great significance: the illusory space of the picture is redoubled and to some extent involves, through the reflection, the space of the observer. The painter's interest in the study of optics and perspective took a different route from the research carried out by Italian artists into the same themes, achieving results that were in many ways more advanced and perhaps unequalled over the course of the 15th century. (S.G.C.)

Van der Weyden

Reconstructing the activity of van der Weyden (Rogier de la Pasture) is difficult owing to the lack of reliable chronological facts: none of his paintings is dated and the information we have on the painter's life is scanty, but a few of his works are mentioned in contemporary sources, and their style is so distinctive that it is possible to identify a consistent and dependable corpus.

It is presumed that Roger van der Weyden was born around the year 1400 at Tournai, and that he was a disciple of Robert Campin (also known as the Master of Flémalle), who passed on to him his taste for realistic and meticulous narration. Van der Weyden also came under the influence of the other great Flemish painter of the time, Jan van Eyck, developing his naturalistic approach and rigorous conception of space. His original style differs from that of both his masters in its greater intensity and drama, and unlike them, found expression especially in works of a religious character. He concentrated his attention on themes of great emotional force and in doing so renewed Christian iconography.

By 1435 Roger had settled in Brussels, and the following year was appointed city painter. It was in this guise, evidently, that he executed (1439) several important murals for the city hall, destroyed over the course of the 17th century. In these years, or sometime around the middle of the century, he painted several panels characterized by the use of warm colors, an accentuated verticality and figures disposed in elegant attitudes, which show a growing interest in the theme of Christ's Passion. Outstanding among these are the *Descent from the Cross* in the Prado and the *Miraflores Altarpiece* in Berlin (Staatliche Museen), of which a replica exists, divided between Granada (Capilla Real) and New York (Metropolitan Museum). The date of the *Annunciation* in the Louvre is still controversial.

A fundamental moment in his formation was the journey to Italy he undertook around 1449. In July of that year Lionello d'Este, marchese of Ferrara, showed a triptych by Roger depicting the *Lamentation over the Body of Christ* to Ciriaco d'Ancona. The link with Lionello d'Este must have continued over the following years as there are records of payments for paintings in the period from 1450 to 1451, some of them relating to works for his study at Belfiore. In 1460, several years after van der Weyden had returned to Flanders, Bianca Maria Sforza sent a Lombard painter, Zanetto Bugatto, to be taught by him.

His Italian experience favored a fertile exchange between the artistic worlds to the south and north of the Alps, and resulted in a marked change in Roger's painting, which became more rigorous in its handling of space, richer in humanity and realism in the presentation of the figures and more distant from the exaggerated dramatic and mystical tones of his beginnings.

Among the more important works executed on his return from Italy are the polyptych with the *Last Judgment* (1450-51, Hôtel-Dieu, Beaune), the *Saint John the Baptist Triptych* (1453, Staatliche Museen, Berlin) and the *Triptych* in the Louvre, presumably commissioned by Catherine of Brabant for her husband Jean Braque, who died at Tournai in 1452. Roger van der Weyden's own life came to an end in Brussels in 1464.

The Descent from the Cross
oil on panel, 220x262 cm
Prado, Madrid

The picture, one of the artist's best known, was painted in 1435 for the chapel of the Confraternity of the Archers in the church of Notre-Dame-hors-les-murs at Louvain, in the Low Countries. Perhaps it is the dedication of the church to the Virgin that explains the unusual importance given to this figure in the composition, where she is represented in the act of slumping to the ground – tenderly supported by St. John and one of the Marys – in an attitude that echoes that of Christ's body. The emphasis placed on the two figures probably serves to underline Mary's importance alongside Christ in the redemption of humanity and, at the same time, generates an unusual composition with a markedly horizontal character. The decision to give the space no sense of depth bestows the solidity of a polychrome sculptural group on the figures, reinforced by the openwork wood carvings painted at the corners of the picture, resembling those of the aedicules and pediments used to house sculptures in high relief. In fact Robert Campin's workshop, where Roger had served his apprenticeship, also produced altars with painted panels and carvings, and it is possible that the artist's idea for this painting derived from those works. Note the painter's great virtuosity in the representation of the fabrics and flesh tones, and the innovation on the iconographic plane of the faces bathed with tears, rather unusual in contemporary Italian painting. This aspect was picked up by the Humanist Bartolomeo Facio in his *De viribus illustribus*, when in a brief assessment of van der Weyden he remarked on the artist's great capacity for the representation of sorrow.

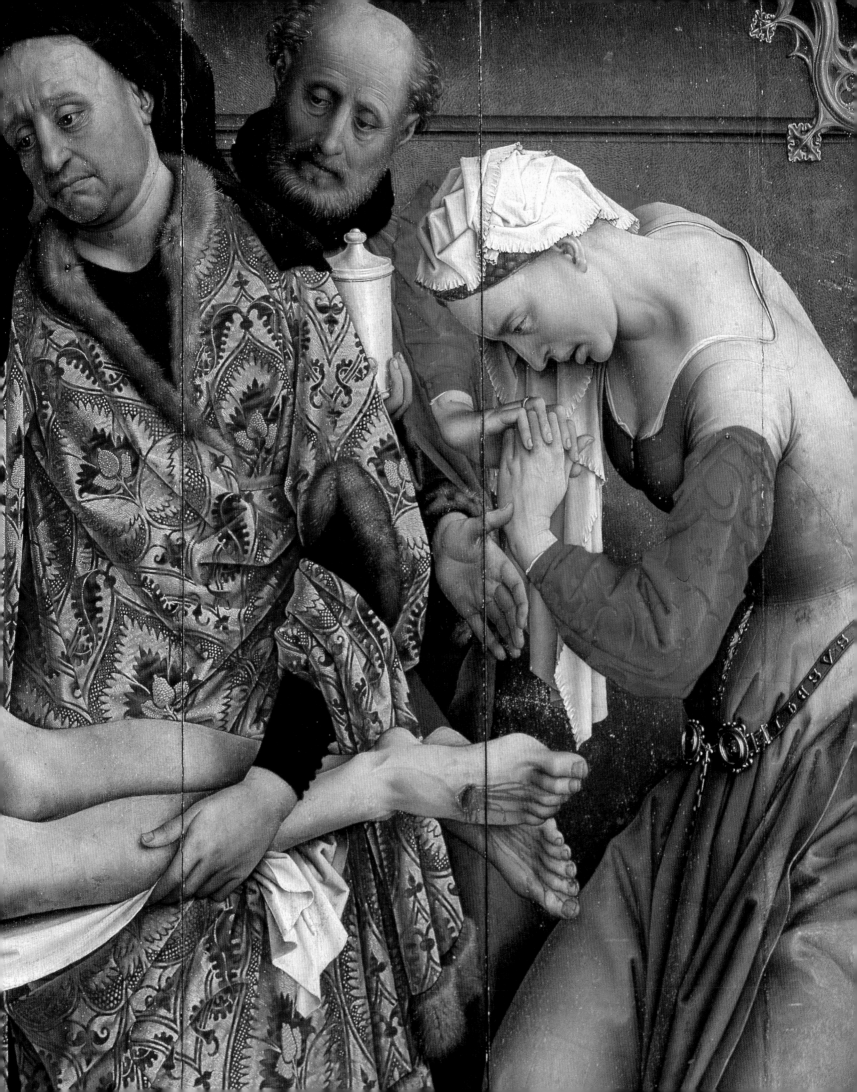

The Deposition in the Tomb
oil on panel, 110x96 cm
Uffizi, Florence

The panel is inspired by a similar painting by Fra Angelico (Alte Pinakothek, Munich) which formed part of the great altarpiece for the church of San Marco in Florence. Van der Weyden seems to share the spirituality of Angelico's work, which was intended to encourage prayer and meditation through display of Christ's body to the faithful in the same manner as the host during the consecration. But he introduces a greater wealth of detail and variety of expressions that attenuate the abstraction of the Tuscan artist's composition. It should also be noted that the subject was foreign to the Flemish tradition, which tended to prefer the theme of the Deposition from the Cross to that of the Lamentation over the Dead Christ so common in Italian art. This does not necessarily imply that the picture was painted during his visit to Italy. On the contrary, it is believed to date from at least ten years later, between 1463 and 1464. The link with Italy appears to lie instead in its commission by the Medici family, *de facto* rulers of Florence at the time. In the view of some scholars, in fact, Nicodemus's face has the features of the most influential member of the family, Cosimo the Elder, who was also responsible for the reconstruction of the church and monastery of San Marco. The connection with the Medici family and Florence resurfaces in the *Madonna and Child with Four Saints* in Frankfurt (Städelsches Institut), where we see Cosmas and Damian, patrons of the Medici, and the lily that symbolizes Florence, in the middle of the predella. (A.F.)

Nativity
oil on panel, 50x37 cm
Capilla Real, Granada

The *Nativity* was originally part of a triptych that also comprised the *Pietà*, housed in the same Capilla Real in Granada, and the *Risen Christ Appearing to the Virgin* now in the Metropolitan Museum of New York. An almost identical version of this work is the altarpiece (now in Berlin) donated in 1445 to the monastery of Miraflores, near Burgos, by King John II of Castile, who had founded the monastery to serve as a mausoleum for himself and his wife, Isabella of Portugal. Today it is thought that this is the older of the two paintings, but that the version in Granada and New York is still van der Weyden's own work.
Particular care has been taken over the setting of the three scenes, which presents several features of interest. In each painting, for example, the color of Mary's dress is different, passing from white to red to blue. In the scene of the *Nativity* the dress is white because the color symbolizes the Virgin's purity, also alluded to by the inscription on the scroll, which is a free adaptation of the apocryphal Gospel of James. The inscription on the border of the mantle also refers to the choice of the Virgin as Mother of Christ, with words taken from the Gospel of St. Luke (1: 46-8) which make up the prayer of the *Magnificat*: "My soul doth magnify the Lord, And my spirit hath rejoiced in God."
The decoration of the portals that frame the individual scenes is highly elaborate, reproducing scenes linked to the main representation.

Memling

The Last Judgment
oil on panel, 221x161 cm
Muzeum Narodowe, Gdansk

We know very little about this artist, but it is presumed that he was born between 1430 and 1440 at Mainz, although his artistic training was Flemish rather than German. In particular, his real education can be traced to a close contact in Brussels, probably as assistant, with Roger van der Weyden, a painter who enjoyed great fame, especially for his capacity to convey emotions. The painters of Brussels belonged to a guild with the usual protectionist aims of regulating the work of its members, defending them against competition and maintaining high standards of quality. Unlike in other cities, the apprenticeship lasted four years and the master painters could only have one apprentice at a time, but provision was made for the presence of assistants, paid by the master and entitled to board and lodging. Memling did not imbibe the disquiet of his master's work: his portraits are set against backdrops of charming scenery and his sentimental tone, which has led to him being considered the Northern European equivalent of Fra Angelico, has resulted over the centuries in recurrent periods of incomprehension and disparagement. In addition, the stylistic uniformity of his works, which show no signs of real evolution, makes their dating difficult.

Van der Weyden died in 1464 and in 1465 Memling became a citizen of Bruges, a city where he would have the opportunity to admire the works of Jan van Eyck and which he was never to leave, becoming the favorite painter of its rich burghers. One of his most fundamental works, in which the artist displayed all his narrative skill, is the *Shrine of Saint Ursula*, in which the relics of the saint and her companions were deposited in 1489 and whose decoration is based on the *Golden Legend* of Jacobus de Voragine, a 13th-century text that for hundreds of years constituted the main source of reference on the lives of the saints for painters and sculptors.

From 1480 to 1490, a fatal decade for Bruges, swept by the winds of history, Memling went on painting pictures that were remote from the chaos of the world, right up until his death in 1494.

In the central panel Christ the Judge is seated on a rainbow, surrounded by the twelve Apostles and by Mary and John the Baptist, intercessors on behalf of humanity. Angels in flight display the instruments of the Passion and sound the trumpets of the Apocalypse. Alongside Christ, who is showing his wounds (to be saved it was necessary to have embraced the Christian faith, which was made manifest in the marks of the Passion), the lily of innocence is set above his gesture of benediction, while the sword of justice corresponds to the gesture of his left hand, turned downward. The rainbow separates the two worlds; on the plane of the earth St. Michael Archangel, at the boundary between the green meadow and the bare ground, weighs the souls: the damned are herded by black demons toward Hell, represented on the right wing of the triptych, while the souls of the elect are welcomed by St. Peter into Heaven, on the left wing. There are no distinctions of race: among both the damned and the blessed appears a figure with black skin.

From the stylistic viewpoint, the figure of Christ, for the one and only time in Memling's career, is almost a copy of the Christ in a polyptych by van der Weyden. The painter has taken great care over representation of the perspective, the light and the reflections (especially on the globe and on the archangel's armor). Many of the elect have realistic features, suggesting that some personages had had their portraits inserted into the painting. The adventurous history of the triptych, painted around 1467-71, commences with its commission by Angelo Tani, director of the branch of the bank owned by the Florentine family of the Medici in Bruges, probably on the occasion of his marriage to Caterina Tanagli, as the representation of the clients on the outer shutters of the wings suggests. It must have been intended for the Tani Chapel dedicated to St. Michael in the Badia of Fiesole near Florence, a church that the Medici had had built to celebrate the glory of the family and the power of the

bank: in fact all the chapels in the south aisle were set aside for its agents. Tani would not be reappointed and his place was taken, in 1465, by Tommaso Portinari, who provided the Burgundian court with large sums of money and was in exchange authorized to levy duties on the import of wool into the Low Countries. And Portinari is the man portrayed on the balance on the side of the blessed: his head has been painted over the one that was there before, suggesting that he may have contributed to the financing of the picture. Portinari also acquired three unused galleys from the duke of Burgundy and converted them into merchant ships flying the Burgundian flag but crewed by Italians. In 1473 Memling's *Judgment* was loaded on board the galley *San Matteo*, sailing for England with a cargo of merchandise from Italy: alum, gold brocade, satin, damask and gold thread. But the vessel was attacked by a warship of the Hanseatic League commanded by the privateer Paul Benecke, who took part of the booty to Danzig. Among the spoils was the triptych, which was donated to the city's cathedral. The adventures of the altarpiece were not over yet: in 1806 it was requisitioned by Napoleon's troops, taken to Paris and hung in the Louvre, then called the Musée Napoléon. Attributed at that time to van Eyck, it was much admired by visitors. The only dissenting voice was that of the writer Stendhal: "One Sunday, go to the museum. You will find, at a certain point in the gallery, your passage blocked by the crowd gathered in front of a picture: and every Sunday in front of the same picture. You will think it must be a masterpiece. Not a bit of it. It is a daub of the German School: it represents the *Last Judgment*. People enjoy looking at the grimaces of the damned."

The Passion of Christ
oil on panel, 56.7x92.2 cm
Galleria Sabauda, Turin

An example of simultaneous narration (datable to around 1470-71) in which, through a cunning use of perspective, the various moments in the Passion of Christ are arranged in succession in the painting. The unifying elements are Jerusalem, represented as a medieval city, and the lighting of the scene: the sun is rising at the top right, a device which allows the front part on the left to remain in shadow, permitting the simultaneous representation of different times of day, from dawn to night. The donors are portrayed in the foreground on the right and left, in the customary attitude of prayer: they can be identified as Tommaso Portinari, a Florentine banker in Bruges, and his wife.

In 1470 a friend of Portinari's, Anselm Adornes, had made a pilgrimage to the Holy Land and his son had written down a detailed account of the journey. The painting appears to be a reconstruction of the holy places at which the pilgrim could obtain indulgences and is connected with the *devotio moderna*, a movement that urged the believer to participate mentally in the life of Christ: even an "imaginary pilgrimage," made by looking at a painting, was valid for the acquisition of indulgences.

At the top, from the left, we see the *Entry of Christ into Jerusalem*, then the *Expulsion of the Merchants from the Temple*. *Judas's Betrayal* of Jesus and the *Last Supper* are illuminated by the light of torches. And then, in the foreground on the left, the *Agony in the Garden* and the *Arrest of Jesus* take place at night. The peacock on the wall of the city symbolizes the Resurrection and eternal life; the spear of the soldier on the left indicates the direction of the narrative. Peter denies Christ, who is taken before Pilate and then scourged. Christ is crowned with thorns and shown to the people (*Ecce homo*), while the cross is constructed. The procession continues outside the walls of the city on the road to Calvary, with Christ stumbling and looking toward the observer. Christ is nailed to the cross, whose position on the ground

shows us the direction to follow. And it is the *Crucifixion* that dominates the scene. The descent from the cross is followed by the *Deposition in the Tomb* and then the *Resurrection*, with the successive apparitions of Christ, *Noli me tangere*, the *Pilgrims at Emmaus*, and *Christ on the Sea of Galilee*, immersed in the landscape.

Adoration of the Magi (*Triptych of Jan Crabbe*)
oil on panel, 147x96.4 cm (central panel), 98.2x63.3 cm (left panel), 98x63.6 cm (right panel)
Museo del Prado, Madrid

The central part of the triptych, painted around 1470-72, represents the *Adoration of the Magi*, in the same architectural setting as the left-hand

panel with the *Nativity*, while the panel on the right depicts the *Presentation in the Temple*. The arrangement of the figures is simple and clear. In the *Adoration* the Virgin is placed in front of a column that recalls her function as pillar of the Church. On the left we see the blue flag with gold stars of the European king, on the right the blue one with the crescent moon and star of the Oriental king and the white one of the

African king, represented, unusually, as a man of color: the kings symbolize the three known continents, as well as the three ages of man. The donors are probably portrayed in the *Presentation*, in the guise of the prophetess Anna and the young man on the right, perhaps related to each other and linked to Ter Duinen Abbey, one of the most powerful of the Cistercian Order. Its abbot was Jan Crabbe, a great patron of the sciences and arts and political adviser to Mary of Burgundy and Maximilian of Austria. (E.F.)

Piero della Francesca

Piero della Francesca was born at Borgo San Sepolcro (now Sansepolcro) around 1415. He probably received his training in Florence, in the workshop of Domenico Veneziano, as we are told by a document of 1439. In 1445 he was commissioned to paint a polyptych for the Confraternita della Misericordia of Sansepolcro, but did not finish it until around 1460. He was active at the castle of the Este in Ferrara, and at the Tempio Malatestiano in Rimini. It was probably at the court of Sigismondo Pandolfo that he came into contact with Leon Battista Alberti, who had a great influence on Piero, both as a painter and as a theorist on art. Between 1452 and 1458 he executed the work that can be considered his masterpiece, the frescoes in the choir of the church of San Francesco in Arezzo representing the *Legend of the True Cross*. Then he set off for Rome, where he painted in the Vatican for Pope Pius II Piccolomini (but the works of the Roman period have not survived). In the 1460s and '70s he worked in Urbino, at the court of Federico da Montefeltro, for whom he painted some of his most celebrated pictures, such as the *Flagellation* (Galleria Nazionale delle Marche, Urbino), the portraits and triumphs of Federico and his wife Battista Sforza (Galleria degli Uffizi, Florence) and the *Brera Madonna*. In the last years of his life he was forced to stop painting by the progressive loss of his eyesight. He died at Arezzo in 1492.

Piero was one of the great innovators of the early Renaissance: his use of light and color to create a spatial effect, in what Roberto Longhi called a "perspective synthesis of form-color," constitutes one of the highest meditations on painting of the 15th century in Italy, in dialogue with the most advanced experiments of the Flemish artists, including the technical ones. Piero was also an eminent theorist and mathematician: his most important treatise is the *De perspectiva pingendi*, probably written in the early 1470s, on the use of mathematical perspective in painting, and significantly addressed to the "many painters who deprecate perspective, as they do not understand the force of the lines and angles that are produced by it." Other works are the *Libellus de quinque corporibus regularibus*, a short treatise on solid geometry, and the *Trattato d'abaco*, which deals with problems of mathematics and elementary algebra and is aimed largely at merchants.

Baptism of Christ
tempera on panel, 167x116 cm
National Gallery, London

One of Piero's early works, perhaps painted before 1450, it was intended for the Badia Camaldolese at Sansepolcro. Here the influence of the Florentine painting of the thirties still appears very strong: an echo of Masaccio's nudes in the Brancacci Chapel can be seen in the catechumen getting undressed in the background on the left, while the coloring harks back to Piero's master, Domenico Veneziano. The figures in the background, wearing tall hats in the Greek manner, are a reference to the Byzantine prelates and scholars who had come to Italy for the Council that agreed on a reunion of the Catholic and Orthodox Churches in 1439. The fact that the picture was painted for a Camaldolensian abbey renders this reference more credible, since one of the principal proponents of the accord with the Eastern Church was Ambrogio Traversari, general of the Camaldolensian Order. The balance of the composition, with the tree marking the golden section of the panel, seems to have already been influenced by Leon Battista Alberti's treatise on painting, although it may be the fruit of a parallel meditation on the same themes by Piero.

Legend of the True Cross: Death of Adam
fresco, 390x747 cm
San Francesco, Arezzo

The decoration of the chapel of the choir of San Francesco was commissioned in 1447 by the Bacci family from the elderly painter Bicci di Lorenzo, who died in 1452 after painting the frescoes on the ceiling. Piero della Francesca then took over the job. The internal chronology of the cycle is fairly controversial, but it is likely that the work was completed before the artist's journey to Rome in 1458. The paintings illustrate the story of the wood from which the Cross was made, as related by Jacobus de Voragine in the

Golden Legend. Shortly before his death Adam sends his son Seth to ask the angel guarding the garden of Eden for the oil of mercy needed to cure him; Seth obtains a sprig of a miraculous plant, but on his return finds his father already dead. The scene illustrated here shows Adam on the right, supported by Eve, entrusting his son with the task; in the background we see Seth in conversation with the angel and then, on the left, the death of Adam, while in the middle stands the tree that grew from the sprig. From that tree would be hewn a piece of wood that, because of a prophecy on the fall of the kingdom of Israel, was discarded during the construction of the Temple and used as a bridge over a river. When the queen of

Sheba comes to visit Solomon she has a premonition that the wood will be used to make the Cross and kneels in adoration of it. The narration then moves on to the episodes following the Crucifixion: after the dream of Constantine and his victory over Maxentius, his mother Helena finds the true cross, which had been buried, and proves its authenticity by a miraculous resurrection. The final scenes represent the *Victory of Heraclius over the Pagan Chosroes*, who had stolen the Cross, and the *Exaltation of the Cross*, or the entrance of Heraclius into Jerusalem with the sacred relic. The *Death of Adam* was the first scene to be painted and can therefore be dated to around 1452, in years not too distant from his Florentine

training. The fact that this still exercised a strong influence over Piero is apparent from the incisive drawing, close in some ways to that of Andrea del Castagno. But here we are looking at the work of a mature painter, capable of following his own, highly original course of artistic development, in search of a perfectly balanced composition, and above all a light and coloring that clearly define the forms. The citations from antiquity, like the figures of the young man leaning on a stick and of Seth, in the scene on the right, drawn from Scopas's *Pothos* and from the so-called *Condottiere of Tivoli* respectively, or again, the mourning figure with her arms spread, are inserted naturally into the context of Piero's fresco, which is never "archeological" but a fully "classical" work.

Madonna di Senigallia
panel, 61x53.5 cm
Galleria Nazionale delle Marche, Urbino

Painted for the church of Santa Maria delle Grazie extra Moenia at Senigallia, the panel is datable to the 1470s, during the time the painter spent in Urbino. The representation of the Virgin with the Child in her arms flanked by two angels conceals religious symbols in the depiction of its elegant Renaissance setting, a practice typical of the paintings of the period: the sunlight that filters through the window on the left is meant to signify the immaculate conception, the wicker basket on the shelf on the right is a reference to Moses as a prefiguration of Christ, while the box for the Host, located just above, alludes to the sacrifice of Jesus, as does the coral hanging around the Child's neck. The work is of great technical and stylistic interest: the use of oil as a medium testifies to Piero's exposure to Flemish art at the Montefeltro court, where Justus of Ghent (Joos van Wassenhove) was active. In the works of these years the influence of Flemish painting was not limited to the technique, but also affected his style: the light

entering through the window, for instance, would not have been conceivable without the example, however indirect, of van Eyck, and the painstaking representation of the objects, almost as if they had been examined through a lens, also appears to be of Flemish derivation. Northern European art provided Piero with the means he needed to take the research into light that had characterized his work right from the beginning to a new and unprecedented level.
(S.G.C.)

Antonello da Messina

I t is thought that Antonello was born in Messina between 1420 and 1430. We know nothing of the years of his training, but it is presumed that he served an apprenticeship around 1445 with the painter Colantonio in Naples, under Aragonese rule at the time and a cosmopolitan place that drew artists and works from Spain, Provence, Burgundy and Flanders.

In fact his earliest work can be traced in a picture by Colantonio, the *Altarpiece of Saint Jerome* (1445), where he is believed to have painted the pillars with *Blessed Franciscan Souls*. There is no question about his authorship of the *Crucifixion* in Bucharest (*c.* 1450, Muzeul de Arta), a work in which the influence of Flemish painting is still strong and that is therefore thought to date from the beginning of his career. Two more small panels, *Visit of the Three Angels to Abraham* and *Saint Jerome in His Study* (Museo della Magna Grecia, Reggio Calabria) were painted around 1460. After 1465 he left Sicily and did not return until 1471: it may have been during this undocumented period that Antonello came into contact with works that exemplified the new conception of space and light developed by the Italian painting of the Renaissance, possibly in Rome where Piero della Francesca and Fra Angelico were present.

The last decade of his activity probably opened with the *Ecce homo* in the Metropolitan Museum of New York, datable to 1470. The *Portrait of a Man* (Museo Mandralisca, Cefalù), considered one of his first portraits, may date from the same year. The pictures of this period show the maturation of his style under the influence of the art of Central Italy. The artist proposes a new figurative language capable of fusing the meticulous description of reality, clearly derived from Flemish painting, with the new handling of space and perspective typical of Piero della Francesca.

The last years of his career are better documented: the *Portrait of a Man* (Staatliche Museen, Berlin) and the *Ecce homo* (formerly in Vienna, lost during the Second World War) have been dated to 1474. His subsequent visit to Venice in 1474-75 brought the luministic and spatial rigor of his painting into contact with the soft colors and lyricism of Giovanni Bellini. It is likely that Antonello concentrated on portrait painting while in Venice, which would have earned him broader and more rapid approval. Marco Antonio Michiel, a Venetian writer who lived in the first half of the 16th century, mentions two portraits by Antonello that no longer exist, "Alvise Pasqualino" and "Michele Vianello," and also recalls having seen a *Saint Jerome in His Study* at Pasqualino's house. If, as seems plausible, this *Saint Jerome* is the same as the one now in the National Gallery of London, the panel would not date from his youth, as has long been thought, but from 1475, and the influence of the works of Jan van Eyck that is evident in the painting should be considered a sort of homage to the great master on the part of an already established artist with a style all of his own.

In Venice Antonello also painted the *Christ Giving His Blessing* (1475, National Gallery, London), the *San Cassiano Altarpiece* (1476, Kunsthistorisches Museum, Vienna), and the *Saint Sebastian* (1476, Gemäldegalerie, Dresden). By the September of 1476 the artist was already back in Messina, and his last dated work is the *Portrait of a Man* (Staatliche Museen, Berlin) of 1478. Antonello died in Messina in February 1479. The exponent of a new and complex figurative language, he was to exercise a lasting influence on European Renaissance art.

Portrait of a Man
Museo della Fondazione
Mondralisca, Cefalù

ANTONELLO DA MESSINA

Portrait of a Man

oil on panel, 30x25 cm
Museo della Fondazione Mandralisca, Cefalù

The three-quarters position in which the mysterious personage is presented constitutes an innovation for Italian portraiture, given that hitherto it had been used solely for known figures in compositions of various kinds (such as the self-portrait of Masaccio in the *Scenes from the Life of Saint Peter* in the Brancacci Chapel, Florence). In Europe this new approach had been introduced by Jan van Eyck in celebrated works like the so-called *Tymotheos* (1432, National Gallery, London), and *Cardinal Albergati* (1438, Kunsthistorisches Museum, Vienna). These paintings, and many others of the Flemish school from the same decades, also have in common with Antonello's work the use of oil as a medium, the black background and a marked predilection for the limpid representation of details. Such elements were not in themselves a novelty in Italian painting, but the fact that they all recur in the portraits executed by Antonello highlights the importance of his role as the principal propagator of the Northern European style of painting in Italy. According to some, this is Antonello's earliest portrait. It is certainly the only one to have survived in Sicily and is thought to have been acquired on Lipari by Baron Mandralisca around the middle of the 19th century.

Salvator mundi

oil on panel, 38.7x29.8 cm
National Gallery, London

The principal model of reference for Antonello's composition, highly unusual for Italian painting, seems to have been the central panel of van der Weyden's *Braque Triptych* (Louvre, Paris) representing *Christ Giving His Blessing between Mourners*. In fact the work of the Flemish painter was well known and widely imitated in Northern Europe, and there are many paintings derived from it that present similarities with Antonello's panel. However, there is one element that

characterizes and differentiates the Sicilian painter's *Salvator mundi* from these northern works: the position of the blessing hand, represented with a very strong foreshortening that seems to project it out of the plane of the picture. Through this bold handling of perspective – also used for the *Virgin Annunciate* in Palermo (Galleria Regionale della Sicilia) and the Madonna of the *San Cassiano Altarpiece* (Kunsthistorisches Museum, Vienna) – Antonello sought to bring observers into the painting and arouse

their wonder at his ability to imitate reality. Even the scroll that bears the date and signature of the painter, a genuine *trompe-l'œil*, responds to the same criteria of imitation of the real. Antonello seeks to deceive observers by inducing them to believe that the small sheet of paper with numerous folds has simply been stuck onto the painting rather than being part of it. The inscription also gives the date, which has been read either as 1465 or 1475; recently the reading of it as 1475 has prevailed.

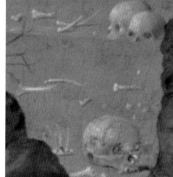

Dead Christ Supported by an Angel
(*Man of Sorrows*)
oil on panel, 74x51 cm
Prado, Madrid

In this splendid painting depicting Christ supported by an angel, the artist has renounced a faithful representation of the biblical text in favor of a fervent meditation on Christ's sacrifice. The theme was popular in 15th-century Italian painting and was made famous by Giovanni Bellini, who produced numerous versions of it, the oldest of which is in the Museo Correr in Venice.
All the pictures of this subject painted in the Venetian area before 1470, inspired by Donatello's bas-relief for the church of Il Santo in Padua, present the figure of Christ in a frontal position. But Antonello sets it diagonally both in the *Man of Sorrows* he painted in Venice (Museo Correr) and in the later version in the Prado, also begun in the lagoon city but probably finished on his return to Messina. It is not certain that Antonello was the first to break with the established tradition of the frontal position because Giovanni Bellini, in the *Dead Christ Supported by Angels* in the Vatican Museums, placed Christ at a marked angle. But the controversial dating of this work does not yet allow us to assign the credit for the innovation to either of the artists.
The panel in the Prado presents features of interest with regard to the landscape as well, where the barren area on the right is strewn with shattered tree trunks, skulls

and human bones, probably a reference to the transience of life. The broken tree from which a new branch is sprouting – also present in the *Crucifixions* in Bucharest and Antwerp – seems to allude to the sacrifice of Christ, who died so that believers could be born into a new life. In the background we see Jerusalem, whose representation may be based on the city of Messina. It is possible that some parts of the landscape should be ascribed to the

painter's son, Jacobello.
Once again the greatest merit of the work lies in the fusion between the Flemish taste for detail and the monumentality and plasticity of the figures, typical of the Italian figurative language. (A.F.)

Mantegna

B orn in 1431 at Isola di Carturo, between Padua and Vicenza, in 1441 he entered the workshop of Francesco Squarcione, who legally adopted him the following year. At the age of just seventeen, having already broken his ties with the head of the Paduan workshop, he was given the prestigious task of participating in the decoration of the Ovetari Chapel in the Eremitani Church in Padua. The scenes entrusted to him, completed by 1453 and largely destroyed during the Second World War, revealed to his contemporaries one of the greatest talents of the age. The confidence he showed in the use of perspective, with bold *sotto in su* foreshortenings to enhance the monumentality of the figures, and the display of a knowledge of archeology hitherto never seen in Northern Italian painting (undoubtedly influenced by his father-in-law Jacopo Bellini's book of antiquarian drawings) immediately made the young Mantegna a favorite with Humanists. Ludovico Gonzaga summoned him to the court of Mantua in 1457: Andrea moved there in 1460, and stayed in the city until his death, in 1506. He produced one of his finest works, the *Camera degli Sposi* for the Gonzaga between 1473 and 1474: on the walls of a small room, he painted *trompe-l'œil* spaces in perspective, exteriors and interiors peopled with life-size figures, in a virtuosity of illusion that reached its peak in the wonderful invention of the mock oculus on the ceiling, from which, against the background of the sky, peer down winged putti. The hard and sharp drawing that characterized his early works was tempered over the years into a more mellow naturalism, culminating in the masterpiece of the latter part of his career, the *Triumphs of Caesar*, climax of a now mature classicism that foreshadowed the "grand manner" of the 16th century and that was destined for lasting fame. In the last years of his life Mantegna was called on by Isabella d'Este, even though she preferred younger and more up-to-date artists, to contribute to the decoration of her celebrated Studiolo. Right from the outset Andrea had become a model for painters from not just Northern Italy but other parts of the peninsula as well, and was considered the greatest master of themes from antiquity of the time. Many of his compositions were highly influential and were diffused through engravings, sometimes made by the artist himself.

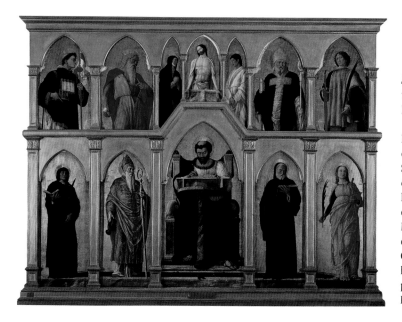

Saint Luke Polyptych
tempera on panel, 178x227 cm
Pinacoteca di Brera, Milan

Painted between 1453 and 1454 for the chapel of San Luca in the church of Santa Giustina at Padua, the polyptych, despite the archaic character of the layout, probably requested by the clients, reflects the first evolution in Mantegna's style following the revelation of the Ovetari Chapel in the Eremitani Church. The assured and complex handling of perspective adopts a low point of view that harks back to the Paduan frescoes, but this is combined with a chromatic and luministic sensibility that already appears to have been influenced by his contacts with the Venetian workshop of the Bellini. In fact it was in 1453 that Mantegna had married Jacopo Bellini's daughter Nicolosia. Note for example St. Justina's cloak on the right, or the very fine pieces of painting in the pluvials of St. Prosdocimus, in the lower row, and St. Augustine in the upper one. The depiction of the faces of the mourners in the *Pietà* with the Madonna and St. John testifies to the attention Mantegna paid to the dramatic and pathetic representation of human expressions.

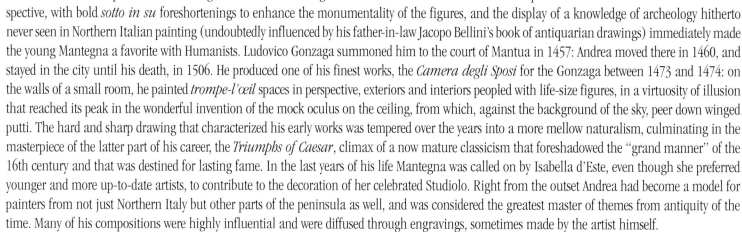

Portrait of Francesco Gonzaga
oil on panel, 25.5x18 cm
Gallerie Nazionali di Capodimonte, Naples

Portrait of Carlo de' Medici
tempera on panel, 40.5x29.5 cm
Galleria degli Uffizi, Florence

As court painter to the Gonzaga, Mantegna was often required to paint official portraits. The young man depicted in the panel in the Gallerie Nazionali di Capodimonte is probably Francesco Gonzaga, who was made a cardinal at the age of just sixteen, in 1462. In reality the dress worn by the figure is that of an apostolic protonotary, and the work must date from around 1460 (it may be the first picture to have been commissioned from Mantegna by Ludovico Gonzaga). The panel is badly worn, but still reveals the artist's ability to capture his sitter's appearance and psychology in the genre of the portrait in profile, which became almost obligatory around the middle of the 15th century, on the example of classical coins and medals.

The picture of Carlo de' Medici, who was also made an apostolic protonotary in 1463, as well as rector of Prato, was painted during Andrea's brief stay in Florence in 1466: here the sitter is portrayed in three-quarter profile, in the Flemish manner, and great attention is paid to the red drapery, from which emerges the face, minutely described with the graphic force typical of Mantegna in these years. The naturalistic observation of the bleary eyes allows the painter to base the work on a few variations of the warm shades of color and further emphasize the intensity of the prelate's gaze.

ANDREA MANTEGNA

Triumph of Caesar: Triumphal Chariot, Trophies and War Machines
tempera on canvas, 267x278 cm
Hampton Court, England

The series of nine canvases with the *Triumphs of Caesar* was commissioned from Mantegna by Francesco Gonzaga around 1485 for Mantua Castle and was probably intended to decorate the large hall that precedes the *Camera degli Sposi* on the *piano nobile*. However, seven of the canvases were soon moved to the Palazzo of San Sebastiano and hung alongside other scenes, painted by Lorenzo Costa, celebrating the marchese's own triumphs. From a letter written by Francesco Gonzaga in 1489 we learn that the canvases were considered the work of Mantegna's hand and mind, and so it is likely that he was also responsible for the iconographic program. The theme was one of the favorites in Humanistic culture: the main source was Suetonius, who describes Caesar's five triumphs, here united in a single parade. The artist also had access to learned texts on antiquity, such as Roberto Valturio's *De re militari*, published in Verona in 1472. Mantegna devoted many years to the execution of the work, interrupted by his stay in Rome from 1488 to 1490, and did not

complete it until 1494. In this masterpiece the artist, as Giorgio Vasari pointed out, succeeded in combining a naturalism and a softness of line not to be found in his early works with the Humanistic and archeological style of painting in which he remained unsurpassed. Even the conception of the series of canvases, with the triumphal parade proceeding from one to the other, appears innovative, especially in the emphasis placed on the movement of the figures, almost life size, which take up the whole of the composition without leaving any room for hints of the setting. The idea of a classicism that is dynamic rather than static constitutes one of the main reasons for the success of the work, already admired by the artist's contemporaries: Mantegna himself was very proud of it and, writing to his son Francesco from Rome to tell him to take care of the conservation of the paintings, declared "in truth I am not ashamed of having done them." The *Triumphs* became one of the very few masterpieces of the 15th century to retain a high reputation right up until the 17th: Rubens was greatly impressed by them and cited them in his *Triumphs*, and Charles I of England decided to acquire them for his collections in 1629. (S.G.C.)

IMP·IVLIO·CAESARI
OB·GALLIAM·DEVICT·
MILITARI·POTENCIA
TRIVMPHVS
DECRETVS·INVIDIA
SPRETA·SVPERATA·

Giovanni Bellini

Giovanni Bellini, son of the painter Jacopo, was born in Venice, probably in 1433. For over fifty years, up until his death in Venice in 1516, he was the greatest figure in Venetian painting, showing himself capable of constant stylistic innovation right up to the last years of his very long career. His early works are close to his father's style and influenced by the production of the Vivarini workshop, commencing with the altarpiece for the Gattamelata Chapel which he signed along with Jacopo and his brother Gentile in 1460. The work carried out in Padua by Andrea Mantegna, who had married his sister Nicolosia in 1453, played a decisive role in Giovanni's artistic development. On several occasions the artist attempted to emulate Andrea's example, in pictures like the *Transfiguration*, now in the National Gallery of London, or the *Presentation in the Temple* in the Galleria Querini Stampalia in Venice. Yet his artistic interests were to take him down very different roads from those trod by his illustrious relative, in search of a style of painting that would explore the atmospheric effects of light and color. His encounter in 1475 with Antonello da Messina, who had quite independently gone in a similar direction, marked a turning point in Giovanni's art: the mutual influence of the two artists, in an inextricable relationship of give and take, was one of the central factors in the history of the Venetian painting, and the art of the Renaissance in general. Even in his maturity and old age, however, Bellini never ceased to renew his style, eventually foreshadowing, in his use of light and color, the tonalism that was to be fully developed by Giorgione and Titian at the beginning of the 16th century. Giovanni had considerable success in his lifetime, and set up a workshop that produced, under his supervision, pictures for a very large number of clients. In 1483 he was appointed official painter of the Repubblica Serenissima, and in the last years of his life the invitation from Isabella d'Este to participate in the decoration of her Studiolo and the admiration of him expressed by the German painter Albrecht Dürer, who regarded him as "still the best of all," were a testimony to the level of fame and recognition he had attained among his contemporaries.

Presentation in the Temple
tempera on panel, 80x105 cm
Galleria Querini Stampalia, Venice

According to St. Luke's Gospel (2: 22-38), once the time of purification was over, Jesus was presented at the temple in Jerusalem for the ritual sacrifice, as prescribed by Jewish law. At the temple Simeon and Anna recognized the Child as the Messiah. Painted at the end of the 1460s, the work is an almost exact copy of a picture of the same subject executed not long before by Andrea Mantegna. The figures in the painting have traditionally been identified as members of the artist's family, with the last on the right a self-portrait and the woman on the left a portrait of his mother. In comparison with Mantegna's composition, enclosed on all four sides by a marble frame, Bellini's work has more relaxed rhythms, with the figures arranged behind a broad parapet. The greater attention paid to effects of light and the search for a warm coloring open to atmospheric effects, still discernible today from the best-preserved parts such as the priest's cowl, reflect the artistic maturity that had been attained by the young Bellini.

Transfiguration

oil on panel, 115x151.5 cm
Gallerie Nazionali di Capodimonte, Naples

The work was painted for the Fioccardo Chapel in Vicenza Cathedral and arrived in the Capodimonte Galleries as part of the Farnese collection. Datable to around 1480, it is signed IOANNES BELLI(NUS) on the small scroll hanging on the fence

in the foreground. Like other pictures painted by Bellini in these years (e.g. the *Saint Francis in Ecstasy* in the Frick Collection, New York, dating from a few years earlier), the *Transfiguration* is wholly centered on the theme of sunlight and its chromatic and atmospheric effects. In the foreground the rocks are tinged with warm tones, as are the walls of the city on the right, while cold colors dominate in the sky, as often happens in the early hours of the morning, as the sun rises (and in fact the light is coming from the bottom left). On Christ's robe, which, caught by the light, appears "white and glistening" (as it is described in Gospel according to Luke, 9: 29), his right hand casts a reddish shadow, an idea that anticipates the tonalism of 16th-century Venetian painting. In the same way, on the right, St. John's dark cloak is tinged with purplish glows. At top left gather darker clouds which, again following the Gospel account (Luke 9: 34-5), represent the manifestation of God the Father: "And there came a voice out of the cloud, saying, This is my beloved Son: hear him." The work has been subjected to some restoration: the heads of St. James and St. Peter have been repainted, along with details of the landscape.

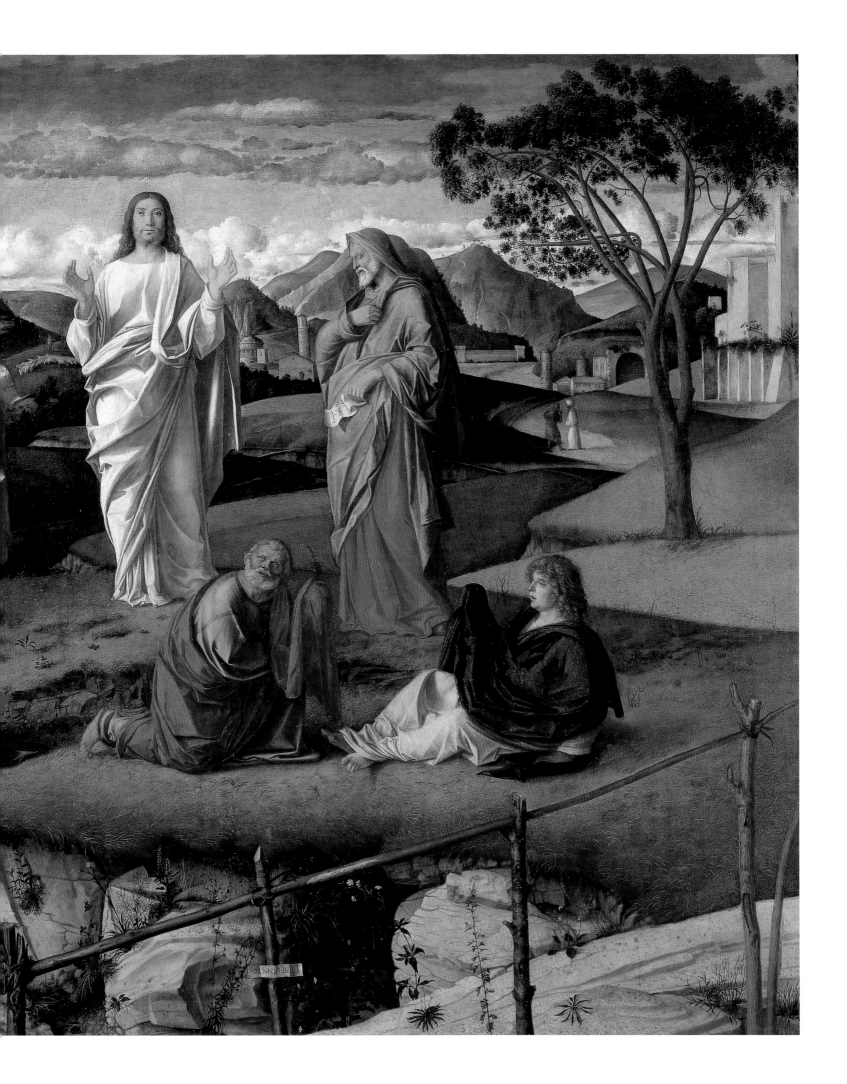

San Zaccaria Altarpiece
(*Enthroned Madonna with Four Saints*)
transferred onto canvas from panel,
500x235 cm
San Zaccaria, Venice

The masterpiece of Bellini's late activity, the work is signed and dated 1505. It is a *sacra conversazione* set in a loggia closed at the back by an apse with a conch decorated with mosaic. At the top hang a lamp and an ostrich egg, symbol of Mary's virgin motherhood. Alongside the Virgin and Child, seated on a throne at whose feet an angel is playing the *lira da braccio*, are represented, from left to right, St. Peter, St. Catherine of Alexandria, St. Lucy and St. Jerome. The picture, originally arched, was painted on panel and transferred onto canvas in the Napoleonic era, when it was taken to Paris. It marks the culmination of Bellini's long quest for an atmospheric kind of painting and a classical and magniloquent balance of composition. The architectural setting is in a style close to that of the Lombardo family of sculptors who were active at the time in Venice, and must originally have looked as if it were a continuation of the chapel's real architecture. The broad arches at the sides open onto a daytime landscape, dominated by a blue and cloudy sky: so the scene is at once indoors and outdoors, and the sunlight penetrates between the figures, illuminating the Madonna on her tall throne, her blue cloak and the face of the Magdalen on the right, while elsewhere deep and warm shadows gather, as in the beautiful foliage of the mosaic. The parallel figures of St. Peter and St. Jerome, with their faces lit from behind in an unprecedented and bold solution, mark the distance between the foreground and the rest of the composition and appear to be set in the same warm semidarkness as the interior of the church from which the observer admires the work. Rightly considered the first great Venetian altarpiece of the 16th century, the work should be seen in relation to the emergence of Giorgione, who may have had an influence on the late manner of the elderly painter.
(S.G.C.)

Bosch

Hieronymus Bosch was born around 1450 in 's-Hertogenbosch, now in the Netherlands, and remained there until his death, in 1516. He belonged to a family of painters, and probably served his apprenticeship in the family workshop. He worked for various local churches, upper middle-class families and aristocrats like Count Henry III of Nassau, who probably commissioned the *Garden of Earthly Delights* (Prado, Madrid). His fame must have already spread wide by 1504, when Philip the Fair ordered from him a *Last Judgment*, from which a fragment now in the Alte Pinakothek of Munich may have come. His works were also collected by Isabella the Catholic, queen of Spain, and the high prelate Philip of Burgundy, who owned *The Cure of Folly* (Prado, Madrid). While it is evident that his works were widely appreciated at the time, it is less clear whether the understanding of their deeper significance was equally widespread. Bosch was the most eclectic and enigmatic Flemish painter of the 16th century, and the atmosphere and iconography of his religious works differ profoundly from the analogous pictures of his contemporaries. References to astrology, alchemy, local folklore and witchcraft are mixed with scenes from the exemplary lives of saints and themes from the Bible, contributing to the creation of a dense web of late medieval symbolism. Today it is no longer possible to assign a precise meaning to each of his fantastic images, but a recurrent theme can be identified in his painting: the human propensity for sin, wanton pleasure and lust, with its consequent eternal damnation.

The earliest works of Bosch to have survived depict biblical scenes like the *Ecce homo* (Städelsches Kunstinstitut, Frankfurt, and Museum of Fine Arts, Boston) and the *Road to Calvary* (Kunsthistorisches Museum, Vienna), datable to around 1480. Subsequently he painted *The Seven Deadly Sins and the Four Last Things* (Prado, Madrid). *The Ship of Fools* (Louvre, Paris) should be dated to around 1490.

His later works, of which there exist numerous replicas of controversial date, can be classified on the basis of iconographic criteria. The most common theme is undoubtedly the Last Judgment: in addition to the painting commissioned by Philip the Fair in 1504, the subject appears in four panels representing *Paradise and Hell* (Doge's Palace, Venice) and in the triptych in Vienna (Akademie der bildenden Künste), whose wings show affinities with those of the triptych of the *Haywain* (Prado, Madrid).

Another theme in which he displayed an interest on several occasions was that of the hermit saint: *Saint John the Baptist in the Wilderness* (Museo Lázaro Galdiano, Madrid) and *Saint Jerome* (Musée des Beaux-Arts, Ghent). He represented St. Anthony several times, in the left wing of the *Crucifixion of Saint Julia* (Venice, Palazzo Ducale), in the *Temptation of Saint Anthony Triptych* (Museu Nacional de Arte Antiga, Lisbon) and in the *Temptation of Saint Anthony* (Van Buuren Collection, Brussels).

With the triptychs of his maturity Bosch reached the peak of his expressive capacity, drawing on an extraordinary range of figurative and literary sources and proposing a rigorous and unitary structuring of space that still permits a minute description of the reality represented, with an impassioned narration that gives rise to a dense and rigorous web of gestures, actions and chromatic and proportional relationships.

The Ship of Fools
oil on panel, 57.9x32.6 cm
Louvre, Paris

The theme of the painting has often been linked with the poem of the same name by the Alsatian Sebastian Brant, published in 1494. This was a biting satire of the infinite varieties of human stupidity and the customs of the time, and proved extremely popular, with translations into several languages. However, the subject of the work was not original and had precedents in the literature of the 14th century, so it is not possible to establish with certainty a connection between the poem and Bosch's picture.

The composition, as in all the artist's paintings, is filled with closely interrelated symbolic representations that are intended as a condemnation of lust, denoted by the sea on which the vessel sails. Numerous images allude to licentiousness, from the mast transformed into a greasy pole, a reference to the wild village festivals that led to debauchery, to the crescent moon represented by the boat. A madman seated on a branch that appears to serve as a tiller seems to have taken command of the ship; he is greedily drinking wine from a bowl. The small craft carries a barrel and even one of the men in the sea is demanding his share. Among the figures on the boat there are also a monk and a nun seated in front of a dish of cherries, yet another allusion to lewdness, who are trying to bite an unidentified object hanging from a cord. Although it is difficult to interpret each individual scene or figure, the general idea remains of the condemnation of a world ruled by sin from which not even the religious are immune.

The date of the painting is also controversial, but many tend to assign it to the artist's maturity.

The Haywain
oil on panel, 135x100 cm (central panel), 135x45 cm (wings)
Prado, Madrid

This triptych with movable wings can be dated to around 1490. There is another version of the work in the Escorial, but

the one in the Prado is considered the original.

When the wings are open the triptych presents the *Triumph of the Haywain* in the middle, scenes of the *Earthly Paradise* (from the *Creation of Eve* to the *Expulsion*) on the left, and *Hell* on the right; with its wings closed it depicts the *Wayfarer*. In the *Paradise* great emphasis is given to the birth of Evil, illustrated by the swarm of insects that represent the rebel angels and are set underneath God the Father. On the right wing we see a building in flames, writhing demons and alchemical symbols. The fire has been interpreted as the fire of alchemy, while the tower that the demons are building is seen as an *athanor*, an alchemical furnace. The *Wayfarer*, visible on the outside of the shutters, alludes to the dangers that threaten the faithful, from physical ones, illustrated by the man robbed by brigands, to moral ones, represented by the dance of the shepherds to the sound of the bagpipe. The main image, that of the haywain, may have been inspired by a Dutch song dating from around 1470, which says that the stack of hay represents what God has given for the benefit of all humanity, and it is folly to try to hoard it. As hay is not costly, the parallel expresses the scarce value of the earthly things over which some are willing to fight, and translates essentially into a criticism of greed. The image of the haywain was widely used in Flanders, appearing in engravings, folk songs and poems, as well as in the

Flemish proverb "the world is like a haywain, everyone takes what he can." We know too that Bosch, as a member of a religious confraternity, had contributed on several occasions to the decoration of wagons for processions, and it is possible that this firsthand experience had inspired the composition.

Above, Christ observes everything, but only an angel turns his gaze on him, a sign of the scanty attention paid to the divine example. Among the people that throng the scene, there is even a pope on the left, identified by some as Alexander VI Borgia.

Garden of Earthly Delights
oil on panel, 220x195 cm (central panel), 220x97 cm (wings)
Prado, Madrid

The triptych, perhaps Bosch's best known work, is regarded by critics as a work of his late maturity, dating from between 1514 and 1516.

With the wings open it depicts the *Garden of Earthly Delights* in the middle, *Hell* on the right and *Paradise* on the left. When closed it presents the *Creation of the World* on the outer faces of the two shutters. While the representations of *Hell* and *Paradise* do not generally cause major problems of interpretation, the significance of the central panel in which the painter seems to have given free rein to his own inexhaustible fantasy is much more controversial. Perhaps the most plausible explanation is that it is a moralizing satire – like the *Haywain* – intended as a denunciation of lechery, but couched in an ambiguous iconography. The fact that the allegorical meaning of

the work could be misunderstood is testified by the description of the picture made by the canon Antonio de Beatis, secretary of Bishop Roger of Aragon, on a visit to the Low Countries. In his account of the journey (1517) he recalls having seen the painting in the palace of Henry III, count of Nassau, showing that he had not grasped its moral significance but had appreciated the artist's unbridled imagination: "[...] things so pleasing and fantastic that in no way is it possible to describe them well to those who have no knowledge of them."

The *Creation of the World*, painted with the grisaille technique, offers a poetic vision of the Earth viewed through a crystal sphere. For it Bosch draws on traditional iconography, although he curiously confines the figure of the creator to the top left-hand corner. The divine act is summed up by the words taken from the Psalms and reproduced on the two panels: *Ipse dixit et facta sunt, Ipse mandavit et creata sunt* ("For he spake and it was done; he commanded, and it stood fast"). The moment represented corresponds to the third day of creation, when the light was separated from the darkness, the lands emerged from the waters and the trees appeared. (A.F.)

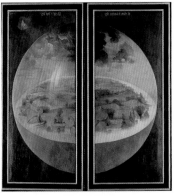

Botticelli

Alessandro Filipepi, whose byname Botticelli may have derived from his elder brother's, was born at Florence in 1445 and trained in the workshop of Filippo Lippi, between 1459 and 1462. After Lippi moved to Spoleto, he entered Verrocchio's workshop, where he further honed his drawing skills and got to know the young Leonardo. He received the commission for the *Fortitude* for the Tribunale della Mercanzia in 1470: orders began to pour in and Botticelli met them with the aid of a well-organized workshop, producing paintings and illuminations, wedding chests, headboards and banners, along with designs for embroideries, church vestments, stamps and plaques, in confirmation of the unity of the arts, not yet classified into major and minor. The artist's earliest documented work for the Medici is in fact a standard, made for the joust held in Piazza Santa Croce in 1475 and celebrated by Politian in his *Stanze*. In 1478 the Medici were to entrust him with a more dramatic task. In April, a group of conspirators led by the Pazzi family attacked the Medici during mass at Santa Maria del Fiore, killing Lorenzo the Magnificent's brother Giuliano. The conspirators were hanged and their images painted above the Porta della Dogana in Palazzo Vecchio as a warning to the citizenry and a mark of shame for the betrayers of Florence. The job was given to Botticelli, who represented them hanging by the neck or feet. Among those executed was the archbishop of Pisa, a fact that exacerbated Florence's already difficult relations with Pope Sixtus IV. Once peace had been reestablished between Florence and the papacy, a group of Florentine painters went to Rome in 1481 to fresco the walls of the Sistine Chapel. Botticelli supplied the drawings for the series of *Popes* and painted three dynamic scenes in which he demonstrated his knowledge of antiquity.

In 1482 Botticelli returned to Florence, where he resumed his illustration of Dante's *Divine Comedy* and, in the refined cultural circles of the Medici, painted his great profane works, the *Primavera, Pallas with the Centaur* and *The Birth of Venus*. They are the paintings for which he is universally renowned and about which we have the least information, not knowing their dates, clients or true significance.

In 1492 Lorenzo died, an event that was heralded, according to tradition, by extraordinary natural phenomena: comets and a bolt of lightning striking the lantern of the cathedral. Around 1496 Botticelli painted his tumultuous *Calumny of Apelles*. These were years dominated by the changing fortunes of the Medici, Charles VIII's invasion of Italy and the ardent preaching of the Dominican Girolamo Savonarola. In his "bonfires of the vanities" books and works of art considered immoral were burned, while Savonarola and his followers, the *piagnoni* or "wailers," preached a return to the simplicity, temperate behavior and piety of the original Christians. In 1498 the friar was hanged and then burned. Sandro's brother, Simone, was among the friar's strongest supporters, but the artist does not seem to have been one of the *piagnoni*. But his paintings did display a new unease, as is apparent in the *Mystic Nativity* of 1501. At the beginning of the 16th century Leonardo, Michelangelo and the young Raphael were all in Florence, while Botticelli's workshop carried on with its repetitive production. Botticelli died in 1510 and was buried in Ognissanti. The painter whose works thousands of people now make long journeys every year to see had hardly ever left Florence.

The Birth of Venus
tempera on canvas, 184.5x285.5 cm
Galleria degli Uffizi, Florence

Presumably linked to the cadet branch of
the Medici, the painting, dating from *c.*
1484-85, sprang out of the same cultural
climate as the *Primavera*. Amidst a
swarm of gilded highlights, Venus is
carried to the shore on a shell, driven by
the breath of two winged figures, the
Winds, where a handmaiden, probably
one of the Hours, waits for her with a
large cloak studded with little plants. The
numerous interpretations of the picture
that art historians have come up with
assign it different dates, clients and
subjects, as there is no reliable
information to draw on. The most widely
accepted version connects the painting
with the neoplatonic circles of Marsilio
Ficino and sees it as the birth of
Humanitas, stemming from the union of
spirit and matter. There is also a close
parallel with the description of the birth
of Venus in Politian's *Stanze per la
Giostra*, written around 1475-78: "A
damsel not with human face / By the lewd
Zephyrs driven ashore / Turns on a shell;
and heaven seems to rejoice."
The story has ancient origins, but the
pose of the goddess does not refer to the
classical image of the maiden wringing
the water from her hair, but to another
ancient source, the *Venus Pudica*
concealing her nakedness with her hands.
The hair blowing in the wind is
reminiscent of Leon Battista Alberti's
advice to artists in his treatise to paint it
wafting freely in the air: "it turns in
spirals as if wishing to knot itself, waves
in the air like flames, twines around itself
like a serpent, while part rises here, part
there."
In the 19th century, the painting that now
draws people from every part of the
world was not to the taste of the grand
duke, who relegated it to the storeroom
of Palazzo Vecchio: it was the director of
the Uffizi who requested the work for his
museum, rescuing it from inevitable
oblivion.

Saint Augustine in His Study

fresco (transferred to canvas),
152x112 cm
Ognissanti, Florence

On the wall that divided the space of the choir from that of the congregation in the church of Ognissanti, Botticelli painted *Saint Augustine* (*c.* 1484) for the Vespucci family, opposite the *Saint Jerome* painted by Ghirlandaio. During the renovation of the church in the 16th century, the partition was demolished and the fresco transferred to its present location. The saint is portrayed in his study, whose green walls call to mind Filarete's recommendations for libraries, surrounded by his books, including a treatise on geometry, and scientific instruments, an armillary sphere and a clock indicating more or less the hour of sunset. Light plays over the pensive expression on his face, while, as we are informed in an apocryphal letter attributed to the saint, he meditates on the nature of the glory of the saints in joyful communion with Christ and decides to write to St. Jerome to ask his opinion. But it is the moment of St. Jerome's death in Jerusalem: St. Augustine is surprised by an ineffable light and perfume, while a voice tells him that it is easier to halt the stars in their tracks than describe the bliss of the saints without having experienced it, as he is experiencing it now.

A few words carefully concealed between the lines of the open volume confirm Botticelli's fondness for jokes, something he had already demonstrated with the cunning prank he had played on his pupil Biagio. They can be rendered as follows: "Where is Fra Martino? He has fled. And where has he gone? He is outside the Porta al Prato." But the gate known as the Porta al Prato is close to the church of Ognissanti, and poor Fra Martino's flight must have been a very brief one.

Madonna della Melagrana (Madonna of the Pomegranate)

tempera on panel, diam. 143.5 cm
Galleria degli Uffizi, Florence

In the eighties Botticelli continued to produce religious paintings for public and private devotion, from the *Madonna del Magnificat* and the *Madonna della Melagrana* (*c.* 1487) to the numerous pictures of the *Madonna and Child* that the workshop would go on churning out after the artist's death, using his models. Even taking into consideration the repetitive character of the painter's female faces, the features of the Virgin are so similar to those of his Venus that the two works must have been painted only a short time apart. The picture was executed for the audience chamber of the Magistrati di Camera in Palazzo Vecchio, a public location that was underlined by the original frame, decorated with golden lilies (the symbol of Florence) on a blue ground. "*Ave Gratia plena*" is written on the band of the angel on the left, while the lilies and roses allude to the purity of Mary, "rose without thorns," woman without sin. The pomegranate, on the other hand, is a symbol of Resurrection, and derives from the ancient world in which it was an attribute of Persephone, who returned every spring from the underworld to the earth to regenerate it. The composition was studied in a concave mirror which, through its optical distortion, enlarges the bodies of Mary and the Child, lending a greater sense of majesty to the scene, just as the *Madonna del Magnificat* betrays the use of a convex mirror, a mark of the painter's interest in experimentation. (E.F.)

16TH CENTURY

Leonardo

Leonardo, born at Vinci, near Florence, in 1452, commenced his career in the 1460s in the Florentine workshop of the painter and sculptor Andrea Verrocchio. Around the middle of the seventies he painted the *Portrait of Ginevra Benci* (National Gallery, Washington), a picture that recalls the *Lady with Primroses*, a marble sculpture by Verrocchio now in the Museo Nazionale del Bargello in Florence. In 1481 Leonardo started work on the *Adoration of the Magi* for the church of San Donato a Scopeto, now in the Uffizi and left incomplete because in 1482 the artist left Florence for the court of Ludovico il Moro in Milan. He was to remain there for eighteen years, during which time he worked in the most diverse fields: as a painter, sculptor, architect, city planner, civil and military engineer, organizer of official ceremonies and creator of temporary structures for festivals and stage sets. In 1483 he signed a contract with the confraternity of Santa Maria della Concezione for the execution of the *Virgin of the Rocks*. He would paint two versions of this, one now in the Louvre, in Paris, the other in the National Gallery of London.

Perhaps the most celebrated work of the Milanese period is the *Last Supper*, painted between 1495 and 1497 for the refectory of the monastery of Santa Maria delle Grazie. It is not a fresco but a painting executed in an experimental technique using a special preparation on dry plaster, and it was not long before it began to deteriorate.

Following the fall of Ludovico il Moro in 1499 and the occupation of Milan by the French, Leonardo went first to Isabella d'Este in Mantua, then on to Venice and finally returned to Florence. In the church of the Santissima Annunziata he showed a cartoon depicting *Saint Ann with the Virgin, the Child and the Infant Saint John*, and Vasari describes the reception it received in the city as follows: "[…] in the room, men and women, young and old, flocked to see it for two days, as if it had been a festival, and they marveled exceedingly." The Medici were absent from Florence, having been driven out of the city in 1494, and in 1503 the republican government commissioned him to decorate one wall of the Salone del Gran Consiglio in Palazzo della Signoria with the *Battle of Anghiari*, at which the Florentines had defeated the Milanese troops of Filippo Maria Visconti in 1440. The fresco was supposed to have been set opposite Michelangelo's version of the *Battle of Cascina*, but for various reasons, neither of the works were finished: the two artists abandoned the city, leaving behind a few preparatory drawings which were to influence the art of generations of artists to come.

In 1506 Leonardo went back to Milan at the invitation of the French governor Charles d'Amboise and devoted himself to studies of anatomy, botany, geophysics and engineering. In 1513, following the return to power of the Sforza dynasty, he left Milan to settle in Rome, under the protection of Giuliano de' Medici. The role of painter was now overshadowed by that of the man of science, while the artistic scene in Rome was dominated by Michelangelo and Raphael. In 1516, after the death of Giuliano de' Medici, Leonardo accepted an invitation from King Francis I to come to France and moved to Cloux, near Amboise. He took with him the *Mona Lisa*, the picture probably painted during his last stay in Florence that perhaps illustrates better than any other the expressive possibilities of *sfumato*, the subtle and gradual passage from shade to light that creates an illusion of depth and slowly brings the forms out of a darkness steeped in mystery. Leonardo died at Cloux in 1519.

Portrait of a Musician
oil on panel, 43x31 cm
Pinacoteca Ambrosiana, Milan

It had been the ruler of Florence, Lorenzo the Magnificent, who first sent Leonardo to Milan as a sort of cultural ambassador: together with Atalante Migliorotti, he took to Ludovico a musical instrument, a lyre, being an accomplished musician himself, as well as the author of texts on improvisations. Leonardo's interest in music also found expression in this work, datable to between 1485 and 1487, which is the only portrait of a man attributed to the artist. Various identities have been proposed for the sitter, and critics now favor the hypothesis that he was Franceschino Gaffurio, choirmaster of Milan Cathedral since 1484. However, the identification of the man is irrelevant to the interpretation of the painting, which is not intended to be the portrait of a particular person but a representation of a musician in the act of performing. The singer is holding a sheet of paper on which the score is written, and the rigidity of his pose is contradicted by the movement of the muscles of the face and mouth, half closed as if to control his respiration while emitting a note. The painting shows the influence of Northern European painting in the great precision of the description, and this may stem from the fact that Leonardo had been able to see works by Antonello da Messina in Milan. The dark background, which reappears in other works by the artist but was extremely rare at that time, is typical of the Sicilian painter's portraits, as is the attention paid to the representation of expressions and psychological attitudes, which Leonardo called "the motions of the mind."

Lady with an Ermine
oil on panel, 54x39 cm
Czartoryski Muzeum, Cracow

The painting is a portrait of Ludovico il
Moro's mistress Cecilia Gallerani and can
be dated to between 1485 and 1490. The
picture is also celebrated in a sonnet by
the court poet Bernardo Bellincioni, who
died in 1492, and so we can be certain
that it had been executed by this date. In
a letter sent by Cecilia Gallerani to
Isabella d'Este in 1498, in response to
Isabella's request for the painting, the
woman declared that in the meantime her
appearance had changed and she could
no longer recognize herself in the
portrait. According to some scholars, this
suggests that the picture was painted
when Gallerani was very young, and so
should be dated to around 1485. This is
corroborated by the comparison with a
preparatory study for the *Virgin of the
Rocks*, executed during the artist's first
stay in Milan, which presents surprising
similarities to the face and pose of the
Lady with an Ermine.
The animal has attracted more attention
from scholars than Cecilia herself. Some
believe that it is an allusion to Moro, who
had received from the king of Naples,
Ferrante of Aragon, the decoration of the
order of St. Michael or of the Ermine. In
a sonnet Bellincioni described Moro as
"*italico morel, bianco ermellino*"
("dark Italian white ermine").
The link between Cecilia and the ermine,
a symbol of chastity, appears more

enigmatic: according to some it may lie in
the assonance between her surname
(Gallerani) and the Greek word for
ermine, *gale*.
The composition of the painting is
extremely refined, based on the three-
quarters position of the woman and the
counterpoint of the ermine's movement.
The handling of the forms is sure, and
they are rendered even more evident by
the choice of a dark background.

Virgin of the Rocks
oil on panel, 199x122 cm
Louvre, Paris

Virgin of the Rocks
oil on panel, 189.5x120 cm
National Gallery, London

Leonardo started work on the first version
of the painting in 1483. This was the year

that the members of the confraternity of
the Immaculate Conception commissioned
an altarpiece from the artist to be placed
in their chapel in the Milanese church of
San Francesco Grande. Leonardo was to
paint the central part of the altarpiece
with an image of the Virgin; the execution
of the side panels was entrusted to the
De Predis brothers, who painted two
Angels Playing Musical Instruments.
However, the dating of the painting is still
uncertain, and oscillates between 1486
and 1490. It also seems that the picture
was never delivered to the clients but
remained instead in the studio of the
painter, who in 1493 received an offer for
it from a French collector and agreed to
sell it at a higher price than the one
initially established in the contract with
the confraternity. The circumstances by
which the painting arrived in the
collections of the king of France and was
hung in the Louvre are still mysterious.

The altar of the Milanese church was
adorned with a second version of the
painting, probably begun after Leonardo
had sold the original one and finished by
1499, during his first stay in Milan, or
perhaps during his second visit to the city,
in 1508. The panel was later sold to the
Scottish painter Gavin Hamilton and after
a few years ended up in the National
Gallery (1880), where it can be seen
today with the panels by the De Predis
brothers hung at the sides, as they had
been in the church.
Instead of the subject that had been
commissioned from him, the Virgin
between angels and two prophets,
Leonardo painted the *Virgin with the
Infant Saint John Adoring the Infant
Christ Accompanied by an Angel*. This
was a theme that does not appear in the
Holy Scriptures but echoes the preaching
of a well-known Florentine friar of the
14th century, Domenico Cavalca. On their

LEONARDO DA VINCI

return from the flight into Egypt the Holy
Family encounters the infant John the
Baptist in the desert; John pays homage to
Jesus, who blesses him and prophesies
his baptism, something to which the water
in the foreground in the version in the
Louvre also seems to allude. The meeting
between the two children served
Leonardo as the cue for a composition
based on a refined exchange of glances,
denoting a depth of psychological analysis
highly unusual for the time.

This is one of the very few paintings of the
period in which the Christ Child and the
Infant St. John are depicted together. The
iconographic theme was to return in
other Florentine works by Leonardo and
would later be taken up by both
Michelangelo and Raphael.

There are several differences between the
versions in the Louvre and the National
Gallery: in the one in England the angel is
not indicating John, while the pointing
finger is clearly visible in the painting in
France; the haloes and John's cross are
missing from the French version, and may
not in fact be Leonardo's work but 18th-
century additions. In general, in the
version in the National Gallery the
centrality of the Virgin and Child is
reaffirmed and the role of the Baptist
diminished, as requested by the members
of the confraternity.

The painting is known as the *Virgin of
the Rocks* because of the natural setting
that forms its backdrop: this was perfect
for the chapel in which it was to be
located, as it had been erected on top of
the Christian catacombs. Leonardo had
already proposed a rocky background in
the *Saint Jerome* in the Pinacoteca
Vaticana, and the *Mona Lisa* in the Louvre
also has a naturalistic setting, reflecting in
the attention to detail the scientific studies
of the artist, who in that period was
showing a growing interest in the
composition of the earth's mantle. (A.F.)

1498

Das malt Ich nach meiner gestalt
Ich was sex vnd zwenzig Jar alt

Albrecht Dürer

Dürer

Dürer was born at Nuremberg in 1471. After serving his apprenticeship, he undertook his first journey for the purposes of study, as every good craftsman was supposed to do. In 1494 he left Nuremberg again, drawn by the rediscovery of the classical world that had for some time been taking art in a new direction in Italy. This marked the beginning of a custom that was to become widespread among artists and art lovers: the visit to Italy, which was to culminate in the 18th century in the "Grand Tour," considered an indispensable part of the education of people of culture. His destination was Venice, a rich trading center linked to Nuremberg by regular carrier services and home to a flourishing publishing industry. German merchants had a strong presence in the city, based around the Fondaco dei Tedeschi. It was through the sale of prints in a Northern European style to these merchants that the young and still unknown artist earned a living, while he studied and copied Mantegna's personal interpretation of antiquity and the works of Giovanni Bellini, from which he drew a new feeling for atmosphere and light. In Venice Dürer also tried his hand at representation of the nude according to exact canons of proportion, producing the first female nude for which a woman was professionally hired to pose as a model. In 1495 he opened a studio in Nuremberg, where he carried out an intense activity both as a painter and an engraver. In 1498 his woodcuts (prints made from wooden blocks) of the *Apocalypse* met with immense success in Europe: published in two editions, in German and Latin, they represented the visions of St. John, a mirror of the religious disquiet that was to culminate in the Protestant Reformation, in a concrete manner that was made possible by his previous study of classical models. His later series of woodcuts depicting religious subjects, such as the *Great Passion* and the *Little Passion*, also had the aim of presenting the Gospels to the people in a clear and concrete form.

In 1505, at the height of his fame, Dürer went back to Italy, partly in order to deepen his understanding of the theoretical knowledge that he now regarded as indispensable to artistic creation: perspective and the proportions of the human body. Stopping at Augsburg on his way to Venice, he accepted the commission to paint an altarpiece entitled *The Feast of the Rose Garlands* for the German community, perhaps from the rich Fugger trading house that gave financial support to the policies of Emperor Maximilian. In Venice Dürer, now esteemed and admired, encountered hostility from his fellow artists (with the sole exception of Bellini), who criticized him for not knowing how to use color. He also brought an action for violation of copyright against Marcantonio Raimondi, accused of having engraved some of the artist's woodcuts on copper and utilizing Dürer's universally known monogram in the copies instead of his own mark. The fact was that he made more money out of the sale of prints than he did from his painting.

It was in Nuremberg, between 1513 and 1514, that he produced his masterpieces of engraving *Knight, Death and the Devil*, *Saint Jerome in His Study* and *Melencolia I*, a sort of allegorical triptych based on the medieval classification of three types of virtues connected with three ways of life. He went on to make a series of engravings for Emperor Maximilian that were intended to glorify the Habsburgs, receiving in exchange an annual pension from the city of Nuremberg. The painter sought to have this renewed by his successor Charles V and made a journey to the Low Countries in 1520 to see him. Given a triumphal welcome in various cities, he met artists and scholars, including Desiderius Erasmus in whom Dürer was to place his hopes on hearing a false report that Luther had been killed: "My God, if Luther is dead, who is going to explain the Holy Gospels clearly to us in future?" The painter had supported the Reformation while rejecting its iconoclastic excesses and claiming the right to paint religious pictures: "a Christian will not be led into superstition by a painting or an image, any more than an honest man will commit a murder because he carries a weapon." Returning to Nuremberg the painter put his theoretical studies to good use, compiling treatises on art and continuing to work right up until his death in 1528.

Self-Portrait with Gloves
oil on panel, 52x41 cm
Museo del Prado, Madrid

"How much I shall desire the sun, in the cold: here I am a lord, and in my own country nothing but a parasite": thus wrote Dürer during his second stay in Venice. The artist from Northern Europe was well aware of the different status enjoyed by his German colleagues, still under the control of the guilds that protected their interests but regulated their activity along with the crafts, in comparison with the Italians, more conscious of the value of their work and ready to assert it. The artist wanted to be recognized as a man of culture, a master of the rules of composition and the laws of optics, geometry and perspective. He held that his income ought not to depend

on external factors such as the number of figures in a picture, the time required for its execution and the quality of the gold and blue paint that was used, but exclusively on his talent. Buoyed up by the success attained in 1498 by the publication of his *Apocalypse*, that same year Dürer portrayed himself as a richly attired, refined and proud gentleman, of a much higher social standing than a mere craftsman, thereby celebrating both himself and the role of the artist.
This self-celebration was to reach its peak in 1500, when Dürer portrayed himself in a rigidly frontal position, according to the scheme customarily adopted for the representation of Christ, reflecting his belief that the genius of the artist, his creative power, came from God. A further mystical identification of the artist and God came from the widely circulated book entitled the *Imitation of Christ*, which argued for the need to imitate the life of the Savior: a doctrine that, taken

literally, could even lead to clients requesting artists to represent them with the cross on their shoulders.

Paumgartner Altarpiece
oil on panel, 155x126 cm (central panel), 157x61 cm (side panels)
Alte Pinakothek, Munich

The triptych, called the *Paumgartner Altarpiece* after its clients, is made up of a central panel with the *Nativity* and two leaves whose inner faces are painted with large-scale, full-length figures of *Saint George* and *Saint Eustace*, probably portraits of the brothers Lukas and Stephan Paumgartner. The altarpiece, painted *c.* 1498-1504, reflects Dürer's studies on the proportion of the human figure in the wings and of perspective in the central panel, where the lines of the walls seem to converge on a point in the background of the picture.

The composition is structured around diagonals: the one determined by Joseph's stick and three of the seven small figures of donors in the foreground, and the one linking Mary's head with Joseph's, the wooden roof and the planks at the top. St. Joseph is holding a lantern, traditional symbol of the earthly light that is outshone by the spiritual light of Jesus, just as the rising of the sun symbolizes the birth of the Savior, the sun of Justice. In the background, an angel announces the birth to the shepherds.

Adoration of the Magi
oil on panel, 100x114 cm
Galleria degli Uffizi, Florence

The scene, painted in 1504, is constructed with a sure grasp of perspective and displays Italian influences in the light and the handling of the atmosphere. His study of Leonardo is evident in the characterization of the expressions of the figures and probably in the agitation of the horsemen in the background as well. The image is framed in an unusual way, with the Virgin shown in profile, while the crumbling buildings around her seem to allude to the dissolution of the pagan world or of the Old Law, which had lapsed with the coming of Christ, although it is also possible, in 16th-century culture, that they are simply a reflection of the renewed interest in antiquity. The presence of plantain, a herb reputed to have the property of healing wounds, is a reference to the blood shed by Christ on the cross. In the same way the butterfly symbolizes immortality and salvation, while the donkey baring its teeth, a symbol of stubborn resistance, can be interpreted as the Old Law menacing the New Revelation.

The Feast of the Rose Garlands
oil on panel, 162x194.5 cm
Národní Galerie, Prague

With this picture, painted in 1506, during his second stay in Venice, Dürer claimed to have silenced those who accused him of being a good engraver but unable to handle color: even the doge and the patriarch had gone to admire it. Hung in San Bartolomeo, the church of the German colony in Venice, it represents the Dominican devotion to the Virgin through the prayer of the rosary, symbolized by the distribution of wreaths of white and red roses: the former correspond to the smaller beads and the recitation of the Ave Maria, the second to the large beads and the Pater Noster; the ring that links the flowers alludes to the recitation of the Credo and symbolizes the Christian faith. St. Dominic takes part in the distribution of the garlands. Laymen and churchmen are present, in an ideal of universal brotherhood, but while the clergymen are in direct relation with Christ, the laymen have access only to the Virgin. The Child, in fact, places the wreath on the pope's head, while Mary crowns the emperor. The faces are strongly characterized, but not all of them have been identified yet: the emperor is undoubtedly Maximilian of Habsburg, so powerful that it was thought, in 1505, that his coronation in Rome was imminent. At the same time the Virgin is crowned, in the final mystery of the Rosary, and her crown, a precious piece of goldwork, recalls the imperial one, while the stars that adorn it evoke the Apocalypse.

Leaning against a tree, on the right, a figure looks out of the painting, toward the observer. He is holding a scroll in Latin that tells us the altarpiece had been executed in five months by the German Dürer: in fact the figure is that of the artist himself, who signs the work on the scroll and introduces his self-portrait into the religious painting, a further affirmation of his dignity as a painter. (E.F.)

Grünewald

I n the same years in which Michelangelo was painting the ceiling of the Sistine Chapel and Raphael the Stanze in the Vatican, to the north of the Alps another great artist, Mathis Grünewald, was working on his masterpiece, a picture very different from the Italian works of the day: the *Isenheim Altarpiece*. We do not know much about the life of Mathis Neithardt Gothart, known as Grünewald from the 17th century onward: born in Würzburg between 1465 and 1480, he was court painter in the service of two consecutive archbishops of Mainz: Uriel von Gemmingen and then Albert of Brandenburg, a great patron of the arts and powerful prince of the Church.

In 1524 the discontent of the German peasants, infuriated by the contrast between their own poverty and the wealth of the Church, the princes and the merchants, spilled over in a violent revolt that sucked in part of the urban population as well. The rebels had political and social objectives as well as utopian aims of Christian love and divine justice. At first Luther espoused the peasants' cause, but then sided with the traditional authorities and, in his broadsheet *Against the Murdering and Thieving Hordes of Peasants*, supported the bloody repression of the rebellion in 1525. Artists who had backed the uprising were persecuted, thrown into prison, tortured or, in the best of cases, sent into exile. It is likely that Grünewald too had sided with the peasants and for this reason lost his position at Albert of Brandenburg's court, like all the other supporters of the revolt and the Protestant Reformation. In 1526 the painter took refuge in the imperial city of Frankfurt. Following threats from the archbishop, who demanded that all those who had taken part in the rebellion be handed over, he went to Halle, where he found work as a hydraulic engineer and died in 1528. In Frankfurt he had devoted his attention to a variety of activities, including the manufacture of a medicinal soap and perhaps the sale of paints. Among the documents, destroyed by bombs during the Second World War, relating to the painter's possessions were several writings by Luther and the *Twelve Articles of the Christian Faith* that are supposed to have constituted the demands of the rebellious peasants, as well as two rosaries, many paints and a pot for making soap, a rich wardrobe and a few items of jewelry. Grünewald had given up the profession of painter, perhaps because he could no longer find suitable clients or because he had embraced the more extreme wing of the Reformation, which was so radically opposed to the religious use of images that it went as far as iconoclasm, with the removal and destruction of paintings in churches.

The visionary quality, the irrational space, the unreal, livid and dazzling light and the intense and emotive color of his painting were to resurface in the great artists of early Mannerism, Pontormo and Rosso Fiorentino, at a time when the certainties of Humanism were being swept away by the spiritual and human crises stirred by the Reformation.

Isenheim Altarpiece
Musée d'Unterlinden, Colmar

Isenheim Altarpiece: *Crucifixion*; *Resurrection*

oil on panel, 269x307 cm, 269x143 cm
Musée d'Unterlinden, Colmar

In Germany, the altarpiece frequently assumed the form of a polyptych with movable wings, in which the leaves, open or closed, displayed different scenes to meet different liturgical requirements, like an immense *Biblia pauperum*, or Bible of the Illiterate, for those who were unable to read the Holy Scriptures but could be taught religious precepts by means of images. These were works of art in which painting, sculpture and architectural design were profoundly interrelated, and in which the artists were strictly conditioned by the requirements of clients and the instructions of theologians. The *Isenheim Altarpiece* has large shutters, painted on both sides, which can be opened and closed to form three combinations: with the leaves closed it is dominated by the dramatic *Crucifixion*, while *Saint Sebastian* and *Saint Anthony of Egypt* are represented on the fixed wings and the *Lamentation over Christ* is depicted in the predella; the second combination, with the leaves open, presents on the contrary a world of joy: the *Annunciation*, the *Incarnation of Christ*, the *Allegory of the Nativity* and the *Resurrection*; the final combination, with the wings opened even further, displays the *Meeting of the Hermit Saints Anthony and Paul* and the *Temptations of Saint Anthony* at the sides, while the central compartment and the predella house wooden sculptures dominated by the figure of St. Anthony of Egypt.
The polyptych was painted around 1512-16 for the church of the Antonite monastery-hospital in the Alsatian town of Isenheim, which reached the height of its splendor under the preceptor Jean d'Orliac, who commissioned the sculptural part of the altar, and, later, the Sicilian Guido Guersi, Grünewald's patron. The Antonites were highly skilled physicians, famous above all for their treatment of erysipelas, known as "St. Anthony's fire," but also of epilepsy and syphilis. Whereas nowadays research is directed toward defeating disease, the practice of medicine at the time was

essentially defensive, aimed at alleviating suffering and treating symptoms rather than curing the patient. With the reform of the Antonite Order, in 1478, prayers and church attendance became part of the regime of treatment. The huge polyptych was set on the main altar of the church and formed part of the hospital's program of healing: in particular circumstances the patient was taken to the altar, which therefore performed a therapeutic and spiritual function.
With the polyptych at the third level of opening, patients would have recognized the symptoms of St. Anthony's fire in the figure in the foreground of the *Temptations of Saint Anthony*, with its dilated stomach and red pustules, while in the meeting between the saints they would see herbs used for medicinal purposes. In the second combination they would have encountered the mystery of the incarnation of Christ and the certainty of the *Resurrection*: a Christ of pure energy, blazing with light in the starry night. With the shutters closed, on the other hand, they would have placed their trust in St. Sebastian, invoked against the plague, and St. Anthony of Egypt, to whom sufferers from "St. Anthony's fire" prayed for solace. But above all they would have been faced with the *Crucifixion*, with suffering and death, but also comfort and hope. There can be no doubt that the patients at Isenheim believed man to be sinful and that illness was often a punishment for sin, but with the sacrifice of Christ the redemption of humanity had been brought to pass and the cross had to be accepted as an example of patience. At the sides of the cross stand the two St. Johns, invoked against epilepsy: the Evangelist supporting the Madonna and the Baptist, alone, indicating Christ. Behind him there is water, a symbol of baptism and spiritual salvation, but perhaps also an allusion to the spa waters of the region of Vosges, less than five kilometers from the monastery. The inscription is taken from the Gospel according to St. John and refers to the words of the Baptist: "He must increase, but I must decrease." The blood of the lamb spurts into the chalice, an allusion to the mass at which the sacrifice of the cross is repeated, while the Magdalen,

kneeling, despairs. The figures are out of proportion and a violent expressionism underlines the crude representation of the Crucified Christ. His body is ashen from loss of blood, the stomach caved in, the mouth half-open and smeared with blood, the arms stretched to support the inert body that bends the cross under its weight, the fingers outspread, the feet strained: it is the vision of the Crucifixion presented by St. Bridget, the Swedish mystic of the 14th century, in her *Revelations*, a source of inspiration that resulted from the presence, at Isenheim, of a convent of Dominican nuns dedicated to the veneration of the holy "mouthpiece of God," founder of the Order of the Most Holy Savior ("Bridgettines") and counselor to churchmen and politicians. In the *Revelations*, the Madonna describes the dramatic moments of the Crucifixion to the saint in ecstasy, with violent details and vivid images of torture to which Grünewald gave visual expression. Other painters were to use the *Revelations* as a source for their paintings, especially for the representation of the Nativity: the Virgin with her long hair unbound and the naked Child lying on the ground, so flooded with light as to render the earthly illumination of St. Joseph's candle superfluous. (E.F.)

Venus and Cupid
Borghese Gallery, Rome

Cranach the Elder

Born in 1472 at Kronach, the small town from which he took his name, the painter moved to Vienna at the beginning of the 16th century. By the end of 1504 he was in the service of the elector of Saxony, Frederick the Wise, at Wittenberg, where he was to remain for almost fifty years as court painter to three successive electors. In 1508 Frederick the Wise granted him a coat of arms (a small crowned and winged snake with a ring in its mouth), which Cranach used to mark his pictures.

In 1508 the former Augustinian monk Martin Luther, professor of theology since 1512, was appointed court preacher. He persuaded the reluctant elector to relinquish his collection of relics. Cranach formed a relationship of profound esteem and friendship with the reformer, borne out by the affectionate letters he sent to the artist. And according to legend it was at Wittenberg that Luther nailed his *Ninety-Five Theses* against the trade in indulgences (they were being sold, among other reasons, to raise money to complete St. Peter's Basilica) and the corruption of the Church to the door of the cathedral in 1517: an act that is regarded as marking the official birth of the Reformation. In the meantime the painter grew wealthy, holding the post of senator in alternate years from 1520 onward and that of burgomaster of the city from 1537 to 1544. His sons Hans and Lucas helped him to fulfill the numerous orders received by the workshop. In 1550 Cranach joined the elector John Frederick in Augsburg, where he was held prisoner by Emperor Charles V following the defeat of the Protestant Schmalkaldic League at the battle of Mühlberg in 1547. He then went to Weimar, where he died in 1553. A brilliant chronicler of life at court, Cranach painted portraits, religious pictures and classical myths, hunting scenes, Germanic legends and female nudes in the guise of Venus, Diana or nymphs. These were often inspired in their composition, but not their style, by Italian models. To meet the incessant demand from his workshop he commenced the mass production of works with small variations, as in the case of the portraits of the reformers Luther and Melanchthon, or of Luther and his wife. Despite his support for the Reformation, he did not disdain working for Catholic clients, such as Luther's enemy Cardinal Albert of Brandenburg, for whom Cranach painted a large number of pictures, including a portrait of the archbishop praying beneath Christ on the cross, silhouetted in diagonal against a stormy sky.

Crucifixion
oil on panel, 138x99 cm
Alte Pinakothek, Munich

Both Cranach and Altdorfer set their religious scenes in special sacred spaces, surrounded by nature in the wild state: they are places of solitude outside the ordinary flow of life, suited to mystical revelations, meditation and moments of transition, places in which nature reveals her power. In this work of 1503, with a bold asymmetrical arrangement of the crosses, Cranach isolates the figure of

Christ against a sky of stormy clouds, while a strong wind snatches at his loincloth: nature is responding to the drama that has just taken place, in accordance with the words of the Gospel: "the sun was darkened and there was a darkness all over the earth." The dead branches of a tree reach toward Christ, recalling the crown of thorns, while at the foot of the cross the remains of a skeleton refer to the name of the place of crucifixion – Golgotha, the skull – and to the mortal remains of Adam, from whom according to tradition the tree of life,

Christ, was born. Blood still flows from the wound in his side: "blood and water" according to the Book of John, interpreted by St. Augustine as symbols of the Eucharist and of baptism, for the redemption of man. A living tree, instead, forms the backdrop to Mary and John, at the center of the composition, separated from Christ and alone in their sorrow: the Dominicans had emphasized the role of the Virgin's compassion and meditation on her suffering had assumed a fundamental role in a mystical movement that was widespread in Germany.

Portrait of Luther; Portrait of Katharina von Bora
oil on panel, 37x23 cm, 37x23 cm
Galleria degli Uffizi, Florence

To meet the growing demand for portraits of Luther, Cranach's workshop organized the mass production of works characterized by small variants and clean and incisive outlines that were easy to reproduce.

Cranach had very close relations with the reformer, standing as his best man at his marriage and as the godfather of his firstborn, while Luther, for his part, was godfather to one of the painter's daughters. The first parallel portraits of Luther and his wife Katharina von Bora, dating from 1526, were probably painted on the occasion of their wedding. The portraits reproduced here date from 1529. Luther is presented in a very simple manner, as a man who could be trusted where questions of faith and the Church are concerned. Cranach helped the spread of Protestantism through the publication and diffusion of Luther's writings and translation of the New Testament, while one influence of the

Reformation on the painter's art can be
detected in his choice of particular
themes: original sin, redemption, Christ
blessing the children. Luther had not
expressed himself clearly on the role of
images, which more radical reformers,
such as Andreas Karlstadt, wished to
destroy in order to prevent them from
being worshiped in the place of the
divinity they represented. Luther's
aspiration to turn Germany into a truly
Christian society was based on an
intimate understanding of the Scriptures,
through what he defined as his
"catechism," in its original meaning of
"oral teaching," for a more direct
contact between man and God. The
central concept of his theology was the
grace of God, freely granted to men in
their earthly existence. The reformer was
convinced that all the arts, including
music, should contribute to the service of
God, and asserted that his duty was to
"destroy images first of all by removing
them from the heart through the word of
God and thus rendering them devoid of
value and insignificant [...]. For when
they are no longer in the heart, they can
do no harm if seen with the eyes."

Hunt in Honor of Charles V at Torgau
oil on panel, 114x175 cm
Museo del Prado, Madrid

Cranach painted a series of profane pictures for the decoration of the elector's hunting lodges at Coburg, Lochau and Torgau, drawing on the assistance of numerous collaborators. He often accompanied his patrons on hunts and drew wild boar, wild crows and Bohemian magpies from life. In his role as celebrator of the court, Cranach immortalized the stag hunt organized for Emperor Charles V in 1544: a pastime reserved for noblemen, but also an image of power, regulated by precise rules and involving a multitude of people with well-defined roles.

The slaughter of the deer in the river, in this as in other paintings, is a display of strength and devotion on the part of the prince toward his distinguished guest. The hunt was closely related to politics and the management of the territory, with the control of forests and watercourses, but also had the function of keeping in shape the fighters who would have to demonstrate courage and physical fitness in battle.

A prominent role was played by the hounds, considered the swiftest and most noble of dogs, and gifts of dogs and falcons for the hunt were not infrequent, even to popes. A fundamental figure was the man responsible for the care and breeding of the dogs: he had to be familiar with the bases of veterinary medicine and possess qualities of speed, agility and courage so as to keep up with the animals during the hunts and to attack the prey that was being pursued, before the arrival of the hunters with their spears, or long, fixed lances. They usually carried short arms, which did not get in their way, and hunting horns to summon the hunters and guide the dogs. As for the prey, wild-boar hunts were considered more exciting because of their danger, but the stag hunt was often regarded as the more noble, both because it tested the riding skills of the horseman in exhausting pursuits and because of the symbolic value of the animal.

The pleasure of the hunt generally concluded with a banquet, providing another opportunity for social ostentation and for definition of the accords and alliances that had been outlined over the course of the hunt itself. (E.F.)

Altdorfer

B orn around 1480, the painter became a citizen of Regensburg in 1505. He was to make his career in the city and hold important posts in the local administration. The minute forms characteristic of his early works can be seen in the *Saint George and the Dragon* of 1510, in which the two protagonists, the saint and the dragon, face one another, motionless and tiny, in a wild forest that dominates the scene. In 1511 the painter made a journey up the Danube, reaching as far as Vienna. In the years immediately afterward, in fact, he collaborated on a series of triumphal engravings for the emperor Maximilian, an undertaking in which Dürer was also involved and which recalled the traditional symbols of triumph of the Roman emperors.

Returning to Regensburg, he became a member of the city's Outer Council in 1517 and probably had a hand in shaping the laws that, for economic motives, were to lead to the expulsion of the Jews in 1519 and the destruction of the synagogue, of which the artist made two engravings before its demolition. In 1526 he became a member of the Inner Council and was appointed city architect, constructing the warehouse for wine and the slaughterhouse. In 1528 he renounced the prestigious position of burgomaster to devote himself to his masterpiece, *The Battle of Issus*, and the following year undertook works of fortification of the city, which felt itself under threat from the Turks who were besieging Vienna. In 1533, in a move that was to have grave political and economic consequences, Regensburg earned the emperor's wrath by requesting the presence of Protestant preachers and thus repudiating its loyalty to Catholicism and the Habsburgs: Altdorfer himself would be sent on a diplomatic mission to Vienna in 1535 to exonerate the city and regain the imperial favor. He came back to Regensburg, where he died in 1538.

His painting shows an openness to the innovations of Dürer, the influence of the paintings of Cranach and a familiarity with Mantegna, probably through prints reproducing his works, a means of communication extensively employed by artists themselves to spread their ideas and which workshops used as a reserve of models and motifs on which to draw. The circulation of small Italian bronzes or *objets d'art* also favored contacts with contemporary German painting: an example is the fountain of the *Rest on the Flight into Egypt*, a reworking of Northern Italian Renaissance motifs. In addition, a small picture of 1507, *The Family of the Satyr*, shows an interesting affinity with Giorgione's *Tempest*, confirming the close cultural ties that existed between Venetian painting and the Danube School, of which Altdorfer was one of the finest exponents. In the early 16th century, in both Venice and the Danube Valley a new and atmospheric conception of the landscape was emerging in which the figures, often of modest size, blended harmoniously into the setting. Underlying this was a new philosophy of nature, which saw a correspondence between the microcosm, man and the macrocosm, the universe. This view was connected with the contemporary ideas of Paracelsus, physician and alchemist, sorcerer and scientist, who regarded the universe as a unity through whose animal and vegetable elements flowed the energy, the action of God.

Christ in the Garden of Olives
oil on panel, 130x95 cm
Abbey of St. Florian, Enns

The great polyptych of St. Sebastian, painted for the abbey of St. Florian between 1509 and 1518, is made up of twenty-four scenes from the *Martyrdom of Saint Sebastian* and the *Passion of Christ*.

As in other cycles of the Passion, the first image is the *Agony in the Garden*, Christ's most human moment, the hour of sorrow and anguish of which the Gospels speak, when Christ, with his disciples Peter, James and John asleep, is alone before the angel who offers him the bitter cup: "Father, if thou be willing, remove this cup from me: nevertheless not my will, but thine, be done." It is the threshold between life and death: the soldiers, in the light of torches and lanterns, are arriving, led by Judas. The landscape is a Germanic interpretation of the Mount of Olives, a place described with a vocabulary more suited to the Alps than to the land of the Bible. The flaming sunset with threatening clouds underlines the drama of the moment. This quest for particular atmospheric effects, which the painting of Venice had in common with that of the Danube, was to lead to the spectacular representation of sunsets and stormy skies to be found not just in Altdorfer and Cranach, but also in Giorgione, Lorenzo Lotto and Titian.

Landscape with Bridge

oil on parchment applied to panel,
42.1x35.1 cm
National Gallery, London

No human figure appears in this landscape from *c.* 1516: the only signs of man's work are a footbridge, a small church in the distance and a construction, perhaps an abandoned castle. Altdorfer's sources of inspiration were close to the courtly literature of the circles of Emperor Maximilian I. The painter's Danubian landscapes are not depicted topographically and his trees often have no equivalent in nature, but are hybrids of different species that assume disturbing forms. The wilderness is charged with natural energy; it is a place suited to bringing out the value of the hero, the isolated individual, remote from the civilized community. And these were the years in which Luther preached a personal religion in opposition to the superstition of the masses: religion as chivalrous romance.But they were also the years of a reawakening, around the throne of Maximilian I, of German pride and national consciousness, in hostile opposition to the Italian classical tradition. The sense of patriotism was fueled by the rediscovery, in the middle of the 15th century, of *Germania*, a text written by the Roman historian Tacitus sometime between the 1st and 2nd century AD and published in Nuremberg in 1473, with its celebration of the Germans as an uncorrupted people in contrast to the decadence of Rome. The tendency toward unity and a sense of national identity encouraged the study not just of German history, but also its geography, with the description of cities, rivers and natural resources. Altdorfer became the painter of the Germanic forest, the land of the courageous peoples celebrated by Tacitus.

Alexander's Victory over Darius at the Battle of Issus

oil on panel, 158x120 cm
Alte Pinakothek, Munich

"The heavens declare the glory of God; and the firmament sheweth his

handywork": Psalm 19 of the Bible celebrates the Lord as the Sun of Justice, manifesting divine perfection in nature and in law. At the time the German vision of the world was dominated by the idea of the correspondence between the life of the universe and the life of men, in a period in which it was believed that cosmic manifestations, signs of the power of God, could have an extraordinary influence on terrestrial phenomena. Altdorfer often included in his paintings such inexplicable events as comets, whose approach to the earth was considered a bad omen, a portent of "disaster," a word that originally meant "bad star."
In this case, however, what is portrayed is a struggle between the sun, emblem of Christ, and the crescent moon, symbol and flag of the Turks. The picture, painted for Duke William IV of Bavaria in 1529, represents the victory of Alexander the Great over the Persian king Darius III, in 333 BC. The point of view is located in Anatolia, where the clash took place: the gaze roams over the Mediterranean basin, where it is possible to recognize the delta of the Nile with its seven branches on the

horizon, the Red Sea on the left and the island of Cyprus at the center. The source reworked by Altdorfer was the account of the battle by the historian of the 1st century AD Curtius Rufus, while the text on the panel suspended at the top was probably written by Johannes Aventinus, a historian of the Bavarian court who resided at Regensburg. The glorious sun is low in the west, reflecting the fact that the ancient chronicles state that Alexander's victory took place at sunset. But the painter introduced an element of his own time, competently reproducing the armor and tactics of contemporary infantry and cavalry. It was the year of the Turkish siege of Vienna and Altdorfer was celebrating at one and the same time the victory of the past and that of the present: just as Alexander had defeated the Persians, the modern empire had vanquished the Turks.
Napoleon was so enamored of the painting that he had it requisitioned and hung in his bedroom at Saint-Cloud: the emperor wanted to be able to see it every day. (E.F.)

Giorgione

V ery few facts and even fewer acknowledged works. And yet Giorgione's fame has endured for centuries. In the absence of documented information his myth has grown, building on the image of the painter, excellent singer and lute player presented in the 16th century by Giorgio Vasari.

Born in the province of Treviso between 1477 and 1478, Zorzi da Castelfranco, known as Giorgione (Zorzon in the Venetian dialect, or "Big George") for "his physical appearance and his moral and intellectual stature," moved to Venice, where he quickly made his way into the cultural circles of the aristocracy. Intellectual life revolved around the famous Venetian printing houses, the historic University of Padua and the refined circle of Asolo, founded by the queen of Cypress, Caterina Cornaro, and dominated by the poet Pietro Bembo, author of the *Asolani*. Artistic culture in Venice was particularly lively owing to the presence of Giovanni Bellini and Carpaccio, the circulation of prints, the city's collections with their many works from Northern Europe and the contribution made by painters passing through: at the end of the 15th century Perugino had brought his harmonious classicism to Venice, Dürer had visited the city, returning there as an established painter just a few years later, while Leonardo, in exile from Milan, stayed in Venice in 1499 or 1500. Giorgione's early work was influenced by Bellini and by the soft classicism of Central Italian artists like Perugino, Francesco Francia and Lorenzo Costa. He worked mainly for private clients but, probably between 1504 and 1505, painted one of his rare public works, the "Castelfranco Altarpiece," in which the *Madonna and Child with Saints* are set in an airy landscape, while a warm and golden light bestows unity on the scene. The first reliable reference to the painter, an inscription on the back of the portrait of a woman known as *Laura*, perhaps dates from 1506, while the dating of other works is much debated by the critics: this is the case with *The Tempest*, *The Three Philosophers*, the *Portrait of an Old Woman*, the various versions of the *Madonna and Child* for private devotion and the *Venus* in Dresden, finished by Titian. In 1507-08 he received a commission for the Doge's Palace in Venice and in 1508 one for the decoration of the facades of the Fondaco dei Tedeschi, rebuilt after the fire of 1505. Giorgione was assigned the front facing onto the Grand Canal, while the young Titian, whose work is recognizable by the greater dynamism of the figures, painted the one facing onto the Mercerie. Dissatisfied with the payment he received, Giorgione submitted his work to a board of experts chaired by Bellini.

In 1510 Giorgione died of the plague and Isabella d'Este asked her agent in Venice to obtain for her the painting of a "Nocte" that must have been in the painter's estate. Over a century later, the demand for his work would be so great that it gave rise to a copious production of fakes. He left no workshop behind him, but had collaborated extensively with other painters, including Titian and Sebastiano del Piombo. Following in the footsteps of Leonardo, he had made great strides in the depiction of atmosphere, blurring the outlines with delicate passages of light and shade and using superimposed glazes of color to create a tonal landscape immersed in a warm luminism.

Gabriele D'Annunzio referred to the painter in his *Fire*: "We know nothing, or next to nothing of him; and some even deny his existence. His name is not written on any work; and there are those who recognize no work to be certainly his [...]. In truth, Giorgione represents in art the Epiphany of Fire. He deserves to be called 'bringer of fire,' like Prometheus."

Moses' Trial by Fire; *The Judgment of Solomon*
oil on panel, 89x72 cm, 89x72 cm
Galleria degli Uffizi, Florence

Previously attributed to Bellini, the two small panels, datable to *c.* 1505, are now considered early works by Giorgione, apart from the figures and a few elements of the landscape in the *Judgment*, painted

by a less gifted artist. The theme of justice present in both the works has led to the suggestion that they were commissioned by a member of one of the various Venetian magistracies for his residence. In the first picture, to prove the innocence of the baby Moses, who has knocked the pharaoh's crown to the ground and trampled on it, the child is offered two bowls, one filled with gold, the other with

burning coals. Moses chooses a coal and lifts it to his mouth, burning himself, but is saved. In the second picture, two women are contending for the same child, both claiming to be its mother. In order to discover the truth, King Solomon orders the child to be cut in two and divided between the women. On hearing the sentence, the real mother renounces the child so as to save its life and the king

gives it to her. The treatment of the landscape shows Northern European influences. The city is confined to the background and the figures look very small in comparison with the soaring trees: characteristics that are close to the Danube School and Altdorfer's lush depiction of nature.

Judith with the Head of Holofernes
oil on panel transferred onto canvas,
144x66.5 cm
Hermitage, St. Petersburg

Acquired by the tsarina Catherine II for
the Hermitage in 1772, the painting dates
from *c.* 1504 and was probably the door
of a cabinet, to judge by the piece of

wood that has been inserted to fill what
must once have been a keyhole. Attributed
to Raphael for its classical composition,
the picture shows the influence of
Perugino and the heroine's face recalls
that of the Virgin in the "Castelfranco
Altarpiece," while the atmospheric veiling
that blurs the landscape in the distance
reveals a familiarity with Leonardo.

After the battle of Fornovo in 1495, at
which the Venetians defeated the army of
Charles VIII, Judith came to be identified
more and more often with Venice in the
guise of Justice. In fact Judith is the
biblical heroine who saved her city,
Bethulia, under siege by the Assyrian
general Holofernes, by seducing him and
cutting off his head. A symbol of the
Church triumphant over unbelievers and
prefiguring Mary's defeat of the devil,
Judith is the personification of various
virtues and of the strength of God that is
made more manifest in the weakness of
men: it is a woman, Judith, who frees the
Jewish city of Bethulia from the threat of
tyranny and an adolescent, David, who
kills the giant Goliath, permitting the
victory of the Israelites over the
Philistines. The woman's bare leg is an
allusion to the seduction of her enemy in
order to achieve her aim and is taken
from Dürer's engraving *The Doctor's
Dream*. As in traditional images of
triumph, the victor stands over the loser.
The heroine rests her foot on the head of
Holofernes, a crude image that contrasts
strongly with the serenity of the landscape
and of the expression on the woman's
face. It is likely that Giorgione portrayed
himself as the general, just as, a century
later, Caravaggio was to give his own
features to the Goliath killed by David.

The Tempest
oil on canvas, 83x73 cm
Gallerie dell'Accademia, Venice

According to Pliny, the legendary Greek
painter Apelles "even painted what cannot
be painted, thunder, flashes, lightning."
Dürer too would be praised by Erasmus
for his ability to reproduce fire, a ray of
light, thunder and lightning. And
Castiglione, in the *Cortegiano*, alludes to
Giorgione's capacity to capture natural
phenomena, storms and the night. The
painter accepted the ancient challenge
and with this small painting of *c.* 1505
created a work whose meaning has left
critics permanently divided. The earliest
reference to the picture is its description
by Marcantonio Michiel, who saw it in
1530 in Gabriele Vendramin's collection
in Venice: "The small landscape on canvas

with the tempest, with the gypsy woman
and soldier, was the work of Zorzi from
Castelfranco." Thus the myth was born of
Giorgione the painter without a subject,
who simply depicted a landscape with a
soldier and a gypsy nursing her child
under a threatening sky. Interpretations
have ranged from allegory to myth
(Mercury and Isis, Jupiter Stator and the
Great Earth Mother), religion (Adam and
Eve, the flight into Egypt), history (the war
of 1509 that engulfed the cities of Veneto
and in particular Padua, identifiable by
the symbol of the Carrara family frescoed
on one of the gates and the lion of St.
Mark on a tower), esotericism and a
search for classical sources. Interesting
parallels have been drawn with Francesco
Colonna's *Hypnerotomachia Poliphili*,
published in 1499 by the famous Venetian
printing house of Aldus Manutius, a work
that circulated in the city's refined and
exclusive cultural circles, fond of hidden
and erudite references comprehensible
only to the initiated. Beneath the figure of
the young man, who in any case is not a
soldier, X-rays have revealed the presence
of a nude woman bathing in the pool;
further analyses have brought to light
details that differ from the final version:
the woman's dress, the presence of
another tower. All in all, the painting may
be an example of the new Venetian genre
of *poesie*: lyrical works which bring
together various literary and visual
sources familiar to readers or observers,
but which leave them free in their
interpretation and emotional response.
Giorgione's research is consistent with
that of Altdorfer's contemporary Danube
School. But *The Tempest* bears no trace
of the untamed nature of Germany, to the
point where it has been seen by recent
critics as an Italian response to
primordial landscape of Northern
European: it presents an archaic world,
but one that is civilized and steeped in
classical values, close to the bucolic
images of Sannazzaro's *Arcadia*. (E.F.)

Titian

Titian (Tiziano Vecellio) was born at Pieve di Cadore in *c.* 1488-90. The early part of his career was closely linked to the activity of Giorgione. Together, they painted the frescoes on the Fondaco dei Tedeschi in Venice, between 1508 and 1509, of which little now remains. Titian also shared Giorgione's thematic and stylistic preferences, and in his youthful work their style is so close that the attribution of a painting like the *Country Concert* (1509, Louvre, Paris) has long oscillated between the two. Titian's first documented independent commission was for the frescoes in the Scuola del Santo in Padua, on which the painter worked in 1511. By 1513 the reputation he had attained in Venice was such that Titian became a sort of state painter, a role that was further consolidated following the death of Giovanni Bellini, in 1516. In that year he received the commission for the *Assumption* for the church of Santa Maria dei Frari, and the altarpiece was unveiled in 1518. With Giorgione and Giovanni Bellini vanished from the scene, Titian showed himself to be a worthy heir, breaking his ties with the local tradition and looking instead to Raphael and Michelangelo, interpreting painting chiefly in terms of color and at the same time constructing a composition of great dynamic and dramatic effect. Those years saw a succession of masterpieces, including the celebrated *Sacred Love and Profane Love* (*c.* 1515, Galleria Borghese, Rome,) and new and prestigious commissions, such as the one in 1518 from the duke of Ferrara, Alfonso d'Este, for the first of a series of three paintings – probably *The Worship of Venus* (Prado, Madrid) – to be hung in his study, the "Camerino d'alabastro." Thus Titian established himself as the absolute master of the Venetian scene and a leading figure on the Italian one: after Raphael's death in 1520, only Michelangelo enjoyed similar prestige. His career continued, with works of a religious character, public commissions and portraits. In 1520 he received the commission for the *Averoldi Polyptych*. Completed in 1522 it can still be seen in the Brescian church of Santi Nazaro e Celso. In 1523 he went back to Venice, where he worked for the doge Andrea Gritti. In 1533 he was appointed official painter to Emperor Charles V, a post that spread his fame throughout Europe. In 1538 he painted the *Venus of Urbino* (Uffizi, Florence) for Guidobaldo II della Rovere, duke of Urbino. Over the next two decades Titian continued to be the most sought-after

Country Concert (*Concert Champêtre*)
Louvre, Paris

portraitist in Europe. He worked for Pope Paul III, Emperor Charles V and his successor, his son Philip II. The scheme of his portraits, at half-length, with the hands visible and continuously varied in its solutions, was highly innovative and allowed him to elevate the psychology of his sitters, transforming them into absolute and ideal types. In 1545 Pope Paul III invited him to Rome, where the following year he painted *Paul III Farnese and His Grandsons* (Capodimonte, Naples). In 1548 he joined the emperor in Augsburg and painted the equestrian portrait *Charles V at Mühlberg* (Prado, Madrid). In the same city, in 1551, he executed the *Portrait of Prince Philip* (Prado, Madrid), at full length and in armor. One of his last works was the *Pietà* in the Gallerie dell'Accademia in Venice, intended for his own tomb and finished by Palma il Giovane. At the end of his career the painter abandoned the meticulous representation of details and the color laid on in large expanses in favor of a style based on broad brushstrokes, in which the final touches were added by smudging the paint with his fingers. The great colorist died in Venice in 1576.

Country Concert (*Concert Champêtre*)
oil on canvas, 105x136.5 cm
Louvre, Paris

The *Country Concert*, long attributed to Giorgione, is now regarded as a work by Titian datable to 1509. The subject of the picture has always prompted questions and arguments. It depicts two women, almost completely nude, one pouring something from a jug and the other playing the flute. With them are two young men seated side by side, one of them playing a lute. In the background a shepherd tends his flock in the shade of some trees, with a few houses further back that seem to form a village. Some scholars hold that it is an allegory with its roots in neoplatonic culture. Among the more recent and accredited

interpretations is the one put forward by Elizabeth Buckley, that the subject was inspired by a text by Sannazaro, the *Arcadia*, published in Naples in 1504, although an unauthorized edition was already in circulation in Venice in 1502. At the beginning of the sixth part of the *Arcadia* a group of shepherds, including Sincero, is about to leave the tomb of Androgeo, located near a spring. Sincero sees a shepherd coming toward him who reminds him of the Trojan Paris but is actually Carino. Sincero tells him of his ill-starred love, and the shepherd asks him to write songs for his beloved. The two women in the painting could be the nymphs that Sincero meets in a dream in the twelfth part: they do not participate in the dialogue between the two youths; indeed, they appear to be invisible to their eyes.

Portrait of Pietro Aretino
oil on canvas, 96.7x77.6 cm
Galleria Palatina, Florence

The painter was a close friend of Pietro Aretino, who in the *Cortigiana* (1534) wrote "[in Venice] there is the glorious, wonderful and great Titian, whose

coloring breathes no differently from the flesh tones, which have pulse and vigor," and in 1537 had called the *Death of Saint Peter Martyr* for the church of Santi Giovanni e Paolo in Venice "the most beautiful thing in Italy." So it is only natural that Pietro Aretino should have turned to Titian for his own portrait, which was delivered in 1545. The painting did not fully meet the writer's expectations, but in a letter sent to Cosimo I, then duke of Tuscany, he was unable to refrain from describing it as follows: "it breathes, the pulse beats in the way I do in life." Pietro gave the picture to Cosimo with the aim of getting into his good graces, but the duke, who kept up a frequent correspondence with him, does not mention the work in his letters. In reality his silence was due to the fact that the canvas had been intercepted by his majordomo, Pierfrancesco Riccio, and hidden from Cosimo for at least three years. Probably the majordomo had guessed that Aretino

wanted to win himself a position at the Medici court with this gift and thought this would come at the expense of his own power. In addition, at the very time the picture was sent, Bronzino, who can be considered Riccio's protégé, was painting the first official portrait of the duke, and Titian's work might have upstaged it, jeopardizing his possibility of becoming the official court portraitist. Later, in 1551, the misunderstanding with Cosimo was cleared up and the portrait was hung in the first room of his private wardrobe along with the Medici's most important pictures. It was seen there by Giorgio Vasari, who mentions it in his *Lives*.

Portrait of a Lady (*La Bella*)
oil on canvas, 89x75.5 cm
Galleria Palatina, Florence

On May 2, 1536, the duke of Urbino, Francesco Maria della Rovere, wrote to his agent Giacomo Leonardi asking him to

put pressure on Titian: he was waiting for the painter to finish "that portrait of that Woman in the blue dress" and send it to him. It is thought that the duke did not see the completed painting until the January of 1538, when he was in Venice with his wife Eleonora Gonzaga and was about to be made commander-in-chief. The picture, known today as *La Bella*, represents a woman in a luxurious and elaborate dress, embellished with golden embroidery. From the cuff of the sleeves, adorned with little roses, protrudes a lace border, the same that runs around the neckline. She is also wearing a long necklace of gold. The use of one of the most costly of pigments, lapis lazuli, for the dress helps to reinforce the impression of richness and opulence. The painting is one of his non-formal portraits, works in which Titian was able to express himself with greater spontaneity, and can be compared with the *Girl with a Fur Wrap* (Kunsthistorisches Museum, Vienna), for which he seems to have used the same model, as he may have done for the *Venus of Urbino* (Galleria degli Uffizi, Florence) as well. For many decades scholars have sought to identify the person portrayed, but nowadays critics tend to favor the hypothesis that she was an anonymous model.

Christ Crowned with Thorns
oil on panel, 303x180 cm
Louvre, Paris

Christ Crowned with Thorns
oil on canvas, 280x182 cm
Alte Pinakothek, Munich

The picture was painted between 1540 and 1542 for the chapel of the confraternity of Santa Corona in the Milanese church of Santa Maria delle Grazie, which housed a precious relic, a thorn from Christ's crown. It formed part of a cycle of frescoes with *Scenes of the Passion* painted by Gaudenzio Ferrari. The highly dramatic composition, characterized by the extreme dynamism of the bodies that converge on the figure of Christ, includes some references to Greco-Roman antiquity: in the bust of Tiberius, for example, who was emperor when Jesus was crucified and whose name is inscribed on the architrave, but also in the representation of Christ, where the face and the position of the legs are citations of the *Laocoön*, the ancient statue in the Vatican Museums whose discovery (1506) had stirred a great deal of interest. Other elements of the painting, however, show the influence of the most recent artistic developments: the rustication of the building in the background, which recalls the Palazzo Te in Mantua, and the twisting of the bodies of the two torturers, which is reminiscent of the frescoes executed by Giulio Romano in that same palace.

Some thirty years after the painting in the Louvre, Titian again tackled the theme of the *Crowning with Thorns*. The composition presents no noteworthy differences as far as Christ and the figures around him are concerned. However, the bust of Tiberius at top right has disappeared, replaced by a large skylight that radiates a shimmering and immanent light and helps to dramatically dematerialize the personages represented: the glimmering reflections fall on the bodies and clothing, producing surprising effects of immateriality on the cloth next to Christ's feet. It is a painting made up of luminous filaments in which the color, powdery and inconsistent, seems to congeal, by now serving no descriptive function and used exclusively to convey the emotional tension. This was to become a typical feature of the last decade of Titian's activity. (A.F.)

Michelangelo

Michelangelo Buonarroti was born at Caprese, near Arezzo, on March 6, 1475. The son of Ludovico Buonarroti, the town's podestà or administrator, he soon moved to Florence with his family. At the age of thirteen he entered the workshop of the painter Domenico Ghirlandaio and, while still an adolescent, studied under the sculptor Bertoldo and frequented the garden of San Marco, where the Medici had installed part of their collection of ancient statuary. Here he came into contact with Lorenzo the Magnificent and other members of the Medici family, as well as Humanists like Marsilio Ficino and Politian, who often visited the garden. Before the age of sixteen he had carved two bas-reliefs that revealed the extraordinary depth of his talent: the *Battle of the Centaurs* and the *Madonna della Scala* (now both in the Casa Buonarroti, Florence).

Following Lorenzo's death in 1492, and on the eve of the expulsion of the Medici from Florence, Michelangelo went to Bologna. He stayed in the city until 1495, executing several sculptures for the *Tomb of Saint Dominic*. In 1496 he went to Rome, as a guest of the banker Jacopo Galli, and obtained prestigious commissions from the pope's nephew, Cardinal Raffaele Riario (the *Bacchus* now in the Bargello, 1497-98), and from Cardinal Jean Bilhères (the *Pietà* in St. Peter's, 1498-1500).

Returning in 1501 to Florence, then under a republican government headed by the gonfalonier Pier Soderini, he was commissioned to carve a statue of *David*: the major sculptural undertaking of his youth, it was completed by 1504. The statue was originally intended for one of the external buttresses of the cathedral, but was then erected, as a symbol of Florentine freedom, in front of the Palazzo della Signoria. The other major public commission of those years was a large fresco depicting the *Battle of Cascina*, which was to decorate one of the walls of the Sala del Maggior Consiglio, in competition with Leonardo, who had been entrusted with the execution of the *Battle of Anghiari* in the same room. The work was never finished, but Michelangelo's cartoon stirred great admiration among his contemporaries and soon became the object of enthusiastic study by Florentine and foreign artists, with the result that, according to Vasari, it was quickly torn to shreds. In the same years Michelangelo painted the most important of his panel pictures, the *Doni Tondo* (1507), for the wealthy Florentine merchant Agnolo Doni, who was also Raphael's patron.

In 1505 Pope Julius II had entrusted Michelangelo with the grandiose project for his tomb, a work originally intended to comprise a total of forty life-size statues. But on his arrival in Rome in 1508, the artist, despite his lively protests, was given the task of decorating the ceiling of the Sistine Chapel: this marked the beginning of what Michelangelo himself was to call "the tragedy of the tomb," with the execution of the ambitious project, to which he attached great importance, always postponed and progressively pared down until it was reduced, in 1545, to the wall monument in San Pietro in Vincoli adorned with the celebrated statue of *Moses*. The decoration of the Sistine Chapel, an undertaking that he initially accepted with reluctance (Michelangelo considered himself a sculptor and not a painter), engaged him until 1512: it is the artist's greatest pictorial masterpiece and one of the most important works of the Italian Renaissance, destined to exercise a decisive influence on Italian and European art.

In 1515 he returned to Florence, where he had been commissioned to build the facade of the church of San Lorenzo by Pope Leo X, the son of Lorenzo the Magnificent. But this too, the first major architectural project entrusted to Michelangelo, was never completed. However, again at the behest of Leo X and then his cousin Clement VII, the artist did realize some works linked to the complex of San Lorenzo: in 1519 the New Sacristy, with the Medicean tombs of Duke Lorenzo of Urbino and Duke Giuliano of Nemours, and in 1524 the Library with its celebrated grand staircase.

In 1534 Michelangelo left Florence for good and went back to Rome, where Paul III, in 1535, entrusted him with the execution of the *Last Judgment* on the rear wall of the Sistine Chapel and, in 1541, the decoration of the Pauline Chapel with the *Conversion of Saint Paul* and *Crucifixion of Saint Peter*, finished by 1550. In 1538 he was commissioned to reorganize the square on top of the Capitoline Hill, and in 1546 placed in charge of the construction of St. Peter's, for which he submitted a design for the basilica and above all for his greatest architectural masterpiece, the dome, completed after his death. Despite his advanced age, Michelangelo went on working on his sculpture right up until the last days of his life. He died in Rome on February 18, 1564.

Deposition in the Tomb
tempera on panel, 159x149 cm
National Gallery, London

The authorship of the panel has long been debated by critics, ever since the attribution to Michelangelo was first proposed, around the middle of the 19th century. It is one of the very few paintings by Buonarroti that is not a fresco: the artist distinctly preferred the medium of sculpture to that of painting. Like the so-called *Manchester Madonna* (also in the National Gallery of London), the *Deposition* was executed in Rome, in the same years in which Michelangelo started work on the ceiling of the Sistine Chapel. The picture was never finished, and several parts are missing, like the figure on the right or the arm of the woman kneeling on the left. Comparison of the completed sections with such an undisputed masterpiece as the *Doni Tondo* has led to the recognition, in the drawing of the figures as well as the choice of colors, of Michelangelo's authorship. The sculptural contraposition of Joseph of Arimathea, on the left, putting his weight on his bent leg and turning his head on its massive neck to the other side, is typically Michelangelesque and reminiscent of the powerful torsions of the figures in the Sistine Chapel, while the old man supporting Christ echoes the St. Joseph in the *Doni Tondo*.
The beautiful anatomical study of Jesus's lifeless body, just lowered from the cross and held upright by the bands, is a theme that was to hold the interest of Michelangelo the sculptor right up until his very last work, also left unfinished, the *Rondanini Pietà*.

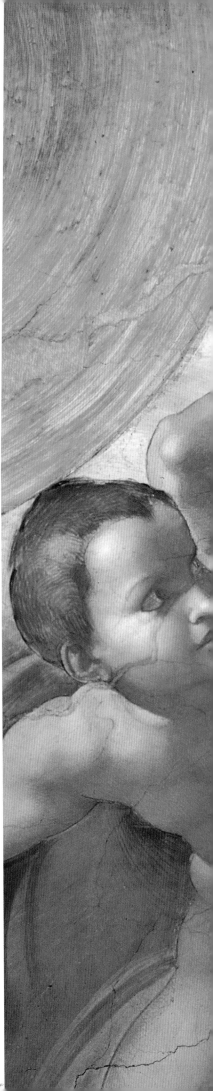

MICHELANGELO

Ceiling of the Sistine Chapel

The chapel, consecrated in 1483, had been built for Sixtus IV, and the pope had summoned the most famous artists of those years to decorate its walls: Botticelli, Perugino, Ghirlandaio and Signorelli. The ceiling was painted with a starry sky, and Julius II entrusted Michelangelo with the task of frescoing it, asking the painter to temporarily set aside the grandiose project of the papal tomb. Michelangelo agreed with ill grace, and rejected the pontiff's request for a decoration rich in gold and precious materials. The painter came up with a highly ambitious iconographic program, which comprised scenes from Genesis and representations of prophets, sibyls and the ancestors of Christ. The ceiling was divided into panels by a grand framework of painted architecture. At the center are four larger panels alternating with five smaller ones: *Separation of Light from Darkness, Creation of the Sun and Moon, Separation of the Water and the Earth and Creation of the Animals, Creation of Adam, Creation of Eve, Original Sin and Expulsion from Paradise, Sacrifice of Noah, The Flood* and *Drunkenness of Noah*. In front of the mock pilasters that separate the scenes from Genesis are the *Ignudi*, nude adolescents holding festoons tied to bronze medallions. Between the vaulting cells *Sibyls* and *Prophets* are represented on a gigantic scale (originally their places

were to have been taken by the twelve apostles). In the corner cells are frescoed four miracles worked to preserve Israel (*The Punishment of Haman, The Brazen Serpent, Judith and Holofernes, David and Goliath*). In the cells and the lunettes above the windows are set the *Ancestors of Christ*, each represented with his family, always made up of three people like that of Jesus to underline their function as a link between the scenes from the Old Testament on the vault and the Christological episodes on the walls. Michelangelo took about four years to complete the frescoes, between 1508 and 1512. The whole of the cycle, from the viewpoint of not just style but also iconography and doctrine, was conceived by the artist himself. Evidence for this is provided by Vasari, who was able to hear the story from Buonarroti at first hand. Pope Julius II had told him: "Have the chapel enriched with colors and gold, in which it is poor." To which Michelangelo had replied by reminding him of the poverty of the "holy men who despised wealth." The work made his fame, and was straightaway admired and studied by other artists, exercising a powerful influence on the evolution of Renaissance art. Raphael, who had been able to see it, not yet complete, in 1509, was so deeply impressed that he modified his own style in the decoration of the Vatican Stanze.

The *Creation of the Sun and Moon*, reproduced here, is one of the most striking of Michelangelo's inventions, with the gesture of God the Father marking the depth of the space with his outstretched arms, a compositional theme that the painter was to develop years later, in the Pauline Chapel. Remarkable, and iconographically daring, is the idea of the figure of the Eternal Father viewed from behind, moving away into the background, in a beautiful foreshortening. The recent restoration of the ceiling, whose results have stirred a great deal of controversy, has freed the frescoes from centuries of grime that had dimmed their colors. While it is true that Michelangelo's art is, even in painting, essentially plastic in nature, and so based on shading and drawing, the cleaning of the Sistine Chapel has revealed an extremely varied palette, in which color is used in a way that anticipates Mannerist painting, with the variation of shades in relation to the incidence of the light. (S.G.C.)

Raphael

Raphael (Raffaello Sanzio) was born in Urbino in 1483, the son of Giovanni Santi, a painter and poet active at the court of Federico da Montefeltro and author of an interesting chronicle in verse that refers to some of the greatest artists of the 15th century. Raphael soon entered the workshop of Pietro Perugino, one of the most renowned painters of the day who was to have a great influence on his formation. In the years between 1500 and 1504 Raphael moved between Perugia, Siena, Orvieto, Venice and perhaps Florence and Rome, studying the works of his contemporaries, and in particular Luca Signorelli and Pinturicchio. From 1504 to 1508 he was in Florence, during the culturally lively years of the republic headed by Soderini, and saw Michelangelo and Leonardo at work on the decoration of the Sala del Maggior Consiglio: the encounter with Florentine art left a profound mark on the artistic evolution of the young but already well-known painter. He also obtained important commissions from the city's most prominent families, bolstering his reputation.

In 1508 Pope Julius II called him to Rome to fresco the papal apartments (the Vatican Stanze). Raphael finished the Stanza della Segnatura by 1511, the Stanza di Eliodoro in 1514 and the Stanza dell'Incendio di Borgo in 1517; the Stanza di Costantino was completed in 1520 by his assistants, who had already made a major contribution in the previous room. Over the years he was working on the grand undertaking of the Stanze, Raphael received commissions and posts of great prestige. In 1514 Leo X appointed him architect in charge of the construction of St. Peter's. In 1515 he was commissioned to design the cartoons (now in the Victoria and Albert Museum, London) for a series of tapestries to be hung in the Sistine Chapel. In 1519, with his pupils and collaborators, he painted the *Scenes from the Old Testament* in the Vatican Logge. The banker Agostino Chigi entrusted him with the decoration of the loggia of his villa (later called the Farnesina) and the family chapel in Santa Maria del Popolo, for which he also designed the architecture. He worked for the most eminent members of the papal court, from Cardinal Bibbiena to Bindo Altoviti and the writer Baldassare Castiglione. Raphael became extremely famous during his lifetime, and was, along with Michelangelo, the most sought-after and highly esteemed artist of his day. Unlike the great Florentine, Raphael quickly surrounded himself with a group of disciples and collaborators (of whom the most talented was Giulio Romano) who permitted him to fulfill the numerous and demanding commissions that he received and who were responsible, through the production of prints, for the diffusion of Raphael's models in Italy and beyond. We know, for example, that Dürer was very keen to acquire a complete series of Raimondi's engravings after Raphael. He also played an important role in the preservation and rediscovery of Rome's classical antiquities: Leo X made him the city's first conservator of antiquities and he was given the task of drawing up an archeological plan of Rome. He died in Rome on April 6, 1520, at the age of just thirty-seven.

Triumph of Galatea
fresco, 295x225 cm
Villa Farnesina, Rome

The fresco was commissioned from Raphael by the Sienese Agostino Chigi, the pope's extremely wealthy banker, for the villa he had had built between 1509 and 1510, later acquired by the Farnese family and for this reason now known as the Farnesina. Baldassarre Peruzzi and Sebastiano del Piombo also took part in the decoration. Raphael finished his share of the work between 1511 and 1512.

Chigi was a great admirer of Raphael's art, and he also entrusted him with the design and decoration of the family chapel in Santa Maria del Popolo. The fresco represents Galatea, one of the Nereids, daughters of Nereus and Doris, who was courted in vain by the Cyclops Polyphemus and loved by the handsome shepherd Acis: the source for the iconography of the fresco is a poem by the Florentine Humanist Politian. Galatea rides across the sea on a shell drawn by dolphins guided by a cupid; tritons and nymphs keep her company, while other

cupids shoot their arrows of love from the sky. A fresco by Sebastiano del Piombo, located to the left of Raphael's painting, represents Polyphemus singing his clumsy love song. The work was greatly appreciated by his contemporaries, who in particular admired the beauty of the figure at the center of the composition. To the praise of his great friend, the celebrated man-of-letters Baldassare Castiglione, Raphael responded: "As for the Galatea, I should consider myself a great master if it had half the merits you mention in your letter. [...] I add that in order to paint a fair one, I should need to see several fair ones. [...] but as there is a shortage of both good judges and beautiful women, I am making use of some sort of idea which comes into my mind. Whether this idea has any artistic excellence in itself, I do not know. But I do strive to attain it." The passage is particularly interesting because it shows how Raphael's fully Humanistic conception of art fits into the current of Neoplatonic thought: imperfect nature can provide a model for art, in this case the representation of the human body, only if it is possible to pick the best characteristics from many women. Consequently, as the philosopher Pico della Mirandola argued, the very idea of beauty is innate. Raphael's art is the highest expression of this conception of ideal beauty, and he was admired by his contemporaries chiefly for the perfection of his painting: in his epitaph for the painter, the poet Pietro Bembo wrote that Mother Nature herself had feared to be surpassed by Raphael. The fresco of the *Galatea* was painted immediately after those of the Stanza della Segnatura in the Vatican, and at the time of its execution Raphael was engaged, with his assistants, in the decoration of the Stanza di Eliodoro. It was around this time that Michelangelo finished the ceiling of the Sistine Chapel, but Raphael had already had an opportunity to see it before its completion: here too we can see the influence of Michelangelo in the sculptural poses of the athletic and muscular nudes used to represent the tritons.

RAPHAEL

Portrait of Baldassare Castiglione
oil on canvas, 82x67 cm
Louvre, Paris

Born in Mantua in 1478, Baldassare
Castiglione was in the service of
Guidobaldo da Montefeltro and then
Francesco Maria della Rovere at the court
of Urbino from 1504 to 1513. Sent as
ambassador to Rome in 1513, he made
friends with Raphael. A refined poet in the
vulgar tongue and in Latin and a
successful diplomat, Castiglione owed his
fame largely to the book *Il cortegiano*
(*The Courtier*), written between 1513
and 1518 and published in 1528. The
work, in the form of a dialogue, is a
discussion of the ideal qualities of the
courtier: the book proved an almost
immediate success at all the courts of
Europe. Raphael painted the portrait of
his friend between 1514 and 1515; it is
one of the painter's finest works in the
genre. The composition, which cuts off
the sitter's arm, normally included in the
framing of the Renaissance portrait,
brings us close to the figure of
Castiglione: our gaze meets the writer's
and we are struck by his expression and
psychology, so accurately caught by
Raphael. The symphony of blacks and
grays in the sleeve and the convincing
representation of the texture of the fur, in
a delicate harmony with the sandy color
of the background, constitute one of
Raphael's most superb achievements.

La Fornarina
oil on panel, 85x60 cm
Galleria Nazionale di Arte Antica, Rome

The painting is a portrait of Raphael's
mistress, whom he also portrayed in *La
Donna Velata* in Palazzo Pitti, Florence,
and who can be recognized in other
works by the artist. The woman has been
tentatively identified as Margherita Luti,
the daughter of a baker in the Santa
Dorotea quarter of Rome called
Francesco Senese (*fornarina* means
something like "baker's little girl"). The
work became very well-known in the
Romantic era, when there was keen
interest in the love affair between the
great painter and the working-class girl
who, according to the pseudo-historical
reconstructions of the 19th century,
entered the convent of Sant'Apollonia
following the death of her lover. It is one
of Raphael's last paintings, datable to the
year of his death, 1520 or a little earlier.
Doubts have been raised about whether
the painting is entirely his work and it has
been suggested that Raphael's most gifted
pupil, Giulio Romano, made a decisive
contribution to the work after his master's
death. But the recent restoration has
shown that the final layers of glaze were
never completed, and so it is likely that it
was left in its present state by Raphael
himself. Originally the background did not
consist of a bush of myrtle, a plant sacred
to Venus, but of a landscape fading into
the distance. The canvas bears Raphael's
signature on the bracelet around the
Fornarina's left arm. (S.G.C.)

Holbein the Younger

orn around 1497 at Augsburg, he started to work independently at Basel in 1515. Here, at the service of the wealthy local burghers, he executed portraits, religious paintings and illustrations for books. He then received commissions for the decoration of the Great Council Chamber in the city hall and of the facade of the Haus zum Tanz, a daring experiment in illusionism. In 1524 he made a journey to France, where he was able to see the works of Leonardo, including, perhaps, the *Mona Lisa* at a castle on the Loire. He then went back to Basel, but the time of major commissions from the Catholic Church, which was struggling for its survival, was over and the Protestant Reformation rejected sacred images: as Erasmus wrote in 1526: "Here art died." So he went to try his luck in England, presenting himself to Thomas More with a letter of introduction from Desiderius Erasmus. He worked for the island's humanists and scholars, foreshadowing the Dutch group portraits of the 17th century, and returned to Basel a richer man. But it was a difficult moment: in February 1529 a frenzy of iconoclasm broke out and works of art were torn to pieces and burned in the streets and in front of churches. There was no room for artists and in 1532 he went back to England. Here too the political situation had changed. His former clients had fallen into disgrace and the artist now sought the patronage of the colony of German merchants, for whom he painted portraits that focused on the features and the resolve of his subjects, presenting them surrounded by the symbols of their social status. His first portrait of King Henry VIII and his third wife Jane Seymour dates from 1536: Holbein had at last found a position as court painter. In this guise he was obliged to make several trips to the Continent, in order to paint portraits of noblewomen from which the sovereign could choose his fourth wife. He went to Brussels, where he portrayed Christine of Denmark, as well as to Le Havre, Nancy and Joinville. He paid a brief visit to Basel, where he arrived, as a contemporary recalled, "dressed in silk and velvet: he who previously could barely afford to buy wine by the glass." In 1539 he left London for the Continent once again, to paint portraits of the sisters Amalia and Anne of Cleves, Henry's future wife. Returning to London, he died there in 1543, perhaps in an outbreak of the plague.

The Ambassadors
oil on panel, 207x209.5 cm
National Gallery, London

The painting, executed in 1533, was presented as an enigma, a "picture with a secret," in line with a custom that was to become common, especially in Germany. In fact the wealth of carefully described details is accompanied by an indecipherable figure in the foreground. The age of the figures is explicitly stated in the painting: twenty-nine is engraved on the dagger of the gentleman on the left, while the book on which the one on the

right is leaning declares that he is twenty-four. The objects and details reflect the private life and political career of the subjects. In addition to the usual places, a portable globe indicates a small town called Polisy, home of the personage on the left: thus he is identified as the French ambassador Jean de Dinteville, wearing around his neck the medal of the Order of St. Michael that he had been awarded by Francis I. The young churchman is Georges de Selve, his friend and the papal ambassador. Both men were on a mission to London in 1533, as we are informed by the floor depicted in the painting: it is, in

fact, the floor of the abbey of Westminster, political and religious symbol of England. The objects represented cover all the disciplines of the "quadrivium," the exact sciences: geometry, arithmetic, music and astronomy. In addition to the terrestrial globe, on which the route taken by Magellan in 1522 is traced, as a proof that the earth is round, there is a celestial globe, positioned in such a way as to indicate a precise date, but with reference to the latitude of Paris or Rome, and therefore alluding to the Vatican. The sundials and the *torquetum* or goniometer, a device used by Nicholas of

Cusa to fix the position of the sun and stars, are a reminder of another portrait by Holbein, that of Nikolaus Kratzer, a German astronomer and friend of Thomas More, Desiderius Erasmus and Copernicus who had moved to London and was an ardent supporter of the idea that the earth moved around the sun. The open books in the painting, on the other hand, are inscribed with two hymns by Luther, in reference to the mission of Bishop de Selve, an advocate of the need for a reconciliation between the Catholic and Protestant doctrines. But this is 1533: the Church of Rome has not accepted Henry VIII's divorce from Catherine of Aragon and marriage to Anne Boleyn, and so the king has declared himself head of the Church of England and the Anglican schism is looming, while Catholic France

is engaged in a struggle with Charles V. A delicate mission, that of the French ambassadors, and one that had to avoid a rupture with England. But the lute depicted in the painting has a broken string and its case lies, upside down, on the ground, a sign of lack of harmony. The clasp of Jean de Dinteville's hat is a skull, a *memento mori* to ward off

earthly vanity. And the strange shape in the foreground is also a skull, which is only revealed when viewed in a particular way: it is an anamorphosis, not recognizable unless looked at edgeways or with the aid of a curved mirror. Such symbols of death were sometimes included in portraits to put people on their guard against false pride and illusion.

The scene is set in front of a rich and heavy drape, like the ones that were generally raised to unveil a sacred vision or a revelation. De Selve believed in a God who could not be reached with reason alone, a God hidden in the heart of the believer: in profile and with the short arm of the cross turned toward us, a small silver crucifix is concealed in the first fold of the drape.

Portrait of Erasmus of Rotterdam
oil on panel, 42x33 cm
Louvre, Paris

At Basel in 1523 Holbein met the Humanist Erasmus of Rotterdam, who that year had composed his *Paraphrase on Mark*. Erasmus wrote of himself: "He was rather fastidious, so that nothing he has written has ever satisfied him, and he was not even content with his own appearance; it is already much that, on the insistence of his friends, he allowed his picture to be painted." So Holbein became the painter of Erasmus, as Cranach was of Luther. From a letter written by Erasmus in 1524 it can be deduced that this was one of two portraits "painted by an artist of great merit" and sent to England, one for the archbishop of Canterbury and this one, probably, for Thomas More, who thanked him for the gift. But the scholar was convinced that his best side emerged from his writings: "What small part of Erasmus would you carry with you, if you took home a painted

or sculpted image of this little body? You can see the best part of Erasmus, every time you wish, in his books, assuming that there be something in me worth looking at." The scholar accepted the value of portraits, but claimed they were unable to reveal the mind, the intelligence and the memory of the person portrayed. He also praised Dürer as an "artist worthy of immortality," as a modern version of Apelles, the legendary artist of antiquity. But on the other hand he criticized the superstitious use of images: in the *Praise of Folly* he deplored the stupidity of those who were convinced "that if they can but see a wooden or painted Polypheme Christopher, they shall not die that day" (it was because of this belief that large figures of St. Christopher were often painted on the outside walls of houses, so they would be visible from a distance), or that they would not die in battle after saluting a carving of St. Barbara. In the portrait the humanist is presented in profile, busy writing the *incipit* of his work. The pose in profile denotes a

classical influence, as it is typical of the images on coins: Erasmus himself, moreover, had had a coin with his effigy struck in 1519 to give to his friends.

Portrait of Henry VIII
oil on panel, 88.2x75 cm
Galleria Nazionale, Rome

The king is portrayed here at the age of forty-nine, at the time of his fourth marriage to Anne of Cleves, an alliance supported by the prime minister Thomas Cromwell as a means of binding England to the Protestant princes of Germany. But the princess was soon repudiated and Cromwell executed, as happened to all those who opposed the king's designs. The picture, datable to 1539-40 and not attributed by all art historians to Holbein, can be connected with the lost mural painting in the Privy Chamber of 1537, and should probably be seen in relation to the portrait of Anne of Cleves in the Louvre: the king's costume, judging by

contemporary descriptions, is the one he wore at their wedding. Generally speaking, the portrait in profile is typical of the clients of a painting, as well as of numismatics and genealogical trees, and recalls the practice of the exchange of portraits between correspondents who did not know each other. This was very common in the case of betrothals, and in such pictures women were represented facing to the left, in analogy with their position in front of the altar. The frontal portrait, on the other hand, is mark of the ruler, whether religious or secular: it symbolizes sovereignty. In this state portrait all the elements, the pose, the clothing, the gaze, combine to underline the majesty of Henry VIII, the king who, with the Act of Supremacy of 1534, created the Church of England, declaring himself its supreme head. (E.F.)

ANNO · ÆTATIS ·   · SVÆ · XLIX ·

Bruegel the Elder

According to the scanty information available to us, Bruegel was born sometime between 1525 and 1530. In 1551 he was registered in the guild of Antwerp as a master and in 1552 set off on a journey to France and Italy, going as far as Sicily, as is demonstrated by his drawing of Reggio Calabria in flames while under siege by the Turks. In 1553 he spent a long time in Rome and by 1555 was back in Antwerp, where prints made from the artist's drawings of landscapes were published by Hieronymus Cock's famous printing house *Aux Quatre Vents*, frequented by people of culture like the geographer and cartographer Abraham Ortelius, author of one of the first modern atlases. Then came the paintings, from *The Netherlands Proverbs* and *Children's Games*, filled with tiny figures engaged in various activities and of particular interest for the history of popular customs, to *The Tower of Babel* or the *Peasant Wedding* and *Dance of the Peasants*, later works in which a few figures of large size occupy the space. It was a particularly difficult time for Flanders, ravaged by fighting, starvation and plunder. These were the years of the Spanish repression carried out by Philip II in the Low Countries, years of tension that were to explode, in 1567, into a long and bloody war. To the famines and the political and economic crises were added Protestant demands for religious freedom, but also the frenzy of iconoclasm that was to lead to the destruction of sacred images and the devastation of churches.

In 1563 the painter moved to Brussels, where he married and where he would die in 1569. His opposition to Philip II was probably the reason for the order he gave to his wife on his deathbed to burn a large number of particularly satirical and caustic drawings, "either because he had repented of them or because he feared that his wife might suffer some unpleasantness as a result of them," commented the Flemish painter and writer van Mander, adding that the painter left him in his will a picture with a magpie on the gallows: the magpie represented the backbiter, deemed worthy of hanging.

Hunters in the Snow
oil on panel, 117x162 cm
Kunsthistorisches Museum, Vienna

In the Netherlands artists, unable to count on the commission of great cycles of religious paintings, devoted themselves principally to the production of easel paintings, which the bourgeoisie hung on the walls of their homes. Both Luther and Erasmus considered the home to be the ideal place to learn the stories of the Bible

and had written about the pedagogic function of its decoration. Proverbs were thought particularly suitable for the adornment of doors, windows and goblets. Representations of the months, on the other hand, were usually located in the dining room. This picture painted by Bruegel in 1565 belongs to a series of *Months* or *Seasons* of which only five panels survive. The most likely hypothesis is that there were six of them in all and that they represented pairs of months: in this case two winter months, perhaps the last in the series and therefore the end of the year, which for the Low Countries began in March. In the European tradition, the months were generally represented by illustration of the human activities typical of the period, often accompanied by the corresponding sign of the Zodiac. Bruegel's paintings underline the seasonal changes in the landscape and the work that permits food to be put on the table, suited to their

location in the dining room. In particular, the hunters are coming home with their bag, passing in front of an inn called "At the Stag" where a pig is being roasted: peasants were generally not allowed to hunt big game and therefore devoted their attention mainly to rabbits, hares, foxes and badgers, partly with the aim, in springtime, of protecting the crops. The "cartographic" layout of the painting may be a reflection of the artist's friendship with the geographer Abraham Ortelius and serves to stress the descriptive character of Flemish painting, in contrast to the narrative style typical of Italian art.

The Parable of the Blind
tempera on canvas, 86x154 cm
Gallerie Nazionali di Capodimonte, Naples

"Can the blind lead the blind? Shall they not both fall into the ditch?": these are the words of the Gospel to which this painting of 1568 refers, and it may also allude to a Flemish proverb that advised people always to walk with great care, be steady on their feet and never put their complete trust in anyone but God. This interpretation is also justified by the presence, in the background, of a small church and the hurdy-gurdy, a musical instrument and symbol of moral blindness. In a device typical of Italian painting and the theater, one of the figures seeks to involve the observer: in fact the beggar who is about to fall over turns his gaze out of the painting, but the diagonal composition suggests that his companions will meet the same fate as the leader of the procession, falling inevitably into the same hole.

Peasant Wedding
oil on panel, 114x164 cm
Kunsthistorisches Museum, Vienna

Bruegel's biographer van Mander relates that the painter often attended fairs and weddings with a friend. Dressed as peasants, they handed out gifts and, passing themselves off as relatives of the bride or the groom, amused themselves observing the people eating, drinking and dancing.

The representation of peasants was generally associated with mockery and a sense of ridicule, perhaps in order to reaffirm the values of the dominant urban classes. But there was another literary tradition that saw the peasants in a more favorable light: Desiderius Erasmus considered them essential to society and the Protestant reformers regarded farming as one of the primary occupations of Christians and contrasted the corruption of the town with the simple lifestyle of the peasants, synonymous with innocence and common sense. A handbook on marriage printed at Bruges in 1561 advised young women not to disdain marriage with a peasant, guarantee of a healthy, prosperous and wholesome life.
In the picture, painted around 1568, the reception takes place in a barn; the bride, who was expected to maintain a modest demeanor at her wedding, sits with her eyes lowered in front of the drape of honor, while dishes made with saffron, traditional at wedding feasts and harvest time, are distributed. Among the guests, who would often arrive with spoons tucked into their hats and knives in their belts, we see a Franciscan monk on the

right in conversation with a bearded gentleman, perhaps the landowner come to honor the banquet with his presence, who closely resembles the portrait of Bruegel himself. The groom cannot be identified, but it was the custom at weddings for him to serve the bride and her family. Two small sheaves of wheat are hung in the form of a cross under a wooden rake: they represent the gleaning, the collection of ears left over after reaping that was a guaranteed right of the poor.
Dutch peasants were famous everywhere for their productivity. Philip II of Spain, ruler of the Low Countries, feared

disorder and outbreaks of violence at the country festivals, which entailed the movement of large numbers of people from one village to another. In 1559 he issued a decree declaring that each community had to limit itself to one festival a year, and that all such festivals were to take place on the same day. At a time of rediscovery of local traditions, Bruegel's painting, favorable to the freedom of the peasant feasts, may have represented a patriotic gesture of protest against Spanish interference. (E.F.)

EL GRECO

El Greco

Domenikos Theotokópoulos called El Greco was born to a Catholic family on Crete, in the city of Candia (Iraklion), in 1541. In 1560 he moved to Venice, where he probably entered Titian's studio, and in 1570 met the Croatian illuminator Giulio Clovio, who recommended him to Cardinal Alessandro Farnese. In 1572 he was in Rome, at a time when debate was raging over the nudes in Michelangelo's *Last Judgment*. Declaring that he could repaint the fresco, "if the whole work were pulled down," "with honesty and decency," he made himself very unpopular with the artists present. From 1572 to 1575 he seems to have been in Venice again, and then moved to Spain in 1576, probably recommended by Pedro Chacon, the canon of Toledo Cathedral who had been librarian of the Palazzo Farnese and whom we know to have owned seven paintings by Theotokópoulos. In Spain he was given the byname El Greco ("The Greek"). After a short stay in Madrid he settled in Toledo, where he soon received numerous commissions, including the celebrated *El Espolio* (*Disrobing of Christ*) for that city's cathedral. In 1579 he was able to meet Philip II on a visit to the city: the next year the king commissioned the *Martyrdom of Saint Maurice* from him for the chapel dedicated to the saint in the Escorial near Madrid. Over the following years the painter enjoyed a degree of success, as is apparent from his standard of living and the prestigious assignments he received. His output was prolific and almost all of it produced for local religious institutions. He became very famous, and his art was celebrated by Spanish writers in his own lifetime. Many conjectures have been made about El Greco's state of physical and mental health, but nothing can be said for certain, except that in 1613 he fell seriously ill and died on April 7, 1614.

Martyrdom of Saint Maurice and His Legions
oil on canvas, 448x301 cm
El Escorial, Madrid

The altarpiece was commissioned by Philip II for the chapel dedicated to St. Maurice in the Escorial and is signed on the sheet of paper in the mouth of the snake in the foreground. The oldest reference to the work in the documents is the king's order to the prior, dated April 25, 1580, to procure for the artist the material he needed, and ultramarine blue in particular. The work was completed on November 16, 1582. It is likely that the task was assigned to El Greco following the death, in 1579, of the painter Fernandez de Navarrete, who had undertaken to supply thirty-six altarpieces for the Escorial. The king was not satisfied with the work and a few years later decided to replace El Greco's masterpiece with a canvas ordered from the Umbrian painter Romolo Cincinnato. The picture was to remain the only royal commission fulfilled by Theotokópoulos. Among the soldiers of the "Theban Legion" can be recognized portraits of some members of the court with high military rank: in the background on the right, we see Emanuele Filiberto, duke of Savoy and grand master of the Order of St. Maurice and St. Lazarus, and Philip's nephew Alessandro Farnese, duke of Parma. St. Maurice was the patron of the Order of the Golden Fleece. The saint was given the features of Philip II himself. The scene in the foreground is the moment when the saint persuades his companions to face martyrdom for their belief in Christ. The martyrdom itself is represented in the background: two soldiers are holding a long pole, symbolizing the yoke under which they were forced to pass as an act of humiliation prior to their execution. In direct conflict with the Roman school (favored by Philip II, always on the

EL GRECO

lookout for Italian artists), El Greco painted a profoundly Mannerist picture with the diagonal separating the scene of the martyrdom from that of the decision, the off-center position of the figure in the foreground and the great differences of scale. The work was found wanting because it was not historically accurate, because it distorted the meaning of the scene by concentrating more on the acceptance of martyrdom than on the martyrdom itself and because it did not invite devotion: in his version, Cincinnato brought the martyrdom of the saint into the foreground and eliminated the portraits of contemporary personages.

The Burial of the Count of Orgaz
oil on canvas, 480x360 cm
Santo Tomé, Toledo

The work, signed and dated 1578, was actually executed between 1586 and 1588. The date is set on the handkerchief peeping out of the pocket of the boy kneeling in the foreground on the left,

identified by art historians as the painter's son Jorge Manuel, and perhaps refers to the year of his birth. The large canvas was commissioned from El Greco by Andrés Núñez, priest of the church of Santo Tomé, and depicts the miraculous burial of Gonzalo Ruiz, a member of the family later to be made counts of Orgaz, who had died in 1323. According to legend the nobleman's body had been placed in the tomb by St. Augustine and St. Stephen, as a reward for the good works he had carried out during his life, and in particular the foundation of a monastery dedicated to St. Stephen and assigned to the Augustinian Fathers in 1312. Further evidence for this miraculous event appears to have come to light in 1583. The burial takes place before a large group of contemporary personages, among whom the figure in the second row looking toward the observer has been identified as the painter himself, and the priest on the right as the client, while the Virgin, the only woman present, may be a portrait of Doña Jerónima de Las Cuevas, mother of El Greco's son. Above,

among the clouds, Christ is surrounded by hosts of angels and saints, with St. John the Baptist and Mary interceding, in a bipartite scheme of composition, with the celestial vision dominating the upper part of the painting in a manner that was typical of Counter-Reformation art and frequently adopted by El Greco.

Adoration of the Shepherds
oil on canvas, 319x180 cm
Prado, Madrid

The *Adoration of the Shepherds* is one of El Greco's masterpieces and is datable to the last years of his life: Luis Trista, El Greco's assistant in 1603-07, claimed to have seen him still working on the picture in 1618. The artist had painted it for his own sepulchral monument, following his acquisition of a family chapel in the Toledan church of Santo Domingo el Antiguo. The architectural frame of gilded wood is original and was designed by the painter himself.

The composition is still influenced by the work of Bassano, from whose *Adorations* he also took the idea of the nocturne illuminated from below by the figure of the Infant Jesus, with the figures in the foreground lit from behind, but El Greco's reinterpretation places greater emphasis on the expression of emotions and the eloquence of the gestures. He makes remarkable use of the light, which moves between the figures, lending depth to the picture. In spite of the nighttime setting the colors are brilliant, and the reddish-orange clothing of the kneeling shepherd and the yellow of St. Joseph's drapery stand out. (S.G.C.)

17TH CENTURY

Annibale Carracci

he son of a tailor, he was born in Bologna in 1560 and took the first steps of his artistic career working for his cousin Ludovico, who was slightly older, alongside his brother Agostino. At the age of twenty, on a visit to Parma, he was greatly impressed by the painting of Correggio, and shortly afterward, through Agostino, came into contact with the work of the great Venetian masters, especially Veronese and Tintoretto. These early experiences were to have a decisive role in Annibale's formation, and over the course of the 1580s he went several times to both Parma and Venice. The first major public commission undertaken by the Carracci was the frieze of Palazzo Fava in Bologna, finished by 1584. In the same years they founded an academy of painting, at first called the Accademia dei Desiderosi and then the Accademia degli Incamminati, on the model of similar literary institutions. The three artists set out to encourage a return to the study of nature, in opposition to the contrived tendencies of late Mannerism, taking as a model the art of the mature Renaissance, from Raphael to Correggio and Titian. In 1595 Annibale went to Rome, where he was soon joined by Agostino, to decorate first the Camerino and then, between 1597 and 1604, the Farnese Gallery. The effect of Annibale's stay in Rome was to take his art in a more classical direction, and in this he was joined by his numerous collaborators, including Domenichino, Lanfranco and Sisto Badalocchio. In these years he had the opportunity to meet the other great reformer of Italian painting at the turn of the century, Caravaggio, who judged him a "worthy man" and "good painter," notwithstanding his totally different conception of art. Annibale died in Rome in 1609.

Self-Portrait with the Artist's Father and Nephew Antonio
oil on canvas, 60x48 cm
Pinacoteca di Brera, Milan

The painter's role and his family roots were questions that mattered deeply to Annibale, who did not agree with his brother Agostino's aspirations to rise in society. Here the painter portrays himself at the easel; behind him we see his elderly father, who had made considerable sacrifices to further the artistic career of his sons, and a youth, probably his nephew Antonio.

On the right appears the profile of a man who may be Agostino. The dignified but essentially modest clothing of Annibale and his father underline their social status, and appear to offer a figurative version of the rebuke the painter had addressed to his brother, who liked to frequent the most refined and influential circles in Rome: "remember, Agostino, that you are the son of a tailor." The picture can also be seen as a family version of the three ages of man, and thus a reworking of a typically Venetian iconographic tradition, dating back to Giorgione and Titian.

From the stylistic viewpoint it is a superb example of Carracci's naturalism, characterized by a bold composition of extreme modernity.

Hercules at the Crossroads
oil on canvas, 167x273 cm
Gallerie Nazionali di Capodimonte, Naples

The canvas was originally hung in the Camerino di Ercole, or "Study of Hercules," in Palazzo Farnese, the residence of Cardinal Odoardo Farnese. The iconographic program for this room,

which was the first decoration that Annibale carried out in Rome, between 1595 and 1597, was dictated by Cardinal Fulvio Orsini and should be interpreted as an exhortation to virtue. It called for the representation of the *Labors of Hercules* in fresco on the ceiling and this canvas with *Hercules at the Crossroads* was placed at its center. The picture shows the hero about to make his choice between the difficult path indicated by the personification of Virtue, on the left, and the easy but illusory one of Pleasure, on the right. The heroic nude of Hercules, leaning on his club as he makes his

decision, is already influenced by Annibale's sight of Raphael's frescoes in the Vatican and his first meditations on classical antiquities, in particular the celebrated *Farnese Hercules*. The style of his painting too, and especially his use of light, appears to have changed since his early works, which were more closely tied to the examples of Correggio and the Venetian artists. The symmetrical and yet varied composition reflects a search for classical equilibrium that also affects the natural setting, with the steep path of Virtue on the left and the forest of Vice on the right, and anticipates the great

renewal in landscape painting for which Annibale was to be responsible in the years to come. An almost identical figure to that of Pleasure, Raphaelesque in the fine view from behind and the elegant drapery, can be found in a picture by Caravaggio, the *Rest on the Flight into Egypt* (Galleria Doria-Pamphilj, Rome), testifying to the contacts and exchanges that took place between the two painters even before their joint decoration of the Cerasi Chapel in Santa Maria del Popolo.

ANNIBALE CARRACCI

Assumption
oil on canvas, 245x155 cm
Cerasi Chapel, Santa Maria del Popolo,
Rome

The panel was painted for the Cerasi
Chapel in the Roman church of Santa
Maria del Popolo in 1601. The decoration
of the chapel was commissioned from
Annibale and Caravaggio, who painted the
Martyrdom of Saint Peter and the
Conversion of Saint Paul. A work from
Carracci's most classical period, the
Assumption is characterized by the
monumentality of the life-size figures,
which occupy the whole of the
composition. The light picks out the
imposing masses of the bodies and the
drapery, while the warm colors reveal the
influence of Venetian painting, always very
strong in Annibale's style. But a decisive
part is also played here by his study of the
great art of the Roman Renaissance, as is
apparent from the Michelangelesque pose
of the angel supporting the Virgin Mary.
The sweeping and eloquent gestures
respond to the need for rhetorical
emphasis and exaltation of the emotions
typical of Counter-Reformation art, which
was to find its most suitable pictorial
language in the work of Annibale and his
followers. (S.G.C.)

Caravaggio

"In the beginning [...] God said, Let there be light: and there was light." This is how Genesis describes the creation of the world: God was originally manifested in the separation of light and darkness. In all religions light is a symbol of spirituality, and it is a supernatural light that bursts into the paintings of Caravaggio's maturity, testifying to divine intervention in human affairs. It is the light that constructs the forms and the painter also made use of mirrors to study it. He painted without making preparatory drawings, reproducing the model from life and laying out his compositions by means of lines cut directly into the wet priming of the canvas.

Michelangelo Merisi was born in 1571 in Lombardy, at Milan or Caravaggio, and took the name of Caravaggio from his family's place of origin. He received his artistic training in Milan, in the circles of Lombard naturalism linked to the culture of nearby Veneto and influenced by Leonardo's investigations of natural phenomena, "motions of the mind" and the representation of expressions. In 1592 Caravaggio was in Rome where, in the studio of the Cavalier d'Arpino, he painted flowers and fruit, contributing in decisive fashion to the birth of a genre, the still life, that was to have a long and successful future. The painter's early works quickly attracted the attention of great collectors like Cardinal Francesco Maria del Monte, his first patron, and Marchese Vincenzo Giustiniani. The *Basket of Fruit* in the Pinacoteca Ambrosiana, the *Bacchus* in the Uffizi and the *Sick Bacchus* in the Galleria Borghese date from his youth, as do the *Rest on the Flight into Egypt* and *The Fortune Teller*. At the end of the 16th century Caravaggio began, as a 17th-century biographer put it, "to strengthen the darks," in other words to accentuate the contrasts of light and shade, a transformation that was to culminate in the *Scenes from the Life of Saint Matthew* for the church of San Luigi dei Francesi, his first major religious commission. It was followed in 1600 by one for the *Crucifixion of Saint Peter* and *Conversion of Saint Paul* for the Cerasi Chapel in Santa Maria del Popolo. From this time on the painter's name was frequently recorded in the police registers for brawls, assaults and acts of indecency: he attacked a man with a stick, drew his sword against a soldier, slandered a painter, threw a dish of artichokes in the face of an insolent waiter at a tavern and insulted a gendarme. In 1605 he was sent to jail again for the illegal possession of a dagger and a sword and was brought before the magistrates for causing offense to two women and assaulting a notary. In arrears with the rent, he was reported to the police by his landlady and, to get his revenge, broke the shutters of her windows with stones one night. Found in bed with wounds to his throat and left ear, his explanation failed to convince the gendarmes: "I wounded myself with my own sword, and so fell down in these streets and I don't know where it happened, nor was anybody else there." In 1606 his violent temper proved fatal. Charged with the murder of Ranuccio Tommasoni, Caravaggio was condemned to death: the sentence could be carried out anywhere and by anyone. Wounded in the fight, the painter took refuge in the fiefs of the Colonna family, his patrons, and then fled to Naples and later Malta, where in 1608 he obtained, with special apostolic authorization, a much-desired investiture as a Knight of Malta. His artistic activity and fame did not suffer as a result of his flights and excesses: in Naples he left *The Seven Works of Charity*, on Malta the *Decollation of the Baptist*, a painting that he signed with the red of the blood spurting from the saint's head. Perhaps as a consequence of an offense caused to another Knight, Caravaggio was imprisoned, escaped – or was helped to escape – and sailed for Sicily, where he continued to paint. From here, in an attempt to return to Rome, he went back to Naples and took ship again, but new problems prevented him from reaching his goal and he died at Porto Ercole in 1610, in the grip of malarial fever.

Few artists have exercised such a profound influence on the history of European art. In Italy, France and Spain, painters were unable to ignore his work, repeating individual motifs or adopting the most revolutionary aspects of his style. And even today Caravaggio remains one of the best-loved of all artists, the same man who had portrayed himself, toward the end of his life, in the agonizing head of Goliath severed by the youthful David.

The Fortune Teller
oil on canvas, 115x150 cm
Pinacoteca Capitolina, Rome

The Fortune Teller
oil on canvas, 99x131 cm
Louvre, Paris

"I don't know who is the greater magician / the woman that you paint, / or you that paint her": this is how Gaspare Murtola underlined the painter's skill in representing the deceitful woman in the verses he devoted to Caravaggio's picture in 1603. In fact in both versions of the painting, in which the artist adopts a three-quarter framing in the Venetian manner, the gypsy girl, while pretending to read the young man's hand, is adroitly slipping off his ring. The canvas in Rome, painted over the top of a picture of the Virgin with her hands joined, is considered by more recent criticism to be the first version of the subject, executed between 1593 and 1594, and displays a greater sense of movement than the more static one in the Louvre, datable to between 1596 and 1597. The woman's dress, with a turban and a cloak tied at the shoulder, is described in the catalogues of costumes of the period as typical of the gypsies, who were already being portrayed in Northern European art as examples of avarice and dishonesty. At the end of the 16th century the streets of Rome were violent places, filled with soldiers and vagabonds, and the city had earned itself the reputation of a "swindler's paradise." The disquieting fascination of this world was often represented in drama and popular literature, but it was also described in treatises on the habits and tricks of rogues, beggars and peddlers. Gypsies had appeared in Italy at the beginning of the 15th century: at first treated as pilgrims, they had then begun to arouse fear and suspicion, but had retained the allure and magic of distant lands. As well as popular songs, their way of life had inspired the *commedia dell'arte*, and it is in relation to the theater that we should see the theme of the two paintings, the slyness of the deception contrasted with the ingenuousness of the young man.

CARAVAGGIO

Head of Medusa
oil on canvas glued onto wooden shield,
60x55 cm
Galleria degli Uffizi, Florence

In Greek mythology, the terrible Medusa
with a head of snakes instead of hair had
the power to turn anyone who looked at
her into stone: a power that her head
retained even when Perseus killed her by
cutting it off.
The image (painted in the last decade of
the 16th century) is set on a round
shield, a "buckler" for use in
tournaments, sent from Rome by Cardinal
Francesco Maria del Monte as a gift to the
grand duke of Tuscany Ferdinando I:
Caravaggio's patron, the cardinal may
have wanted to make the skill of his
painter known in Florence as well. The
choice of subject can be seen as a moral
symbol of the victory of reason over the
senses, and linked to a passage written by
Ludovico Dolce in 1565 that emphasized
its function as a protection "against the
wantonness of the world that turns men
into stones."
Placed in the spectacular setting of the
Medicean armory, the shield was held by
a mannequin mounted on a wooden
horse and dressed in an opulent Oriental
suit of armor that had been donated to
Ferdinando I by the legation of the shah
of Persia, Abbas the Great.
After the explosion of the bomb in Via dei
Georgofili in 1993, the work was
subjected to examination and restoration
that was also designed to arrest the
constant process of deterioration to
which it was subject.
Avoiding the frontal position of the head
typical of theatrical masks, Caravaggio
uses incident light to make the Medusa
stand out, with an expression of horror
and pain that reflects his studies from life.
The staring eyes and mouth gaping in a
blood-curdling scream fit the work into a
series of extraordinary shrieking mouths
stretching all the way from Leonardo's
studies to Edvard Munch's *Scream* and
the silent yell of Francis Bacon, inspired
by Eisenstein's film *The Battleship
Potemkin*.

Saint Matthew and the Angel
oil on canvas, 296.5x189 cm
San Luigi dei Francesi, Rome

In the Gospel, Christ is described as the "light of the world": "he that followeth me, shall not walk in darkness, but shall have the light of life." In the Contarelli Chapel of the church of the French colony in Rome, Caravaggio's figures are picked out from the darkness by a powerful beam of supernatural light. In July 1599 the painter had received an important religious commission for canvases representing *The Calling of Saint Matthew* and *The Martyrdom of Saint Matthew*. When the sculpture of *Saint Matthew and the Angel* ordered for the altar was rejected, a new contract committed Caravaggio to supplying a picture with this subject as well. But the artist's painting was also rejected. The saint, busy writing his Gospel, infringed the rules of decorum: his feet were coarsely exposed to the people and the angel was guiding his hand too confidentially, as if he were an illiterate. So the second version (of 1602) presented the angel in swirling flight at a respectful distance, while the saint, wearing a long robe in the classical style, is seated on a stool tilted toward the observer and writing in a book hanging over the edge of the table: devices designed to make the space of the image encroach on that of reality.

On the death of the client, Cardinal Matteo Contarelli, the program of the decoration was supervised by the Crescenzi family, which had close ties with the oratory of San Filippo Neri. In the contentious attempt to identify Caravaggio's source of inspiration for such realistic visions of the divine, we cannot forget the religious climate in which they were born. With the Catholic Counter Reformation, a much closer check was kept on artists to make sure they did not produce images that were indecorous or too hard to understand. Treatises on art urged painters to imitate visible reality, creating concrete figures, while religious tracts called for them to develop means of rendering the Christian mysteries more tangible and immediate. The religion of the common people reflected in Caravaggio's works is not so different from St. Philip Neri's exaltation of the virtue of humility and the search for Christ in the suffering of the poor. But his paintings ran the risk of causing offense or introducing too many innovations. And so his *Death of the Virgin* and *Madonna dei Palafrenieri* were also rejected. The first version of the *Saint Matthew* was acquired by Marchese Giustiniani and eventually ended up in Germany. All trace of it has been lost since 1945: either it was destroyed in the fire that devastated the storehouse in Berlin where it had been hidden to protect it during the war, or it was carried off by the Red Army as booty before setting fire to the storehouse, quite a common practice in Germany at the end of the war.

Madonna di Loreto (*Madonna with Pilgrims*)
oil on canvas, 280x150 cm
Sant'Agostino, Rome

Greeted by the common people with "great uproar," the picture, painted in 1604-06, represents the Madonna of Loreto, whose cult was very widespread in the closing years of the 16th century. In contrast to the traditional representation of Mary in her Holy House transported by angels, Caravaggio chose to portray a simple woman of the people leaning elegantly against the door of her house to receive the pilgrims, a woman with a dirty and torn bonnet on her head and a man with muddy feet in the foreground. Only the light which picks out Mother and Son in the darkness suggests that they are an apparition. The way Mary's fingers sink into the flesh of the Christ Child emphasizes his human nature: the distance between God and the pilgrims, between God and humanity, has been nullified, while the diagonal composition and the close-up view from below include the observers in the painted scene and invite them to kneel as well. That is what pilgrims did when they visited the Holy House in Loreto, where they believed that the Virgin had been conceived, the Annunciation had taken place and the Infant Jesus had played. These were years which, in reaction to the Protestant Reformation, saw a revival of the passion for pilgrimages and a reinvigoration of the cult of the Virgin. And the church of Sant'Agostino was close to the famous Albergo della Scrofa and a busy pilgrim's way that led to St. Peter's over the Ponte Sant'Angelo. In 1548 St. Philip Neri had founded the Confraternity of Santissima Trinità dei Pellegrini, to which the client of the painting also belonged, to aid the needy pilgrims who arrived in the city from all over Europe. Prelates and aristocrats were involved in this work of assistance for the marginalized, which was to culminate in the Jubilee of 1600. And it was only in this religious climate of renewed faith and compassion for the disadvantaged that poor people could appear, with their dirty feet in the foreground, at the center of an altar. (E.F.)

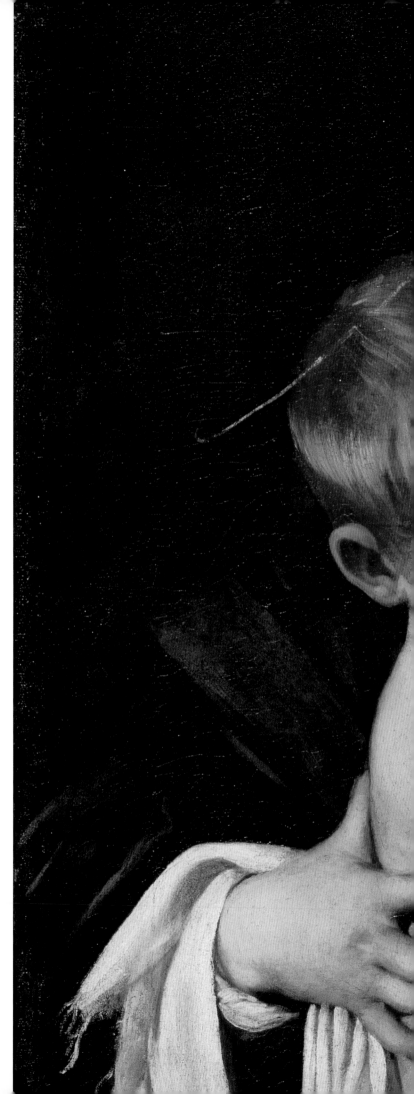

Rubens

"The polite but unbending painter was not willing to accept a lower price than the one fixed beforehand": so a collector was informed by his agent on the outcome of his negotiations for the purchase of a painting by Rubens. Celebrated for his agreeable conversation, great culture, courteous ways and rapidity of work ("the frenzy of the brush"), Rubens earned an international reputation and the most extraordinary sums of money: in his maturity the painter valued his day of work at over a hundred florins, at a time when a working ox was worth ninety.

Born in 1577 at Siegen in Westphalia, Peter Paul Rubens became a master in the Antwerp guild and in 1600 set off on a journey to Italy, staying there for eight years. In Venice he met a gentleman who introduced him at the Gonzaga court in Mantua. He was appointed court painter, a role in which he was required to paint portraits of the noble family, supervise the work of decoration of the palace, copy the most celebrated works of the day and complete the collection of "female beauties," portraits of the most attractive ladies at court, which the duke was assembling in his gallery. In September 1600 Rubens accompanied his lord to Florence to attend the marriage-by-proxy of Maria de' Medici to Henry IV. He then spent time in Genoa and Rome, continuing his study of Italian painters and Roman antiquities. In 1603 he was sent to Spain with gifts (paintings and objects made of crystal, gold and silver) from Vincenzo Gonzaga to King Philip III and his court; the paintings were damaged by rain on the journey and Rubens restored them, replacing some with his own works.

In 1606 he was again in Rome, where he worked for the Oratorian Fathers and started to assemble his own collection. The following year he proposed to the duke the acquisition of Caravaggio's controversial *Death of the Virgin*. In 1608 he returned to Antwerp following the worsening of his mother's illness. He then became court painter to Archduke Albert and Archduchess Isabella, receiving an ample salary and various privileges, including not having to pay his dues to the city guild; in 1630 his exemption from taxes was increased and he was given complete freedom to import wine for himself and his family. By now the artist was at the head of an extremely active studio. From 1620 onward Rubens was engaged in the execution of large cycles of paintings, including the *Life of Marie de Médicis*, but difficult times were just round the corner: in 1626 his beloved wife Isabella Brant died, a distressing event that led him to accept a delicate diplomatic mission that took him to France, the Netherlands, Spain, where he met the young Velázquez, and England. In 1630 he married the youthful Hélène Fourment, of whom he painted numerous portraits, but his life was increasingly burdened by the advance of his gout, up until his death in 1640.

"His figures seem to be fed on roses" the English painter Reynolds would say of Rubens. His strong sense of color, the exuberance of his style and the attention he paid to the scenographic aspect of the presentation of his works made him one of the great precursors of the baroque.

PETER PAUL RUBENS

Vallicella Madonna and Saints
Oil on slate, 425x250 cm
Santa Maria in Vallicella, Rome

"The work of this master is a formidable ode to joy": thus wrote the Belgian poet Émile Verhaeren of Rubens. So it seems only natural that the artist should have worked for the Oratorians, the religious order founded by St. Philip Neri, the saint of joy. In 1606, in fact, he received a commission for the painting over the high altar of Santa Maria in Vallicella. This was the Roman mother church of the order approved in 1575, and was dedicated to the Virgin and St. Gregory. The founders of new orders could not be venerated on altars, so the picture had to represent the Madonna with St. Gregory and the saints whose relics were conserved in the church: Domitilla, Maurus, Papias and Achilleus. The contract specified that the fathers had the right to see the initial design and no obligation to keep the painting if it was not to their liking. And in fact the clients were not happy with it, probably because it did not respect the principles of the Catholic Counter Reformation: the image of the Madonna appeared in a triumphal arch and was too small with respect to the saints. The official version of the incident, however, put the blame on the "unfortunate light" that illuminated the altar and prevented them from appreciating the beauty of the figures. The fathers requested a new work painted on stone or some other material that would absorb the light of the church. So the decision was taken to paint the altarpiece on three panels of slate; the central one incorporated a miraculous *Madonna*, covered by a movable plate of copper on which Rubens depicted another *Madonna and Child*: even today, a mechanism allows the display of the original image on special religious occasions.
In 1608, the year in which the work was finished, the painter departed suddenly for Antwerp on hearing that his mother was gravely ill. He arrived too late and placed the rejected painting on her tomb.

Portrait of Carlo Doria on Horseback
oil on canvas, 265x188 cm
Galleria Nazionale della Liguria, Genoa

In 1606, during his stay in Genoa, Rubens painted the portrait of the nobleman Carlo Doria, who had just received the news that he had been awarded the prestigious Order of Santiago by Philip III of Spain. The genre of the equestrian portrait derived from those of the Roman emperors and was generally reserved for sovereigns; in this case it was adopted to underline the aristocrat's membership of an order of knights.
He is wearing the typical dress of the stag hunt, with puffed and decorated pants and boots of pale leather, his arms protected by long brassards and a tall hat with a wide brim on his head, a fashion that was taking hold in Italy in those years. The red insignia of the order stand out on the corselet of burnished steel. The eagle is the heraldic emblem of the family while the flying storks symbolize his gratitude for the coveted honor. The oak, flowering olive tree and ivy underline Doria's virtues: courage, noble-mindedness and loyalty. The work proved a great success in Genoa and so pleased the prince of Hesse in 1941 that he requested it for Hitler, in spite of the ban on export already imposed by the Italian State. The opposition shown by the minister Giuseppe Bottai, forced to agree to the request for political motives, made it possible for Rodolfo Siviero, who played a leading role in the recovery of the Italian artistic heritage stolen during the Second World War, to get the work back in 1948.

*The Marriage-by-Proxy of Marie
de Médicis; The Coronation of
Marie de Médicis*
oil on canvas, 394x295 cm, 394x727 cm
Louvre, Paris

In 1622 Rubens received the commission
to decorate the gallery of the Luxembourg
Palace in Paris with scenes from the life of
Maria de' Medici, or Marie de Médicis as
she was known in France, representing
real episodes but glorifying them and often
dressing them up as allegorical scenes.
Born in Florence, the niece of Grand
Duke Ferdinando, Maria was beautiful
and rich, but not of noble birth. However,
her marriage was supported by the
Church and by France to avoid the
possibility that the debt-ridden Henry IV
marry his lover Henriette d'Entragues
after the divorce from his wife who had
given him no children. In Florence, on
October 5, 1600, Grand Duke Ferdinando
delivered to his niece the ring sent by the
king of France. Rubens was present at the
ceremony, and when the time came to
represent the scene was able to fill it with
details witnessed at firsthand: the men
wear stockings without garters and with
the upper part covered by breeches, and
the ministrant has placed his cardinal's
hat on the high altar. Hymen, the god
leading the wedding procession, wreathed
with flowers and carrying a torch, holds
Maria's train.
On May 13, 1610, Henry IV celebrated the
coronation of his wife, a ceremony that
was intended to increase the queen's

prestige. The red of the cardinals' robes,
as is often the case in Rubens, serves to
concentrate the attention on the main
motif: Maria in her cloak of blue velvet
strewn with golden lilies. The geniuses
throwing money allude to the distribution
of coins with the effigy of the queen, a
custom at such solemn celebrations.
The day after the coronation the king was
stabbed to death and succeeded by his
son Louis XIII under the regency of his
mother. The assassination handed power
to Maria de' Medici in suspicious
circumstances, with the result that years

later, in order to avoid risky allusions to
the queen, Rubens was obliged to remove
from the *Conferment of the Regency* the
allegorical detail of the Fates cutting short
the king's life. Maria carried on with her
own life amidst struggles for the conquest
of power, betrayals, reconcilements with
her son and flights, up until her exile and
death. Contrary to the initial program of
the cycle, even the more politically
delicate moments in the life of the queen
were included: probably it was not so
much the facts that counted, as the
representation of an adventurous life, in
keeping with the literature of the period
that glorified the deeds of heroes, for
whom not even defeats were a dishonor.
And Maria had presented herself as a
heroine right from the moment of the
signing of the contract, which committed
Rubens to depicting "the heroic exploits
of Her Majesty the Queen."
In 1625 Rubens was in Paris for the
hanging of the canvases. At first supported
and then opposed by Cardinal Richelieu,
he wrote to the scholar and Humanist
Peiresc: "I am fed up with this court." The
gallery was destroyed around 1800, but
the paintings were admired by Watteau,
Fragonard and Delacroix and copied by
an artist who was particularly close to
Rubens: Renoir. (E.F.)

Van Dyck

Anthony van Dyck (Antoon van Dijk) was born in Antwerp in 1599. At the age of ten he entered the studio of Hendrik van Balen, displaying a precocious talent, and just a few years later executed his two earliest dated works: the *Portrait of an Old Man* (Mauritshuis, The Hague) of 1613, and the *Self-Portrait* (Kunsthistorisches Museum, Vienna) of 1614. In 1616-18 he painted a series of *Busts of Apostles* that are now in Dresden (Gemäldegalerie) and Besançon (Musée des Beaux-Arts). He was then inscribed in the Antwerp guild of painters (1618) and became a collaborator of Rubens. The latter's influence molded the style of the young artist, as is evident from the *Drunken Silenus* (Gemäldegalerie, Dresden) and the *Crowning with Thorns* (Prado, Madrid).

In 1620, at the age of just over twenty, he went to England, where his work was highly appreciated and he was granted an annual salary by King James I. But the following February he left the country for Italy, where he stayed until 1627, chiefly in Genoa. The encounter with Italian art, in particular the Venetian school, produced a profound change in van Dyck's style, as he shook off the influence of Rubens and adopted Titian's palette of warm colors and the tonalism and elegant composition of Venetian painting. In Genoa he concentrated on portraiture and painted pictures of members of the most important families: his *Portrait of Marchesa Spinola* (Staatliche Museen, Berlin), and *Equestrian Portrait of Marchese Anton Giulio Brignole-Sale* (Palazzo Rosso, Genoa) are celebrated. He also painted pictures of religious subjects during his stay in Italy, including the *Madonna of the Rosary* (oratory of the Rosario, Palermo).

He then returned to the Low Countries, laden with fame and wealth. Now at the head of a large studio, he devoted himself to the realization of numerous altarpieces and mythological pictures that seemed to anticipate the rococo style, as well as portraits to satisfy the demand from the rich burghers of Flemish society.

In 1632 he went back to England, summoned by King Charles I, his admirer and collector. His activity on the other side of the Channel was prolific: he produced almost 400 works, many of them portraits, and made use of numerous assistants, often limiting his own contribution to the faces and leaving them the job of painting the sumptuous clothing, natural backdrops and gold and silver lighting that was a distinctive trait of his elegant and luminous painting. Van Dyck captured on canvas the suave image of aristocratic English society, with its cult of refinement: the style of his portraits long exercised an influence on that country's painting, leaving lasting traces in the works of Gainsborough and Reynolds.

He also painted various pictures of Charles I, of which the most unusual is perhaps the triple portrait (*Charles I in Three Positions*, 1635, Royal Art Collection, Windsor). The painting depicts the monarch frontally, in profile and at three-quarters, and was executed to serve as a model for a portrait of the king that Bernini carved in Rome in 1636 and sent to England in 1637.

Falling ill at a time when he was thinking of returning to the continent, the artist died in London in 1641.

Self-Portrait
oil on canvas, 116.5x93.5 cm
Hermitage, St. Petersburg

Precocious artist that he was, van Dyck very soon turned his attention to self-portraits. In fact the earliest of these to have survived (Vienna) is datable to 1614, when he was just fifteen. Over the course of his career he painted many of them, and this suggests a marked narcissism. In reality he may have been induced to produce these works simply by the great reputation he acquired with his portraiture. It was an Italian critic, Giovan Battista Bellori, who wrote in 1672 that van Dyck was the greatest portraitist since the time of Titian. Van Dyck undoubtedly knew and appreciated the work of the Venetian painter, and many pages of the sketchbook he used while in Italy are dedicated to the study of one of his portraits, the *Benedetto Varchi* now in the Kunsthistorisches Museum of Vienna. Indeed, some historians regard the *Benedetto Varchi* as a likely source of inspiration for the *Self-Portrait* in St. Petersburg. The wealth of references to Italian art also establishes a link between this canvas and a work by Raphael, a portrait of an unknown man in a cap, and allows us to date it to 1622-23.
In comparison with two similar *Self-Portraits* in New York (Metropolitan Museum) and Munich (Alte Pinakothek), painted a few years earlier, the one in St. Petersburg presents a softer and more elegant handling of the figure.

ANTHONY VAN DYCK

Rinaldo and Armida
oil on canvas, 133x109 cm
Louvre, Paris

The painting depicts a theme from Torquato Tasso's poem *Gerusalemme liberata*, written in Ferrara at the court of Duke Alfonso II d'Este and published in its first complete edition in 1581. Paintings inspired by this work had already appeared by the end of the century, but it was in the 17th century that they became common. The various phases of the meeting between Rinaldo

and Armida were among the themes most often represented. Van Dyck, who painted this picture between 1630 and 1631, had already executed another depicting an earlier moment in the story of the two lovers.
This canvas is inspired by strophes 17 and 20 of the 16th canto and represents the arrival of Carlo and Ubaldo – on the left, almost completely hidden by the fronds – charged with freeing Rinaldo. The hero, captivated by the enchantress Armida, is lost in contemplation of his beloved, who, for her part, is admiring

her own reflection in a mirror.
By 1632 the painting was already in the collection of the governor of the United Provinces, Prince Frederick Henry of Orange-Nassau. A lover of the pastoral themes dear to the Italian poets of the 16th century, he was the owner, and perhaps also the client, of two more paintings executed by van Dyck at this time, based on the verses of Giovanni Battista Guarini's *Il pastor fido*. (A.F.)

La Tour

Georges de La Tour was born at Vic-sur-Seille, in Lorraine, in March 1593, the son of a fairly prosperous baker. We do not know much about his training, but it is likely that he was encouraged to take his first steps in his artistic career by Lieutenant General Alphonse de Rambervilliers, a collector and connoisseur of art. His first teacher may have been the Mannerist Jacques Bellange, who would have introduced his young pupil to the painting of nocturnal scenes by candlelight. It has long been debated whether it is necessary to suppose a journey to Rome by La Tour to explain the obvious parallels, especially in the use of light, with Caravaggesque painting. It is true that many artists from Lorraine did go to Rome, including Claude Deruet, Claude Lorrain and Jean Le Clerc. However, it would have been quite possible for a French painter to have been familiar with Merisi's style through the works of other French or Flemish artists, and more recent critics have preferred to stress La Tour's ties with Northern European rather than Italian painting. Georges's career was in any case, quite apart from any journeys he may have made, linked to the provincial but far from isolated milieu of the duchy of Lorraine. In 1620 he moved to Lunéville, seat of the dukes, and obtained a number of privileges, including a partial exemption from taxes. His marriage to Diane Le Nerf, belonging to a family with ties to the minor nobility of Lorraine, guaranteed the painter close contacts with the ruling class of the duchy, who commissioned the majority of his works. Yet the painter also had some success in Paris, and it has been supposed that Cardinal Richelieu acquired a *Saint Jerome* by La Tour in 1632. In 1639 he was in Nancy, capital of the duchy, and boasted the title of "Peintre ordinaire du Roy," granted to him by Louis XIII for whom he had painted *Saint Sebastian Tended by Saint Irene* during a stay in Paris. In the last decade of his life he was flanked by his son Etienne, whose hand, of inferior quality to that of his father, is discernable in some of the late works. Georges de La Tour died at Lunéville in 1652. The evolution of French painting, which tended to adhere to the classicism of Carraccesque origin, did not contribute to the reputation of the artist, who always stuck to a style based on luministic effects and chiaroscuro, with his celebrated nocturnal scenes lit by a candle. While still appreciated in his native Lorraine, these were remote from Parisian taste, which had for some time abandoned the tenebrism brought to France by painters like Valentin or Régnier. The art of La Tour had no sequel and exercised no significant influence on French painting, and his work soon fell into oblivion, only to be rediscovered and appraised in all its importance in the 20th century.

Cardsharp with Ace of Diamonds
oil on canvas, 106x146 cm
Louvre, Paris

The canvas was painted by La Tour
between 1630 and 1634 and is signed
"Georgius de La Tour fecit." There is

another version of the same subject, in
the Kimbell Art Museum at Fort Worth,
with a few variants (the most significant
being that the figure on the left is
concealing an ace of clubs and not
diamonds). The theme of cheating at
cards was a common one in 17th-century

European painting, and was introduced by
Caravaggio with his famous picture *The
Cardsharps*, painted around 1594 and
also in the Fort Worth museum. In
Caravaggio's work as well as the one
under examination here a young and
richly dressed man is shown being

swindled during a game of cards. In
Merisi's version the cardsharp had a man
as his accomplice, spying on the cards in
the young gentleman's hand, whereas in
this picture the cheat is assisted by two
women, one seated at the table and the
other, a maidservant, pouring wine. The

subject was seen as a warning against gambling, a common practice everywhere in Europe and opposed by the Church, but was at the same time appreciated as a "genre" picture representing, in an amusing way, different human types and modes of behavior, including base or depraved ones. In this sense La Tour's work can be considered one of the most successful of the many pictures of this kind that were painted in those years: the exchange of glances between the two women, who are orchestrating the deception without speaking, is remarkable. Here La Tour displays a great capacity of psychological discernment and a rare narrative skill in telling the story with just a few, highly restrained gestures.

Saint Peter Repentant
oil on canvas, 114.5x95 cm
Cleveland Museum of Art, Cleveland

Signed and dated at top right "Georg de La Tour inve[nit] et pinx[it] 1645," the work is one of the artist's finest nocturnal scenes. The episode from the Gospels it represents is a well-known one: Peter, after the arrest of Christ, denied ever having known him, thereby fulfilling Jesus's prophecy: "Verily, verily, I say unto thee, The cock shall not crow, till thou hast denied me thrice." Realizing what he has done, the apostle repents. This is the moment the painter has chosen to depict. However, only the rooster refers directly to the Gospel story: Peter is presented as an old man, with none of the attributes typical of the saint's iconography, and the setting is reduced to a minimum. The religious message of the work is entrusted to the acute investigation of the expression, to the eyes turned upward, staring at a point outside the canvas, the open mouth and the wrung hands, in a moment of remorse but also of wonder at the prophecy that has just come true. But it is the light that dominates the composition: a symbolic light that descends from above and illuminates Peter's face, and the real light of the large lantern at the bottom. As in other works, La Tour conceals the flame to obtain a realistic effect and places the greatest luministic emphasis on the nearest object,

in this case Peter's right leg: the effect, in the setting cloaked in shadow which fades into total darkness, is that of a dazzling light. Yet the most virtuoso passage is the description of the robe, one of La Tour's finest achievements: the thin cloth lets the light through and becomes translucent, allowing us to make out the shape of the old man's legs, while the rather worn hems are illuminated against the left calf in shadow.

Saint Joseph the Carpenter
oil on canvas, 137x101 cm
Louvre, Paris

Painted between 1635 and 1638, the picture shows the Christ Child assisting Joseph in his carpentry work. The theme, like that of the Virgin Mary learning to read, subject of a later work by La Tour, was connected with the emphasis placed

by the Counter Reformation on the education of children. The Jesuits were particularly committed to this activity, and Father Pierre Fourier had founded the Congrégation de Notre-Dame in Lorraine for the education of girls: the popularity of such compositions should be seen in relation to these pedagogical models. The representation of Joseph as a man of the people was a choice made by other "tenebrist" painters of the time, and in particular Gerrit van Honthorst. The cult of Joseph had been encouraged in the 17th century, and in 1621 Pope Gregory XV had decided to make his feast day, March 19, an official religious holiday. From a stylistic viewpoint the composition is based, in a manner typical of La Tour, on the presence of a single source of artificial light, here the candle held by Jesus. Note the subtle way in which the light shines through the fingers of the Child, a ploy used by the painter in other

works as well. The play of light and shade on Joseph's wrinkled face, with its absorbed expression, and even the human type chosen as a model appear very Caravaggesque, especially when compared with the more summary rendering of Christ's face, the features almost canceled out by the bright light. (S.G.C.)

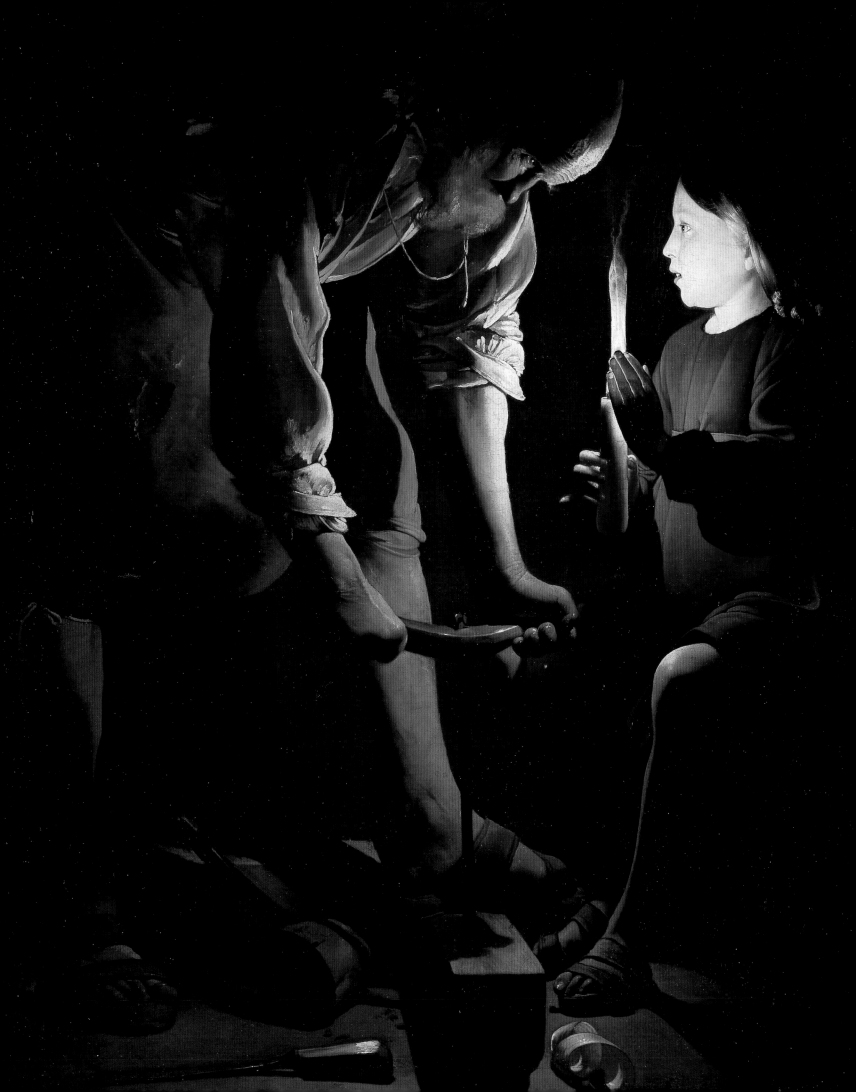

Poussin

Nicolas Poussin was born in 1594, at Les Andelys in Normandy. He may have received his early artistic training in the studio of Noël Jouvenet at Rouen, and then in Paris, under Ferdinand Elle and Georges Lallemant, between 1612 and 1621. In those years he was able to study the paintings in the château of Fontainebleau, and tried, without success, to go to Rome. In 1622 he painted six canvases to celebrate the canonization of Ignacio de Loyola and Francesco Saverio, and was noticed by Cavalier Marino, in Paris at the time. The following year he took part with Philippe de Champaigne in the decoration of the Palais Luxembourg. In 1624 he made it to Rome, where Cavalier Marino introduced him to Cardinal Sacchetti and Francesco Barberini, the nephew of Pope Urban VIII. For the latter he painted, in 1626 and 1627, the *Capture of Jerusalem* (lost) and the *Death of Germanicus*. The prestigious commissions established his reputation in Roman artistic circles and he was asked to execute one of the altarpieces for St. Peter's Basilica, the *Martyrdom of Saint Erasmus*, completed in 1629. The same year he married the daughter of his landlord, a French cook called Jacques Dughet whose younger son Gaspard, destined to become one of the greatest landscape painters of the century, lived with Poussin for several years. However, the marriage put a stop to the social rise of the artist, who also lost a commission for San Luigi dei Francesi. He devoted himself to painting pictures for the private studies of wealthy Italian and French art lovers, including the adventurer Fabrizio Valguarnera, the duke of Créquy and above all Cardinal Richelieu, who acquired some of his works for the château of Poitou. In 1640 Richelieu persuaded him to return to France, and he was given a magnificent reception at Fontainebleau. In Paris he was presented to Louis XIII, who commissioned from him the *Institution of the Eucharist* for the chapel of the château of Saint-Germain; the following year he was appointed first official painter to the king, with overall responsibility for all works of painting and decoration of the royal residences. But his popularity at court was short-lived, and conflicts and jealousies prompted him to go back to Rome in 1642. The deaths of Richelieu, Louis XIII and Urban VIII between 1643 and 1644 deprived Poussin of his most influential patrons. Nonetheless he continued to pursue his artistic career with success, and in 1657 was elected "Principe" of the Accademia di San Luca, although he turned down the post. Nicolas Poussin died in Rome in 1665.

Martyrdom of Saint Erasmus
oil on canvas, 320x186 cm
Pinacoteca Vaticana

In the 1620s the chapels in the nave of St. Peter's, recently constructed by Carlo Maderno, needed to be completed with altarpieces, and the Fabric of St. Peter's decided to entrust the work to a large number of painters, including several foreigners like Valentin Vouet and Nicolas Poussin. Originally the commission had been given to Pietro da Cortona, and was passed on to Poussin only when the Italian artist was assigned the more prestigious task of the decoration of the chapel of the Sacrament. Pietro had already made at least one preparatory drawing, which Poussin must have taken into account, as is apparent from details like the gesture of the priest on the right. Bernini greatly appreciated the work, asserting that it showed a sound and deep ability, and that it would have made him very envious if he had been a painter.

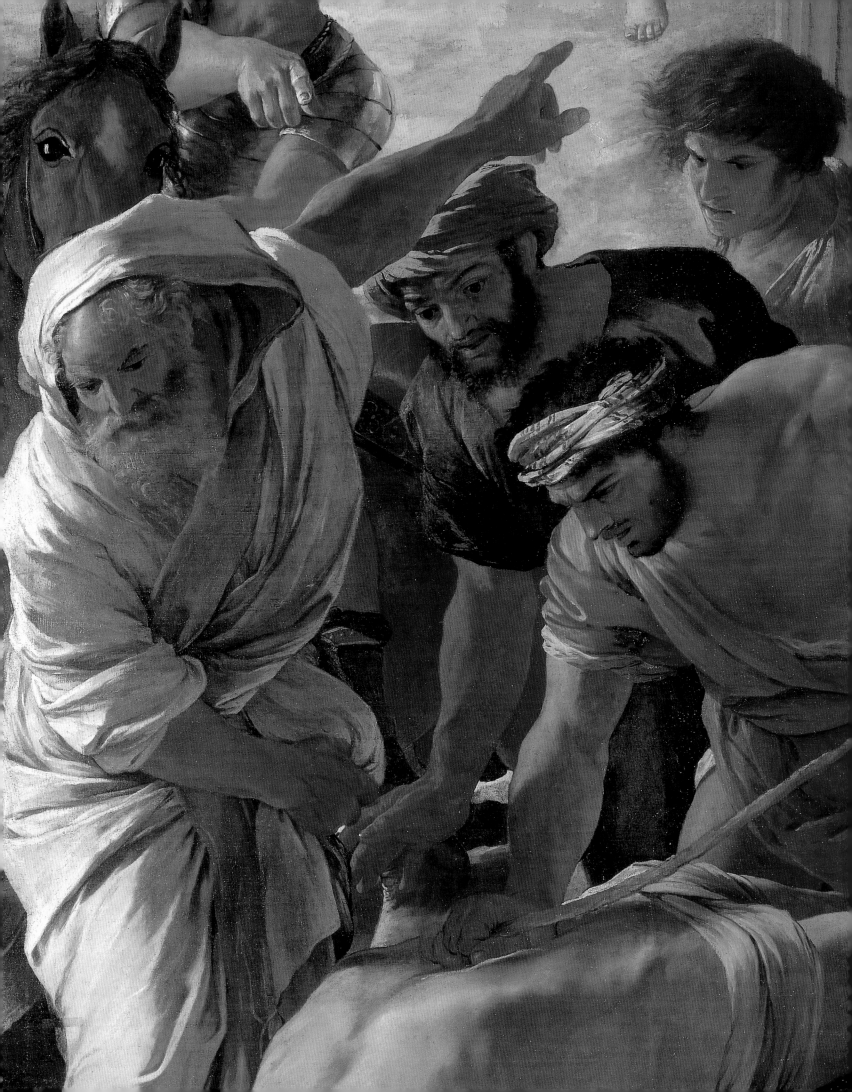

Et in Arcadia ego
oil on canvas, 121x185 cm
Louvre, Paris

The painting was probably executed around 1640. The theme of the tomb in Arcadia had already appeared in Virgil and in the Renaissance was taken up by the Neapolitan poet Sannazzaro in his pastoral poem *Arcadia*, published in 1502. The words ET IN ARCADIA EGO do not have a precise classical source, and have been interpreted in two different ways: they could mean "I [buried here] was in Arcadia too," or refer to Death itself, who says "Even in Arcadia I am": in the first case the composition would be a reminder of the transience of life, while in the second the accent would be placed on the universality of death, which spares nothing, not even the place of happiness *par excellence*, Arcadia. The first representation of this theme is by Guercino (Palazzo Barberini, Rome), and shows two shepherds coming by chance upon a tomb with a skull on top of it. Poussin adopted the same iconography, with a few variants, in a picture painted around 1629-30 and now in the Chatsworth Collection in Great Britain. The version in the Louvre is characterized by the different tone of the narration: here there is no excitement or amazement, and neither does the tomb seem to have been discovered by chance: the shepherds who read the inscription

and meditate on it are accompanied by a woman, who in the earlier work was a youthful Flora in the Titianesque manner but here takes on the reserved and severe appearance of an ancient priestess with a beautiful classical profile.

Landscape with Orpheus and Eurydice

oil on canvas, 124x200 cm
Louvre, Paris

Painted in the early 1650s, it was commissioned by Jean Pointel, the artist's friend and patron, and represents a landscape in Poussin's late manner. The scene portrayed, not a common one in the iconography of the legend of Orpheus and Eurydice, is the moment when the girl is bitten by a serpent, recounted in Book X of Ovid's *Metamorphoses*. Hymen, god of marriage, is summoned by Orpheus to the banks of a river to celebrate his wedding to Eurydice. But the ceremony is not a happy one, and Hymen's torch goes out, causing a great cloud of smoke to rise above the castle where the wedding is being held (Poussin represents it as a fortified building that closely resembles Castel Sant'Angelo in Rome). While Eurydice is walking through the meadows with the nymphs to hear Orpheus's lyre, she is bitten by a snake and dies. The composition, an example of Poussin's late style, after 1648, is closed on the right by a group of trees and opens in the middle onto a distant landscape, while the shaded area in the foreground contrasts with the warm light that illuminates the central section of the picture. Nature is represented as a rational, almost architectural construction, and the interest of the painter is focused not so much on the narration of the episode as on the search for an ideal harmony of composition. (S.G.C.)

Lorrain

I n 1829, the English painter William Turner declared in his will that he wished to leave two of his paintings to the National Gallery in London, on the precise condition that they be hung alongside and at the same height as two pictures by Lorrain, as a mark of both his admiration for the French artist and the prestige he had acquired as a landscapist.

Claude Gellée was born around 1604 at Chamagne in Lorraine, which is why he came to be known as Claude Lorrain. Between 1613 and 1617 he went to Rome, where he probably earned a living as a pastry cook, the trade he had learned at Chamagne. After a stay in Naples he returned to Rome and joined the studio of Agostino Tassi, a painter specializing in stormy seascapes and *trompe-l'oeil* architectural decorations. In 1625 he went back to Lorraine, but two years later had settled among the large community of foreign artists living around Piazza di Spagna in Rome, a city that he was never to leave again. To learn how to represent accurately the variations of light in nature, Lorrain spent whole days observing the Roman countryside. Then, after mixing the appropriate colors on his palette, he went home to paint. Or, as his first biographer relates, he painted sketches in oil from life, a procedure in which he was much ahead of his time, anticipating the work *en plein air*, in the open air, of the Impressionists. His numerous drawings from life reflect a spontaneous approach to nature: they are representations not just of Roman ruins, much in demand by collectors, but also of modern buildings, or simply of the countryside around Rome, and served as a starting point for oil paintings executed in the studio. It is likely that he made use of a black convex mirror, still called a Lorrain glass today, to reproduce the effects of light and atmosphere for which he was to become famous.

The nostalgic atmosphere of the landscape he painted in the 1630s, which seem to conjure up a vanished golden age, recalls that of the *Arcadia*, a pastoral work by Jacopo Sannazzaro published in 1504 and inspired by the *Eclogues* of the Latin poet Virgil. These were the years in which Lorrain consolidated his reputation and attracted the attention of important collectors: ambassadors, aristocrats, churchmen and, above all, Pope Urban VIII, for whom he painted a *Seaport* with spectacular effects of light, and King Philip IV of Spain, who was setting up a gallery of landscapes by contemporary painters at his residence of Buen Retiro. Around 1635 the artist also began the *Liber Veritatis* ("Book of Truth"), intended to protect his works against forgery: in it Lorrain made detailed copies of his paintings, noting on the back the name of the client and sometimes the

date. In fact there was no shortage of forgers of Lorrain and only the previous year a young French painter, Sébastien Bourdon, gifted with a good memory and a versatile hand, had copied a picture by Claude that he had seen unfinished in the artist's studio.

In the 1640s, attracted by the painting of Domenichino and Annibale Carracci, Lorrain's style showed a marked shift toward a clear and harmonious classical composition, in representations of biblical or mythological subjects. The world depicted is often that of Roman antiquity: it is the Italy imagined by foreigners, a rich and fertile land, evoking the perfection of the Garden of Eden and endowed with all the elements that, according to the travel writers of the 17th century, make a landscape beautiful. The final period of his career was dominated by the vision of a remote, heroic and legendary world, re-created principally for nobile Italian families.

In 1682 Claude, who had been ill for some time, died. Thanks to painters like him the landscape, which had previously been regarded as a minor genre, acquired a new prestige. Over the course of the 18th century his works made their way into the collections of the British aristocracy and were considered of such value that no price, however high, was thought too much.

Port with Villa Medici
oil on canvas, 102x133 cm
Galleria degli Uffizi, Florence

Painted in 1637 for a cardinal of the Medici family, as we are informed by the *Liber Veritatis*, the painting refers to the client by the family coats of arms above the clock and on the ships, and above all by the presence of Villa Medici in the background, located by the artist's fantasy on the seashore and not at its real site on the Pincio hill in Rome. It is thought that the client was Cardinal Giancarlo, appointed in those years to the Generalship of the Mediterranean Sea and responsible for ships flying the flag of the

Knights of St. Stephen, an order founded in 1562 by Grand Duke Cosimo de' Medici of Tuscany to combat heretics in the Mediterranean.

Villa Medici owes its name to Cardinal Ferdinando de' Medici, who had acquired and enlarged the existing building in 1576, embellishing it with a precious collection of pictures and ancient sculptures. These included the 1st-century BC statue that came to be known as the *Medici Venus*, which can be seen in the painting, the *Knife Grinder*, the *Wrestlers* and almost all the bas-reliefs on the central section of the facade. The antique sculptures were later transferred to Florence, and over the centuries the villa went through periods of neglect, until Napoleon made it the seat of the Académie de France, an institution that still houses students of various disciplines who have won a scholarship to study in Rome.

The downward slope of the buildings, the vessels lit from behind, arranged like wings in a theater, and the immensity of the sky bestow on the painting that ample sense of space typical of Lorrain,

while our gaze is attracted by the sun in the distance, reflected in a corridor of water on the horizon.

View of Delphi with Procession
oil on canvas, 150x200 cm
Galleria Doria Pamphilj, Rome

An inscription on the bridge indicates the subject of this picture painted around 1650: *Hac itur ad Delphes*, "This is the way to Delphi." Delphi was one of the main religious sites in ancient Greece: considered the center of the world, it was the location of the famous oracle of Apollo, represented in the painting in a manner that recalls Roman buildings of the painter's own time, such as St. Peter's. As usual the composition is organized on parallel planes, with the natural elements illuminated from behind to emphasize their dark silhouettes and to let the sunlight filter through the foliage. The order that governs the composition is typical of the classical landscape: nature, subjected to a process of selection and idealization, is not painted as it is, but how it should be, and its elements are laid out harmoniously in horizontal, vertical and diagonal lines. Yet the impression created is a natural one, thanks to the realistic observation of the light effects which sets the scene at a precise time of day. Lorrain's human figures, on the other hand, are not generally equal to his landscapes: the artist did not follow the custom of having them executed by specialized painters and did the work himself, but never managed to fully master the technique of the figure.

A mythical sense of time is evoked by the pilgrimage to the sacred temple where a sacrifice, in the distance, recalls the customs of antiquity. The Pythia, prophetess of Apollo, was consulted on political as well as religious matters: it was from her personal contact with the god and the tradition of an ancient cult that the response of the oracle came. Thus the yearning for sacred truths known in the past and now lost forever, revealed by the oracle, is combined with the longing for the vanished golden age represented, with harmonious nostalgia, in Lorrain's paintings. (E.F.)

DIEGO VELÁZQUEZ

Velázquez

In Spain the period from 1560 to 1660, marked by wars and by the end of Spanish military predominance in Europe, but also by economic prosperity and an incredible flowering of the arts, is defined as *el Siglo de oro*, the Golden Century. It was the period of Cervantes and his *Don Quixote*, of the plays of Pedro Calderón de la Barca, of St. Teresa of Avila and the painter El Greco. One of the most active centers was Seville, the home of Murillo, Zurbarán and Velázquez and the city to which the works of the second wave of followers of Caravaggio came from Italy, and in particular from Naples, capital of the viceroyalty.

Diego Rodriguez de Silva y Velázquez was born in 1599 and studied painting in the studio of Francisco Pacheco, his future father-in-law and biographer. His early works are realistic pictures of the interiors of kitchens, musicians and drinkers which show the influence of Caravaggio and Flemish painting, with its particular attention to the representation of reflections. In 1617 he was enrolled in the Sevillian guild of painters and in 1622 he made a journey to Madrid, to study the royal collections and probably to try to get himself received at court, where Philip IV had recently ascended the throne. On his second visit to Madrid, in 1623, he was permitted to paint the king's portrait, the first in a long series: from this moment on the artist remained at court, holding increasingly important and well-paid posts over the years and devoting himself principally to portraits of the ruling class. In 1628 Velázquez had the honor of receiving Rubens, at the height of his fame: it may have been as a result of this contact that he decided to visit Italy. He set off the following year, landing at Genoa and visiting Milan, Parma, Venice (where he admired the paintings of Titian), Ferrara, Cento, Loreto and finally arriving in Rome, where he stayed for a year. It was 1630, the time of the explosion of the Roman baroque, but also active in the city were the *bamboccianti*, painters of popular subjects, and the exponents of classicism Domenichino and Poussin. Passing through Naples, he returned to Madrid. With the transfer of many functions to the new royal residence of the Buen Retiro, work commenced on the renovation of the old royal palace, the Alcázar. It was partly to get hold of works of art and artists for the decoration of the Alcázar that Velázquez undertook his second journey to Italy, in the train of the legation sent to Trent to receive Marianna of Austria, the king's new bride. Back in Rome, he painted portraits of Pope Innocent X and various personages of his court. Despite the urgings of the Spanish court, the painter did not decide to return until 1651, probably because he was waiting for a woman painter to give birth to his child. In Madrid he would be appointed *Aposentador major de Palacio*, or chief chamberlain of the palace, a post that made him responsible for the daily running of the royal household, for the upkeep of the accommodations and kitchens, for the ceremonies relating to the movement of the king and queen and for the decorations of the churches which they attended and the scenery for popular festivals. He also supervised the works at the Escorial. Notwithstanding the commitments that distracted him from the work of painting, which he often delegated to his son-in-law, these were the years in which he produced his masterpieces, *Las Hilanderas* (*The Spinners*) and *Las Meninas* (*The Maids of Honor*). In 1659, thanks to a papal dispensation, Velázquez received the Order of Santiago, an honor usually reserved for the nobility: a knight not by birth, but in virtue of his art. In 1660 he went to Fuenterrabía to prepare the royal residence for the marriage of the Infanta Maria Teresa to Louis XIV, setting the seal on peace with France. He then returned to Madrid where, just over a month later, he fell ill and died. The artist, solemnly buried in the robes of a Knight of Santiago, left a great void at court and the sorrowing king wrote two words in a trembling hand: "Quedo adbatido," I am crushed.

The Forge of Vulcan
oil on canvas, 223x290 cm
Museo del Prado, Madrid

Painted in 1630, during his first stay in
Rome, the painting may have formed part
of a trilogy based on the theme of trickery
that included *Joseph's Bloody Coat
Brought to Jacob* and *The Brawl between
Spanish and Italian Soldiers*, pictures in
which the same models can be

recognized. In the first case the trick is
the one related in Genesis, played by
Joseph's brothers on their father, in the
second case a banal quarrel between
cardplayers over cheating. This painting,
however, is based on Ovid's
Metamorphoses, a collection of Greek
and Latin myths written in the 1st century
AD that for centuries would be a primary
source of inspiration for artists. We are in
the forge of Vulcan, blacksmith of gods

and heroes, often represented a little
crooked as a reminder of the fact that he
was lame. He is fashioning a piece of
armor with his assistants the Cyclopes
when he is interrupted by the appearance
of the sun god Apollo, who tells Vulcan of
his wife Venus's infidelity with Mars. The
painter represents the moment in which
the deception is revealed and captures the
different psychological reactions of the
figures, who look as if they are frozen in a

scene from a drama. The composition
reflects Velázquez's study of ancient reliefs
and classical statues, as well as his
familiarity with Raphael's tapestries in the
Vatican and the different academic poses:
the bodies are shown from a variety of
perspectives, frontal, behind and in
profile, and in attitudes of repose or
tension. The conde-duque de Olivares
donated the painting to Philip IV, who
hung it in the Buen Retiro.

Pope Innocent X
oil on panel, 140x120 cm
Galleria Doria Pamphilj, Rome

During his second stay in Rome, around 1650, Velázquez had the honor of painting Pope Innocent X's portrait. "Troppo vero!" (Too truthful!) the pontiff is said to have exclaimed on seeing the picture, in which the painter emphasized the frowning expression and severe features of a man described as surly and reserved, gloomy and mercurial. It seems that Velázquez was offered a handsome payment, which he refused as he was on a mission on behalf of the king of Spain. But he did not turn down a gold chain and the medal of the pontificate, which are even recorded on the plaque. The pope is in summer dress. He is holding a "note" from Philip IV with the painter's name written on it. The freedom of the brushwork and the triumph of reds is reminiscent of Titian, who also contributed to the tradition of the papal portrait with his *Paul III Farnese and His Grandsons*, in which the pontiff, seated, lets his cloth shoe protrude from his cassock for the ceremony of kissing the foot that marked the conclusion, after three bows, of the homage due to the pope. A matter of great debate in the 16th century, beards worn by churchmen posed a number of problems: on the one hand they were a mark of virility, but on the other this might seem inconsistent with the celibacy of the priesthood. The warrior pope Julius II had sworn that he would not shave until he had driven the French out of Italy. Clement VII, by

contrast, had grown a beard as a sign of mourning after the Sack of Rome in 1527, and was imitated by many of the clergy. A treatise entitled *In Defense of Priests' Beards* even came out in 1531, arguing that the beard is a symbol of piety, gravity and dignity, to be preferred to a smooth and effeminate face. Evidently this did not convince Cardinal Carlo Borromeo, later to be canonized as St. Charles, who at the end of the 16th century ordered the priests of his diocese to shave off their beards. Innocent X's not very luxuriant beard probably constituted a sort of compromise between the different positions. The painting has been admired by artists down the centuries, culminating in the dramatic version of it painted by Francis Bacon in 1965.

Las Hilanderas (*The Spinners*)
oil on canvas, 220x289 cm
Museo del Prado, Madrid

Also known as *The Fable of Arachne*, the painting (*c*. 1650-57) records the work of the royal tapestry factory of Santa Isabella, but takes its inspiration from Ovid's *Metamorphoses*. The representation of the myth is set in the background: the young Arachne, proud of her skill with the loom, has challenged

Athena, goddess of wisdom and protectress of spinning and weaving, to a contest. Arachne weaves a tapestry depicting the amorous adventures of the gods, including the rape of Europa, a young woman tricked by Zeus who turns himself into a bull and carries her off through the waves of the sea. Athena is enraged at Arachne's success and tears the tapestry to pieces; the young girl hangs herself, but the goddess saves her from death by turning her into a spider: "You may live, Arachne, but you will hang forever – and do your weaving in the air." What we see here are the final moments of the story, when the warrior goddess Athena, wearing a cuirass, raises her hand against Arachne, standing in front of a tapestry that depicts that very scene: *The Rape of Europa*, painted by Titian for Philip II and copied by Rubens for Philip IV. A picture within the picture and a story within the story: in some 16th-century editions of the *Metamorphoses* the fable of Arachne was presented as the story that the three daughters of Minyas told themselves to distract them from their work.

In the foreground the painting represents an action under way, where the movement is frozen in a manner that long predates Impressionism. The winder is in operation, transforming the skein into

yarn, and the fact that the rotating disc becomes transparent is an optical illusion clearly understood by the painter. So time is the real protagonist here, time that can be represented in painting: and it is the revenge of the artist, in his role of creator, who does not fear comparison with the deity.

Las Meninas (*The Maids of Honor*)
oil on canvas, 318x276 cm
Museo del Prado, Madrid

The theme of the painting and of the gaze in painting has its standard text in this picture of 1656, almost a snapshot of life at court, with the figures in the background out of focus. In a spatiotemporal paradox, the artist stepping back from the easel to compare the painting with reality is the author of the work himself. Velázquez is looking at the scene he is painting, a scene that is situated on this side of the canvas, in the same real space from which we are gazing at the picture, all equally involved in the work. This technique of including the observer in the canvas is typical of the Spanish baroque. The *meninas* are the maids of honor surrounding the Infanta Margarita, potential heir to the throne at the time. On the left kneels María Augustina de Sarmiento, while on Margarita's right we can recognize Isabel de Velasco, curtseying next to the dwarfs Mari-Bárbola and Nicolás Pertusato, who is prodding the big Castilian mastiff with one foot. In the background Marcela de Ulloa, servant of the maids, is conversing with Diego Ruiz de Azcona, while the palace chamberlain José Nieto Velázquez appears in a doorway that opens up a space at the back of the picture. Paintings hang on the walls, including Rubens's *Minerva and Arachne* and Jacob Jordaens's *Apollo and Marsyas*, while a mirror reflects the image of the king and queen of Spain, Philip IV and Mariana of Austria, probably the subjects of Velázquez's painting. The canvas has its back to us and its contents are hidden, but the mirror reveals them, showing to us what is outside our angle of view, capturing the reality that would escape a normal framing. Artists used the mirror both as an element to be inserted in the picture and as an aid in their work, as in the case of self-portraits, and in 15th-century Flanders painters and manufacturers of mirrors belonged to the same guild. In the middle of the 16th century the most widely used type of mirror was still the convex one, but this was gradually replaced by the flat kind, invented in Germany or Flanders and perfected in Venice. Van Eyck had already utilized the mirror in exemplary fashion in the *Arnolfini Marriage Group*, a painting that had been in the royal collections at Madrid and that Velázquez may therefore have seen. With rapid strokes of the brush the painter, who is wearing the noble Cross of Santiago, added after the painting was finished, depicts what the king and queen see while they are having their portraits painted. Born out of a deep trust in the powers of representation, the painting is a literal application of the teaching Velázquez had received from his master and father-in-law Francisco Pacheco: "The image should come out of the picture." (E.F.)

Zurbarán

F rancisco de Zurbarán was born at Fuente de Cantos, Estremadura, in 1598, and served his apprenticeship at Seville in the workshop of the painter Pedro Díaz de Villanueva. In 1626 he was given his first
significant commission, the execution of a cycle of fourteen canvases for the Dominican monastery of
San Pablo in Seville. In 1628 the Mercedarian friars of the monastery of San Fernando in Seville called on
him to paint a cycle devoted to the life of St. Peter Nolasco, and in the same year the painter received the
commission that made his reputation, the continuation of the series of paintings representing the life of St.
Bonaventure for the great Franciscan monastery in the same city. His realistic and penetrating depictions of
monastic life were so highly appreciated that shortly afterward, following a petition made to the municipal-
ity, Zurbarán was invited to move from the city of Llerena (in which he had been living since 1617) to Seville,
where he was appointed official painter.

From the outset his painting shows traces of Caravaggio's style: the influence that Merisi's works had already
had on Spanish painting is well known, and also affected Diego Velázquez in the years of his formation. It
may have been Velázquez, now an established painter at the royal court, who recommended Zurbarán to
Philip IV. In 1634 the king summoned him to paint the *Labors of Hercules* for the Salón de Reinos in the
Palacio de Buen Retiro in Madrid. The pictures reflect a lack of familiarity with the style and composition of
nonreligious subjects, but are still interesting for the landscapes in the
background and the details taken from everyday life. Over the following
years his style reached its full maturity and the artist executed some of
his most famous cycles: in 1637 he began the one in the Jerez Charterhouse, now dismembered and originally made up of the *Battle of Jerez*
(Metropolitan Museum, New York), the *Apotheosis of Saint Bruno*
(Museo de Bellas Artes, Cadiz), and the *Adoration of the Shepherds*
(Musée d'Art et d'Histoire, Grenoble). In the same period he painted a
new cycle of eleven pictures for the monastery of Guadalupe, still in their
original location. In the 1630s Zurbarán was in demand outside Seville
as well, painting pictures that reflected the beliefs of a conservative ec-
clesiastic clientele and producing extremely simplified compositions
with pure, elementary volumes that displayed a marked sense of color.
But in the following decade his reputation began to decline and the
painter, beset by economic difficulties, devoted himself to what almost
amounted to mass production. In an attempt to halt his decline he went
to live in Madrid, but the move did not prove particularly effective and in
1664 Zurbarán died in poverty. His son Juan also painted still lifes that
were closely modeled on his father's work, but met a premature end in
the plague of 1649.

*Apparition of the Apostle Saint
Peter to Saint Peter Nolasco*
oil on canvas, 179x223 cm
Prado, Madrid

The apparition of the crucified St. Peter to
Peter Nolasco is a well-known episode in
the saint's life and appears in all the
representations inspired by it. For some

time the friar had desired to make a journey to the tomb of his illustrious namesake in Rome, but was continually obliged to put it off for a variety of reasons, until the saint appeared to him in a dream for three nights running, consoling him for his inability to make the pilgrimage. On the third night he appeared crucified upside down and

advised him not to leave Spain, where his presence was required to carry out an important task. In fact Peter Nolasco, who lived around the middle of the 13th century, founded an order for the purpose of ransoming Christian captives from the Moors and in 1248 accompanied the king on his reconquest of Seville. Shortly before dying, he established (1249) the

monastery of Nuestra Señora de la Merced Calzada.

The picture, painted in 1629, was part of a series commissioned from Zurbarán by the superior of that same monastery for the cloister of "Los Bojos" to celebrate the canonization of Peter Nolasco, which had taken place that year. The extraordinary realism in the

representation of the individual figures, an evident echo of Caravaggio's painting, and the almost total absence of a setting, reduced to the shadows from which the figures emerge, are what gives this striking image its power.

Still Life
oil on canvas, 46x84 cm
Prado, Madrid

Zurbarán is thought to have painted very few still lifes. According to some scholars only two have survived: the one described here and the one now in Los Angeles (Norton Simon Foundation, formerly in the Contini Bonacossi Collection, Florence)reproduced above. The latter is

signed and dated 1633 and attracted the interest of the great 20th-century art historian Roberto Longhi, who wrote "instead of light that circulates, a dark and abstract background; the objects not set haphazardly on the table of the tavern, but devoutly lined up, like flowers on the altar, strung out in a row like the litanies of the Virgin." These words also apply perfectly to the simple but fascinating composition in the Prado, datable to the

same period or slightly earlier. The style seems to have been influenced by the works of Juan van der Hamen y Leon, an artist of Flemish origin who was much appreciated in Spain at the time for his still lifes. An exact replica of this painting used to be in the Cambò Collection in Madrid, but is attributed to Francisco's son Juan.

Articles of everyday use like the ones in this canvas can often be found in

Zurbarán's large religious pictures as well, and there too are painted with such care and intensity that they can be regarded as still lifes in themselves. This is the case, for example, with the *Childhood of the Virgin* (collegiate church, Jerez) and the *Christ and the Virgin in the House at Nazareth* (Museum of Art, Cleveland).

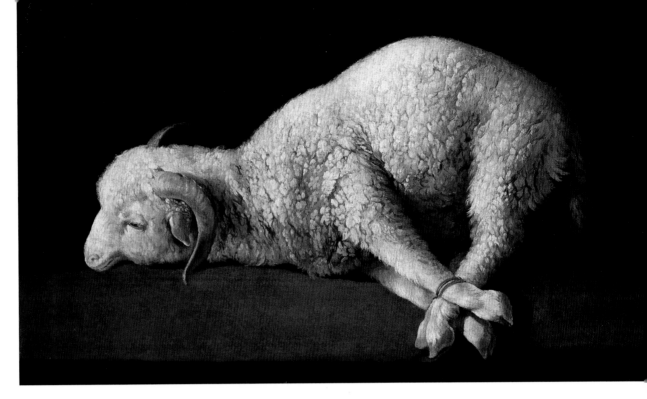

Agnus Dei
oil on canvas, 38x62 cm
Prado, Madrid

The *Agnus Dei* is an extremely rare iconographic subject in religious painting, but one of the most pregnant symbols of Christianity. So it is no wonder that it appears in Zurbarán's painting, where religiosity assumes such a high intensity. Once again the painter interprets the theme in an essential manner, making the animal stand out from the darkness with great plastic emphasis and eliminating any other element.

The *Agnus Dei* is a symbol that links the Old and New Testament. In their epistles Peter (I Peter 1: 18-19) and Paul (I Cor. 5: 7) compare the death of Christ with the sacrifice of the lamb at Passover. John (1: 29), speaking of the Son as the Lamb of God, harks back to the prophesy of Isaiah (53: 7), who said: "He was oppressed, and he was afflicted, yet he opened not his mouth: he is brought as a lamb to the slaughter, and as a sheep before her shearers is dumb, so he openeth not his mouth." (A.F.)

Murillo

Exponent of an everyday and popular form of piety, Murillo introduced images of childhood into religious paintings. His work, free of drama and as remote from the splendor and power of Velázquez as it is from the mystical abandon of Zurbarán, involves observers emotionally, playing on their feelings. Baptized in Seville on January 1, 1618, Murillo was soon left an orphan. We know little of his early career, but his training was influenced by the naturalism of the Sevillian works of Velázquez and Zurbarán. He hardly ever left his native city, with its powerful religious orders and wealth built on trade. In 1646 Murillo made his reputation with the prestigious commission for the small cloister of the Franciscan monastery in Seville. From this moment on his fame continued to grow and in 1655 he was publicly proclaimed the best painter in the city, following the pictures he executed for the cathedral sacristy. In 1658 he visited the court in Madrid, where he was able to study the royal collections, and his style began to shift toward a more vaporous luminosity. The 1660s were marked by important religious commissions: for Santa María la Blanca, the Capuchin church and the Hospital de la Caridad. The painter's success seems to have been unaffected by the dramatic series of disasters that struck Seville. In 1649 the plague had cut the city's population by half in the space of five months, and two years later it was hit by famine and riots over the high price of bread; in 1678 plague and famine descended on the city again, and in 1680 it was struck by an earthquake and then, in 1682, another epidemic, perhaps of typhus.

The exhausted population sought comfort in a humane and consolatory form of religion, emotional rather than dogmatic in character. Murillo himself had probably lost three of his nine children to the plague. His painting is the expression of an intense personal faith. A member of the Confraternity of the Rosary, he entered the Franciscan Tertiary Order in 1662. By the time his wife died, in 1663, only four of their children were still alive. The following year, Murillo joined the Brotherhood of Charity, justifying his request, in the petition, by his desire to serve God through the poor. He devoted himself to helping the needy, distributing bread and probably making donations in money as well. In 17th-century Spain, the rich and the poor lived in close interdependence. In a positive vision of the poor, the favorites of Christ, the rich were obliged to exercise the virtue of charity by helping those in need to gain salvation, while the poor were supposed to accept their sufferings with humility and patience and pray for the wealthy. The poor urchins in Murillo's famous genre scenes are neither sad nor hungry, but are shown eating and playing. They are paupers who stirred the sympathies of the people who looked at them and probably reminded them of the virtue of charity.

In addition to genre scenes, various versions of the *Virgin and Child* pervaded by a sense of great tenderness and his major religious cycles, dismembered and scattered among public and private collections in the 18th and 19th centuries, Murillo's reputation was built on another theme, that of the Immaculate Conception. A dogma held particularly dear in Spain, it was illustrated by the painter in open and dynamic compositions.

The man famous for his pictures of children died in 1682, from the aftereffects of a fall from the scaffolding while painting the central canvas of the Capuchin church in Cadiz.

The Holy Family with a Little Bird
oil on canvas, 144x188 cm
Museo del Prado, Madrid

A touching and intimate scene in a domestic setting: the *Holy Family* (c. 1645-50) viewed in the light of a new and simple piety, accessible to all. St. Joseph and the Child are the true protagonists of the scene, while the Virgin gazes tenderly at her Son. The cult of St. Joseph was relatively recent. Loved but not venerated during the Middle Ages, the saint was viewed in a new light following the publication of the book *Summa de donis Sancti Joseph* by the Dominican Isidoro de Isolano in 1522. St. Teresa of Avila called him "the father of my soul" and dedicated her first convent to him. In 1621, moreover, Gregory XV had given devotion to the saint an official status by fixing March 19 as his feast day. But religious writers had not been able to agree on how he should be represented, elderly and balding or young and vigorous, a man capable of protecting the Virgin, "perfect in the spirit and handsome in the body." And this is how Murillo chooses to present him, youthful, strong and with a thick head of black hair. His greatness lay in his having lived with Jesus, whose perfections he had absorbed. The Child's gesture, reminiscent of Federico Barocci's *Madonna del Gatto*, should be seen in relation to a text on St. Joseph written in 1597 by the Carmelite Graciano de la Madre de Dios, published in three languages and distributed in all the order's monasteries: "He took [...] the Child in his arms and carried him, singing songs, distracted him when he cried and rocked him to sleep [...]. Every time he went out he bought him birds and apples." It is likely that many of the works referring to these episodes were painted for nunneries.

Urchin Hunting for Fleas
(*The Young Beggar*)
oil on canvas, 137x115 cm
Louvre, Paris

Murillo is also famous for his genre
scenes with ragged children, probably
using his own family and those of his
friends as models. This work, dating from
around 1648, is the earliest example of its
kind, and differs from the later ones in
the sense of melancholy and neglect that it
conveys. The genre scene, considered a
mere copy of reality, occupied one of the
lowest rungs in the hierarchy of painting.
Caravaggio and Velázquez had treated it
with the gravity that was usually reserved
for history painting, representing the
figures on a larger scale, while Murillo
paid less attention to the still life – the
objects on the ground – and more to the
figure itself. The artist may have seen
similar paintings by followers of
Caravaggio in collections in Seville, but
these generally depicted more disquieting
subjects than children eating grapes or
playing dice. Such themes were also to be
found in Spanish literature, in the
picaresque novels, but were treated with a
cruel sense of humor and a moralizing
intent that are absent from Murillo's
works. But the world evoked is the same
and the jug of water in the painting is a
reminder of the 1554 novel *Lazarillo de
Tormes*, in which the hero works as a
water carrier in Seville for four years. In
the 17th century Flemish paintings of
mothers ridding their children of fleas
were common. The presence of fleas was
regarded as a good sign and one that,
according to tradition, indicated the
children were in good health: the
parasites would not have attacked them if
they had been sickly. So this painting
emphasizes the solitude of the urchin,
poor but dignified, with his dirty feet left
discreetly in shadow. The kingdom of
heaven belonged to those who accepted
God with the faith of a child. In a religious
vision of the poor as the image of Christ,
the combination of childhood and poverty
constituted a double measure of blessing
and a strong incentive to help the needy.

The Holy Children with a Shell
(*Jesus Offering the Infant St. John
a Drink*)
oil on canvas, 104x124 cm
Museo del Prado, Madrid

The picture, painted around 1670-75, is
probably based on a composition by
Guido Reni of which Murillo may have
seen an engraving. The work is famous
for its tenderness: the Christ Child is
holding a shell filled with water so that the
Infant St. John can drink. When they grow
up, it will be John who will baptize Christ
by pouring water from a shell.
"Verily I say unto you, Except ye be
converted, and become as little children,
ye shall not enter into the kingdom of
heaven." The words of St. Matthew's
Gospel explain the significance of the
work: the veneration of the Infant Jesus, a

model of holiness, virtue and love, and
the representation of the holy children
were intended to kindle an instinctive
faith in the believer, as pure as that of a
child. In the 17th century the Jesuit Juan
Bonifacio praised the perfection of
children: "Children are the flowers of
humanity [...]. Who is not moved by the
sight of a little child? [...] Is there
anything more marvelous in nature than
that serene air and those cheeks that
blush with modesty? [...] And remember
that this delightful appearance is nothing
but a pale reflection of the beauty of his
soul."
The image is the product of the painter's
affectionate observation of children, but
he toned his naturalism down in sacred
scenes for reasons of decorum: the
children are more idealized and, above
all, their feet are clean. In a suffuse

golden light, one of the works of mercy
recommended by Christ is being
performed, giving drink to the thirsty: the
gesture of love and brotherhood
presented in the picture was intended to
persuade adults to imitate the Infant
Jesus. (E.F.)

Hals

Frans Hals was born in Antwerp in 1582 or 1583. His family settled in Haarlem in 1591, and it was in this city that he spent the whole of his life. He was probably a pupil of Karel van Mander, but this does not seem to have had much influence on his art. The earliest work to have come down to us is a fragment of the portrait of *Jacobus Zaffius* (Hals Museum, Haarlem), executed in 1611. In 1616 he painted the *Banquet of the Officers of the Saint George Civic Guard* (Hals Museum), the first of a series of life-size group portraits. In these works of his early maturity the artist already displayed his great gift for portraiture and distinctive capacity to represent movement and fleeting expressions. From the third decade of the 17th century onward, Hals became fairly well-known, obtaining numerous commissions from the Haarlem authorities. But the documents testify to a constantly precarious financial situation that would even lead to the painter being declared bankrupt: in 1662 he was granted a yearly pension by the city, "owing to the insufficiency of his own resources." From the stylistic viewpoint, the range of colors he utilized became less brilliant over the course of the 1630s, abandoning the lively chromatic effects of his early works. In the same years he also started to paint portraits *alla prima*, or "straight off," with rapid brushstrokes, utilizing a technique that he had previously reserved for genre scenes. He died in Haarlem on August 29, 1666. The fortunes of Frans Hals's work, which had quickly fallen into oblivion, were revived in the second half of the 19th century.

Gypsy Girl
oil on panel, 58x52 cm
Louvre, Paris

The Laughing Cavalier
oil on canvas, 86x68 cm
Wallace Collection, London

With this portrait of a gypsy girl, Hals continues in the Caravaggesque tradition of popular subjects which had been imported into the Netherlands by artists like Terbrugghen and Honthorst. Painted around 1628-30, it is striking for its psychological penetration and the liveliness of the expression. Hals has obtained this effect of great immediacy and spontaneity by skillfully constructing a slightly asymmetrical face and emphasizing the prominent features (the eyes, the corners of the mouth) with a strong chiaroscuro: the impression this creates is one of movement, as if the girl's expression were changing before our very eyes. The illusion is strengthened by her pose, in which she seems to have just turned her head to the right, with a dynamism that is underlined by the formless background, also asymmetrical, that grows paler to the right. As always in Hals, the handling of the paint is very brisk, with long brushstrokes laid on without underpainting. Note the beautiful representation of the blouse, one of the artist's finest pieces of work in which he manages to capture the texture and sheen of the material with just a few touches of brilliant and luminous color.

Painted in 1624, the picture is one of the most famous portraits in the world and unquestionably Frans Hals's best-known work. The identity of the sitter is unknown: all we do know, from the inscription at top right, is that he was twenty-six years old at the time. The reputation of the work, purchased by Sir Richard Wallace in 1870 for what was then considered the exorbitant sum of over fifty thousand pounds, is linked to the manner in which the painter has succeeded in capturing the expression on the subject's face, communicating a sensation of immediacy and vivacity. Here, however, Hals's virtuoso exercise is united with a depth of psychological analysis uncommon in his work. The subject of laughter, which he tackled very often in his individual portraits, is a classical one, and shows the artist's skill in handling a theme already discussed in Greco-Roman literature on art and addressed again in the Renaissance. The representation of the clothing owes a great deal to the example of van Dyck, especially in the depiction of the translucent satin, with long and rapid brushstrokes. (S.G.C.)

Rembrandt

Born at Leiden in 1606, Rembrandt Harmenszoon van Rijn abandoned his studies at the city's university to devote himself to painting, completing his training in Amsterdam under Pieter Lastman, an artist specializing in historical and biblical subjects that he represented in a manner influenced by Italian art. Rembrandt then started to work in his own right at Leiden in 1625, although his early paintings, the *Stoning of Saint Stephen* (1625, Musée des Beaux-Arts, Lyons), *Judgment of Brutus* (1626, Stedelijk Museum, Leiden) and *Baptism of the Eunuch* (1626, St. Catherine's Convent National Museum, Utrecht), reveal his debt to Lastman. In fact the artist transposed the themes dear to his teacher into pictures of large format, accentuating their mythological character and infusing them with a passion and sense of tragedy that were unknown to the elegant and measured work of Lastman and revolutionary for Dutch painting. Within a few years Rembrandt had painted such significant works as *Christ at Emmaus* (c. 1628, Musée Jacquemart-André, Paris) and commenced with two masterpieces (1628-29, Munich and Amsterdam) the series of self-portraits that he was to go on producing throughout his career. He taught himself the technique of copper engraving, achieving excellent results: his earliest engravings, the *Bust of an Elderly Woman* and *Face of an Elderly Woman*, which may portray his mother, are dated 1628.

By 1632 he was already a famous artist, and had also begun to work as an art dealer in Leiden, but chose to abandon the career that had got off to such a good start in his native city in order to move to Amsterdam, where he also opened a school that immediately proved a great success: he had pupils right up until his death, and created the most important studio in the Low Countries, which helped to diffuse his style of painting and his innovative aesthetic ideas.

In Amsterdam he started to paint portraits of prominent citizens, and in 1632 was commissioned to paint an anatomy lesson given by Dr. Nicolaes Tulp, praelector of the city's guild of surgeons. The following year he executed two important etchings, the *Descent from the Cross* and *Christ Before Pilate*. Over the fourth decade of the 17th century he returned, in a series of large paintings, to the biblical and mythological themes of his youth, developing a new style of painting, bold in its subjects and use of color, that conveyed a hitherto unknown sense of tragedy, expressive force and sensuality.

In 1642 his wife died, leaving behind a very young son, but this did not prevent him from completing the *Night Watch* that same year. In 1653 he painted *Aristotle Contemplating the Bust of Homer* (Metropolitan Museum, New York) for the Sicilian nobleman Antonio Ruffo, who later commissioned other historical and mythological works from him (*Alexander the Great*, 1655, Art Gallery and Museum, Glasgow; *Homer Dictating His Verses*, 1663, Mauritshuis, The Hague).

In the 1640s the painter put aside the triumphant and dramatic manner that had made his reputation in favor of a more introspective style: in painting this translated into an even more refined and personal use of light and color, while in engraving it was expressed through an accentuation of the contrasts of light and shade and a reduction in the number of objects represented. In the fifties commissions started to grow more infrequent, but despite the drop in his income Rembrandt did not rein in his lifestyle, and in 1656 was forced to apply for bankruptcy. In 1661 he was commissioned to paint the *Conspiracy of Claudius* (or *Julius*) *Civilis* (Nationalmuseet, Stockholm), a work that along with seven others was intended to decorate a large gallery in Amsterdam City Hall. In 1662 he fulfilled another important public commission, the *Syndics of the Drapers' Guild* (Rijksmuseum, Amsterdam). He went on painting masterpieces up until the end of his life, including the last self-portraits of 1669, the year in which he died in Amsterdam.

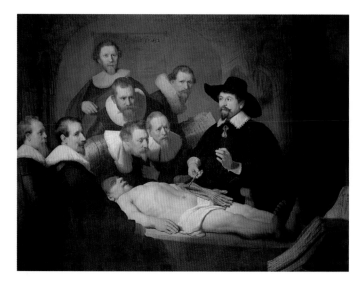

Doctor Nicolaes Tulp's Demonstration of the Anatomy of the Arm
Mauritshuis, The Hague

*Doctor Nicolaes Tulp's
Demonstration of the Anatomy
of the Arm*
oil on canvas, 169.5x216.5 cm
Mauritshuis, The Hague

The picture, usually known as the
*Anatomy Lesson of Doctor Nicolaes
Tulp*, was commissioned for the seat of
the surgeons' guild of Amsterdam. It was
the first large group portrait executed by
Rembrandt at the beginning of his period
in Amsterdam. Tulp had given his first
public lesson of anatomy on January 31,
1631, and the picture was painted on the
occasion of the second lecture open to
the public, in January of the following
year. The demonstrations were held once
a year in chapels of deconsecrated
churches or in a *theatrum anatomicum*
and an entrance fee was charged.
The real subject of the painting is not an
anatomy lesson, but a group portrait that
alludes to an engraving of Vesalius.
Andreas Vesalius (Andries van Wesel) had
attended the universities of Louvain and
Paris, and in 1537 was the first university
professor to practice anatomy personally.
His work *De humani corporis fabrica
libri septem* ("The Seven Books on the
Structure of the Human Body") was
published in Basel in 1543, and almost all
its editions carry an illustration of the
author dissecting a hand. Considering that
Tulp's teacher, Pieter Paauw, had been his
pupil at the University of Padua, the
choice of having himself represented at
work was a way of declaring himself a
follower of Vesalius. This distinguishes the
painting from other group portraits with
anatomists, of which the oldest example
known to us is the one painted by Aert
Pieters in 1603, representing Dr.
Sebastian Egbertsz along with twenty-nine
other people. Around 1656 Rembrandt
painted the *Anatomy Lesson of Doctor
Jan Deyman* (Rijksmuseum, Amsterdam):
here too the operation illustrated, the
opening of the cranium, refers to
Vesalius's book, and constitutes another
declaration in favor of the method
promoted by the physician.

The Flayed Ox
oil on canvas, 94x69 cm
Louvre, Paris

The painting, signed and dated 1655, is
unique in Rembrandt's catalogue. There
is a picture of the same subject in
Glasgow (Art Gallery and Museum), but
recent studies have attributed it to one of
his pupils. Precedents for the painting
already existed in 16th-century Flemish
art, from Aertsen's *Butcher's Stall* of
1551 (University, Uppsala) to
Bueckelaer's *Slaughtered Pig* of 1563
(Wallraf-Richartz-Museum, Cologne) and
the most similar of all these works,
Marten van Cleve's *Slaughtered Ox* of
1566 (Kunsthistorisches Museum,
Vienna). As in other pictures of this
subject, the human presence tends to be
eliminated, and is reduced here to the
face of a woman peeping out from behind
a door, so that some regard the canvas as
a sort of still life.
The way in which the paint is used to
represent the ox is striking: the wrinkled
surfaces of red and white lend the meat
an almost tangible consistency. When the
work was acquired by the Musée du
Louvre, in 1857, it made a great
impression on French painters, especially
Delacroix, and was to remain a source of
inspiration for many artists right into the
20th century.
Some critics have assigned a particular
symbolic significance to the choice of
theme. It has been suggested that
slaughtered animals can represent the
virtue of *Prudentia*, and since the picture
was painted the year before Rembrandt's
bankruptcy, when he must already have
been well aware of his financial
problems, it seems reasonable to link the
choice of subject with the idea of
prudence, something that Rembrandt had
clearly lacked up until them.

Self-Portrait
oil on canvas, 85x61 cm
Galleria degli Uffizi, Florence

Some critics believe that the painting was acquired by Cosimo de' Medici at the time of his visit to the artist's studio in Amsterdam, on December 27, 1667. The work would then have entered the collection of Cardinal Leopoldo, which constitutes the nucleus of the celebrated series of self-portraits on display in the Corridoio Vasariano in Florence.
We know that Rembrandt never ceased to question and analyze himself with pitiless lucidity throughout his life. It was for this reason, perhaps, that he painted around fifty self-portraits in a wide variety of poses and attitudes, even creating a role for himself in some pictures of sacred subjects.
The earliest self-portraits seem to be the ones in Amsterdam (Rijksmuseum)

Above, *Self-Portrait as a Young Man*, Galleria degli Uffizi, Florence

Below, *Self-Portrait as an Old Man*, Galleria degli Uffizi, Florence

and Munich (Bayerische Staatgemäldesammlungen), both datable to around 1628-29; the last ones are in the Mauritshuis in The Hague and the National Gallery in London, and are dated 1669. However, the critics are still divided on the possible motivations for this obsession with painting his own picture: according to Ernst van der Wetering, Rembrandt gained commercial advantages from the proliferation of his image, while for Perry Chapman the self-portrait was a way of continually probing his own place in the world. To the objection that this last interpretation is too modern, it has been pointed out that it appears less anachronistic if we consider the complex questions tackled at the time in works like Shakespeare's *Hamlet*.

The Militia Company of Captain Frans Banning Cocq (*The Night Watch*)
oil on canvas, 363x437 cm
Rijksmuseum, Amsterdam

The painting, finished in 1642, was commissioned by Captain Frans Banning Cocq, portrayed at the center dressed in black with a red sash, next to his lieutenant, Willem van Ruytenburgh. It is presumed that the captain bore the greater part of the expense, but we know that the other people portrayed also contributed to the payment made to the painter: each of the sixteen civic guards represented here paid around a hundred guilders, depending on his position in the painting.
The title *Night Watch* is deceptive, as it is due not to the actual time of the day in which the scene is set but to the fact that in the 19th century the varnish which covered the paint had darkened considerably, creating the mistaken impression of the light of evening or night.
It is not clear what situation is actually represented, and the scene lends itself to multiple interpretations. The payments made by the people in the picture suggest that it was a group portrait, as this was the custom in the second half of the 17th century, at least where militia companies were concerned. It is also possible that it alludes to an important recent historical event, the siege of Amsterdam on January 15, 1641, but without any attempt to provide a realistic description of the place where the episode occurred, the gates of Amsterdam. The backdrop of the scene may also have been inspired by a theatrical set for the play *Gijsbrecht van Aemstel* by Joost van der Vondel.
The work revolutionized the genre of the group portrait, practiced by several other great painters, such as Frans Hals: Rembrandt broke up the group and succeeded in creating the impression that the militiamen were not posed, producing instead a scene that is filled with dynamism. (A.F.)

Vermeer

Jan Vermeer was born in Delft in October 1632, the son of Reynier Janszoon, a manufacturer of silk and an innkeeper who also dealt in works of art. We know virtually nothing about Jan's training, but it is likely that he came into contact with artistic circles through his father's profession, which he also practiced. Enrolled in the artists' guild of St. Luke since 1654, he served as its dean several times, showing that he was already working as a painter in his own right in those years. His earliest dated work is from 1656 (*The Procuress*, now in the Gemäldegalerie, Dresden). Vermeer's output was fairly limited, probably because he mainly produced works on commission, for members of the mercantile middle class of Delft who appreciated his work. This was contrary to the usual practice of Flemish artists, who painted many of their pictures, often genre scenes, for the open market. In 1661 he moved into his mother-in-law's house, where he set up his studio on the upper floor: the room appears in many of his paintings, as do some of the objects that made up its furnishings, such as the heavy oak table or the leather-upholstered chairs. The last years of his life were beset by financial difficulties. He died in 1675.

Vermeer is undoubtedly one of the greatest figures in Flemish painting: his interest in optics constitutes an extremely interesting parallel to the scientific researches and technological inventions that characterized 17th-century culture. At the same time, his art was innovative from a strictly pictorial viewpoint, in its use of *pointillé*, or dots of paint, and its beautiful handing of color, which was to arouse the admiration of van Gogh over two centuries later: "It is true that in the few pictures he painted, one can find the entire scale of colors; but the use of lemon yellow, pale blue and light gray together is as characteristic of him as the harmony of black, white, gray and pink is of Velázquez." His success in life was limited to sales made to a few admirers, although the prices of his works were certainly above the average. During the 18th century and the early part of the 19th he was almost totally forgotten, and it was the French artists of the generation of the Impressionists who rediscovered him and established his modern reputation.

The Milkmaid
oil on canvas, 45.5x41 cm
Rijksmuseum, Amsterdam

Painted between 1658 and 1660, the picture was already considered Vermeer's masterpiece by his contemporaries, as is shown by the valuation of 175 florins placed on it in 1696, when his works were sold by his heirs. The scheme of composition is the same as the one used by the painter in the majority of his pictures: the window on the left lets in the strong light of day, which strikes the figure of a woman at the center of the composition, standing behind the table. Vermeer often used a camera obscura to paint his pictures: this was a technical procedure known since antiquity, but only came into widespread use as an aid to painting in the 16th century. The device made it possible to project the image to be represented onto a sheet of paper or glass: the outlines of the objects were slightly blurred but the precision of the reproduction of the effects of light and shade and of perspective was absolute. Vermeer did not conceal his use of the optical device in this work either. On the contrary, he highlighted its effects by using the technique known as *pointillé*, a method of painting with small touches of the brush that leads to a "crumbling" of the form into small points of light (see in particular the beautiful representation of the bread on the table). In a sense, here as in the painter's other works, the choice of technique results in a choice of style, shifting the attention from the object represented to the seeing of the object itself: it is no coincidence that Vermeer's work was to attract attention again, after a long period of oblivion, at the very time when Impressionist painting was emerging.

The subject of the work, a maidservant pouring milk into a bowl, should also be seen as an allegorical theme, as was frequently the case in 17th-century Flemish art: it is an example of virtue, not devoid of religious allusions to the "sincere milk of the word" (I Peter 2: 2) or the "bread of life" (John 6: 48) and to the Eucharist. Originally a map had hung on the rear wall, used by the artist in other compositions, but the reference to Humility that constitutes the main subject of the picture prompted Vermeer to paint it out, preferring the backdrop of a bare wall, with cracks, holes and nails that are picked out by the grazing light.

JAN VERMEER

View of Delft
oil on canvas, 98.5x117.5 cm
Mauritshuis, The Hague

Painted around 1660-61, this is one of Vermeer's most celebrated works. The urban view had been a fairly common genre in Dutch painting since the beginning of the century: in particular the layout of the composition, with the bank of the Schie River in the foreground and the city extending on the other side of the water, recalls the paintings of Esaias van de Velde or Pieter Bruegel the Elder. But what is lacking here is the eminently topographic interest displayed by the other painters of views of the period: Vermeer has chosen one part of the city, probably framed by a camera obscura on the upper floor of a house. The artist's main interest is the study of light,

and a great deal of space is devoted to the depiction of the sky: stormy clouds darken the buildings that are reflected in the river, while the bank in the foreground appears sunlit; then sky clears in the background, allowing rays of sunshine to fall on the tower of the Niewe Kerk, with a luministic effect that is probably also intended to be symbolic and political, given that William I of Orange had been buried in this church in 1622. Vermeer plays with the harmony of colors with great refinement, with the note of yellow on the houses in the background that relieves the essential uniformity of the painting's tone. This brilliant touch was also to be praised by Proust, who recalled "the patch of yellow wall painted with so much skill and refinement by the artist destined to be for ever unknown and barely identified under the name Vermeer."

The Lacemaker
oil on canvas transferred onto panel, 23.9x20.5 cm
Louvre, Paris

Painted some time around 1670, the picture represents a girl intent on her work with a lace-pillow. The theme should be seen, like the famous *Milkmaid*, as a celebration of female diligence and modesty: the literature of the period on marriage, for example, stressed that needlework and spinning were the activities best suited to a virtuous woman, drawing in part on the passage in Proverbs (31: 10-31) that describes the perfect woman. The subject was fairly common in the Dutch painting of the time, and was seen as an *exemplum virtutis* in contrast to the genre picture, certainly more popular, which, like comedy, preferred to pillory vice. This work too was executed with the aid of a camera obscura and using the technique of *pointillé*, which made the outlines blurred thorough a deliberate imprecision of the focus. What is most striking in the painting is Vermeer's great freedom in the handling of color: note for example the detail, of great modernity, of the red and white threads that spill onto the table from the cushion. (S.G.C.)

18TH CENTURY

Tiepolo

In his novel *Du côté de chez Swann* (*Swann's Way*), Marcel Proust associates Tiepolo's name with a color, the distinctive shade of pink of a dressing gown worn by the character Odette. Tiepolo was the favorite painter of the great European families and courts. He brought the ancient myths to life and the goddesses of Olympus up to date, dressing them in the sensual women's fashion of the time. With Tiepolo, dubbed the "new Veronese," the great decoration of the Venetian Cinquecento was revived. The 18th century was the era of the carnival, of Casanova and Vivaldi, the age of airy rococo, of love affairs and country houses: for some time Venice had no longer derived its wealth from the sea, but from the mainland. Its end, marked by the cession to Austria in 1797, was drawing inexorably closer, but to the last it was seen as the ideal place to savor life's pleasures by the whole of Europe. Giambattista Tiepolo was born in Venice in 1696 and made his debut with religious works in a style close to Piazzetta's Tenebrism, but then gradually adopted lighter and brighter colors along the lines of Sebastiano Ricci, always with an eye on Veronese. In 1719 he married Cecilia Guardi, sister of the Venetian painters Francesco and Antonio. They were to have ten children, but only seven of them, including the painter Giandomenico, would survive. His work found great favor with the conservative society of the day, which commissioned from him grand cycles of murals for the palaces and villas of Venice and the mainland, in which he put his imagination to work on the celebration of triumphs and the creation of a dream world remote in time and space, framed in theatrical settings. He outlined his initial ideas, on the other hand, in rapid and summary sketches in oil, executed in light and lively brushwork of great immediacy. His paintings in the cathedral and Palazzo Arcivescovile of Udine date from the second half of the 1720s. He also worked in Milan, Bergamo, Vicenza and Venice. In the 1740s he painted the frescoes in Palazzo Labia in Venice and at the end of 1750 went to Würzburg with his sons Giandomenico and Lorenzo to decorate the Residenz of the prince-bishop. In 1754 he was working in Venice and in 1757 at Villa Valmarana near Vicenza. In 1762 he went to Madrid at the invitation of King Charles III of Spain, to fresco the ceiling of the throne room of the Palacio Nacional with the *Glory of Spain*. Despite being in great pain from his gout, Tiepolo completed the undertaking with the crucial assistance of his two painter sons and accepted the commission to decorate two more ceilings in the palace. In 1767, still in Madrid, Tiepolo painted seven canvases for the church at Aranjuez, works that were characterized by a greater concern for realism and a deep sense of piety. But the paintings were not a success: installed on the church's altars after the artist's death, they were quickly replaced by works in the neoclassical style. The times were changing and the austerity and restraint of neoclassicism, with its references to the models of antiquity, were supplanting the joy and frivolity of rococo painting. Tiepolo died suddenly in 1770 and was buried in the church of San Martino in Madrid: an artist whose time was past, even the traces of his tomb have been lost.

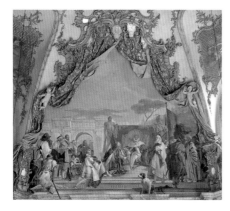

The Investiture of Bishop Harold;
The Marriage of Barbarossa
fresco, 400x500 cm, 400x500 cm
Residenz, Würzburg

In 1750 Tiepolo was invited to Würzburg
to decorate the banquet hall known as the
Kaisersaal in the Residenz of the new
prince-bishop Karl Philipp von

Greiffenklau. He may have been guided in the undertaking by the *Modest Opinions on the Painting of the Prince's Grand Dining Room* supplied by the court council. These had called for the representation of the scenes of the wedding of Emperor Barbarossa to Princess Beatrice of Burgundy, which had taken place at Würzburg in 1156, and the investiture of Bishop Herold of Würzburg as duke of Franconia by Barbarossa in 1168, two quite distant and different events that the painter was required to present as if they were linked by a relationship of cause and effect: in gratitude for the hospitality he had received on the occasion of the fruitful marriage, the emperor invested the bishop as a vassal of the Holy Roman Empire. The painter used the rococo stuccoes of the room to frame the scenes in a theatrical setting on which the curtain is rising, with a markedly illusionistic effect. As was customary, in order to avoid damage to the walls, the decoration commenced from the ceiling, where he painted *Apollo Leading Beatrice of Burgundy to the Genius of the German Nation*. It continued with the scenes at the sides, which were painted in such a way as to make their illumination coincide with the natural lighting of the room. The *Marriage* (1751-53), set in a Palladian-style basilica and with figures dressed in 16th-century clothing, is attended by papal nuncios and prince-electors, the grand marshal of the empire with his sword drawn, located under the imperial insignia as ceremony required, and the grand marshal of Franconia on the far right. On the left, kneeling and wearing an amaranth cloak, is the bride's father, while the officiating bishop has been given the features of the client. The dwarf and court jester, with his baton suspended in the void, connects the painted scene with the real space of the room. But attention is focused on the woman, in a scene that evokes Rubens's *Coronation of Marie de Médicis*. In the *Investiture* (1751-53), Barbarossa offers the imperial scepter to the bishop to be touched in a sign of feudal submission, while the chancellor reads the parchment of

investiture and two pages hold the pluvial and the crown, symbols of the two branches of power, the spiritual and the temporal. The imperial grand marshal with his sword unsheathed and the grand marshal of Franconia are present in this scene too. The page who is staring out of the painting and the dog in the foreground perform the same function as the dwarf in the *Marriage*. The decoration continued on the ceiling of the main staircase with *The Olympus and the Four Continents*, where we can find portraits not just of the client but also of the painter and his son Giandomenico.

The Leave-Taking of Angelica and Medoro; Angelica Carves Medoro's Name on the Tree
Fresco, 250x250 cm, 250x160 cm
Villa Valmarana, Vicenza

It is a more down-to-earth and emotional Tiepolo, a long way from the grandiloquence of his celebratory works, that we find in the frescoes he painted for Conte Giustino Valmarana in his "oasis of peace and quiet," the villa to which he had withdrawn for the "private enjoyment of his leisure." New sentiments and a new style, for a cycle of paintings dominated by the theme of love and the need to

juggle the demands of love and duty in which we see a series of painful renunciations, perhaps a tribute by the count to his deceased wife or a reminder to his sons, to whom he left precise instructions with regard to their treatment of the villa in his will. In the *trompe-l'oeil* settings painted by Mengozzi Colonna, Tiepolo represented scenes from the *Iliad, Aeneid, Orlando Furioso* and *Gerusalemme Liberata* in four small

rooms connected by the central Room of Iphigenia. In the Room of the Orlando Furioso, in 1757, Tiepolo painted scenes drawn from Ariosto's work in an intimate and familiar tone: the episode in which the beautiful Angelica, princess of Cathay, is saved by Ruggero is followed by the story of the girl's love for the humble Medoro. In an idyllic atmosphere, Angelica carves their names "bound together by various knots," on a tree,

while in the scene of the leave-taking the two lovers offer to the peasants who had given them hospitality "a ring of gold, adorned with rich gems" that Orlando had given to Angelica as a pledge of love. The realism of the two peasants is due to Giandomenico Tiepolo, who was also entrusted with the frescoes in the guest quarters. The subjects in the villa were taken from four authors that Conte Francesco Algarotti, a friend of Tiepolo's,

used to recommend to the librettists of operas. The client, moreover, was a lover of the theater and owned a share in the Teatro Novo alla Racchetta in Vicenza, providing yet another motive for the scenographic approach Tiepolo took to the decorations.

Neptune Offering Gifts to Venice
oil on canvas, 135x275 cm
Doge's Palace, Venice

"Under the Ten torture, under the Three burial": this is how Venetians used to sum up the power of the two much-feared magistracies known as the Council of Ten and the Three Chiefs. In the Doge's Palace, the Sala delle Quattro Porte, or Room of Four Doors, was the place through which you had to pass to gain access to the rooms used by the principal organs of government: the Sala del Collegio, Sala del Senato, Sala del Consiglio dei Dieci and Sala dei Tre Capi, reached through the Atrio Quadrato. To replace Tintoretto's fresco in the Sala delle Quattro Porte, severely damaged by the damp, Tiepolo painted a canvas of controversial date (but probably around 1758), that fits in perfectly with the nearby 16th-century paintings and pictures by Veronese. Venice is a beautiful queen leaning on the lion of St. Mark and receiving gifts from Neptune, god of the sea, from whose cornucopia spill gold coins, pieces of coral and pearls. Tiepolo had always taken particular care over the representation of jewelry, and especially pearls and cameos. The pearl, which was extremely popular in the 18th century, had always represented the supremacy of Venice over the sea. Interesting too is the presence of coral, almost ignored by Venetian craftsmen until the 1700s, when a well-known local personage revived its working. Nearing the end of its existence, Venice still celebrated itself as queen of the sea, conjuring up the times when the city could call the Adriatic Sea "our gulf." (E.F.)

Canaletto

Giovanni Antonio Canal, called Canaletto, was born in Venice in 1697. His father and brother were theatrical scene painters, and Canaletto worked alongside them in Venice and Rome from 1716 to 1720.

Later he gave up theatrical painting to devote himself to the execution of topographic and imaginary views, developing an ingenious, highly personal interpretation of a genre that was widely practiced in the baroque period. A stay in Rome (his presence is documented in 1720 but he may have been there since the year before) had brought him into contact with the painting of the Bamboccianti, Northern European artists interested in the life of the taverns, as well as the works of Gaspard van Wittel, a Dutchman who had painted views of the lagoon at the end of the 17th century. But there were painters in Venice too who practiced the genre, and the two that had the greatest influence on him were Luca Carlevarijs and Marco Ricci.

He signed his first contract in 1722 with Owen McSwiney, inventor of the so-called *Allegorical Tombs*, paintings of the imaginary sepulchral monuments of figures from recent English history. Several artists collaborated on each work, and the painter was commissioned with the execution of two allegorical tombs, along with Pittoni, Cimaroli and Piazzetta.

Among the works that commenced his long series of views of the lagoon, it is worth singling out the *Grand Canal Looking from Palazzo Balbi towards Rialto*, the *Rio dei Mendicanti* (both in Ca' Rezzonico, Venice), and *Piazza San Marco* (Thyssen-Bornemisza Collection, Madrid).

Canaletto took the genre of the *veduta* to a new level with paintings of large size in which the meticulous representation of the details of daily life and architectural monuments was united with an attentive observation of atmospheric values, variations in light and the infinite multiplication of the reflections from the water of the lagoon. The intense luminosity and lively coloring created a synergy with the minute depiction of

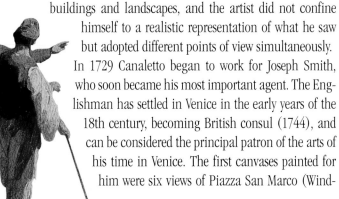

buildings and landscapes, and the artist did not confine himself to a realistic representation of what he saw but adopted different points of view simultaneously.

In 1729 Canaletto began to work for Joseph Smith, who soon became his most important agent. The Englishman has settled in Venice in the early years of the 18th century, becoming British consul (1744), and can be considered the principal patron of the arts of his time in Venice. The first canvases painted for him were six views of Piazza San Marco (Wind-

sor Castle, Royal Collections, 1726-28), followed by a group of twelve views of the Grand Canal, completed by 1730 and later replicated in a series of engravings by Visentini. These were published in 1735 under the title *Prospectus Magni Canalis Venetiarum*. The series anticipated the two collections of twenty-four views of the most celebrated sights of Venice, executed for the duke of Bedford and now at Woburn Abbey, and the seventeen views for the earl of Carlisle at Castle Howard.

Canaletto received numerous orders through Smith and carried out an intense activity in the thirties and forties. From this period date masterpieces like the *View of the Basin of Saint Mark* (Museum of Fine Arts Boston), *The Stonemason's Yard* and the *Feast Day of Saint Roch* (National Gallery, London). In 1746 he went to England, where he stayed for several years, painting about fifty views of London, the Thames and the English countryside, which exercised a deep fascination on him: famous examples are *The Thames and Whitehall from the Terrace of Richmond House* (collection of the duke of Richmond, Goodwood), *Walton Bridge* (London, Dulwich Picture Gallery) and the *Procession of Knights of the Order of the Bath* (Westminster Abbey, London). Canaletto left England for good around 1755, and died in Venice in 1768.

Grand Canal and Palazzo Bembo
oil on canvas, 47x80 cm
Duke of Bedford Collection, Woburn Abbey

This is one of twenty-four views by Canaletto commissioned by the duke of Bedford, Lord John Russell. Between 1729 and 1731 the duke undertook the Grand Tour of the continent, and in the last year of his journey stayed in Venice, where he met Joseph Smith and may have been able to acquire some of the painter's

works. He certainly bought others later on, since several of the canvases in his collection cannot have been painted before 1735. The pictures of the city's most celebrated views remained in his London home for about half a century, and when the building was demolished were moved to the "Canaletto Room" in Woburn Abbey, where they can still be seen today.

Works like this allow us to appreciate the attention paid by the artist to the representation not just of every crack of

the buildings, but also to the quivering reflections in the water. This analytical capacity has led people to believe that the painter made use of a camera obscura and the scholar Decio Gioseffi has recently demonstrated that the drawings in the *Quaderno Cagnola* (Gallerie dell'Accademia, Venice) were in fact realized with the aid of this instrument. Canaletto made sketches and surveys on the spot, and also made notes in his sketchbook for subsequent elaboration. The paintings were executed in the artist's studio, but when transferring the sketches done outdoors onto canvas Canaletto maintained the individual points of view, thereby creating a multiple perspective that increased the fascination of the scene and resulted in a more poetic representation of reality.

The Stonemason's Yard
oil on canvas, 124x163 cm
National Gallery, London

The view of Venice, bathed in bright sunlight, offers us a glimpse of a landscape that has profoundly changed over time, and thus is not immediately recognizable. Canaletto seems to have painted the scene from the second floor of a building that faced onto Campo San Vidal, near the section of the Grand Canal now spanned by the Ponte dell'Accademia. On the other bank, illustrated in the painting, stands the church of La Carità, flanked by the slender campanile that collapsed in 1744; even the small building at the base of the campanile can no longer be seen today.

On the right of the church, the facade of the Scuola della Carità still has its original Gothic appearance: around 1760 it was clad in marble and became the seat of the Accademia di Belle Arti (it is now the entrance to the Gallerie dell'Accademia). Unlike Canaletto's typical *vedute*, this picture does not portray Venice in its immutable beauty, but at a particular moment in time. In fact Campo San Vidal was then being used for work on the new marble facade of the church of the same name, and we can see the stonemasons, rough or half-finished blocks of marble and tools used for cutting stone, such as the large pair of compasses at the center of the composition, represented with the artist's typical attention to detail. On the left the picture is enlivened by a sort of genre scene, with a child who has fallen over helped by a woman under the eyes of another child.

The painting, which was already in England, in the collection of Sir Beaumont, by 1808, can be ascribed to the early part of Canaletto's career and dated to around 1730. (A.F.)

Watteau

"There has been another death that, while not so significant, is of great interest to Dealers. It is that of M. Watot, excellent Painter, at the age of just thirty-six." It was with these words that the *Gazette d'Utrecht* announced the artist's death in 1721. The inventor of the genre of *fêtes galantes*, the painter who created images of gaiety in a frothy rococo style, had been ill for some time. The description of him furnished by his contemporaries is very different from what we might expect: the man who as a boy had used every free moment to draw comic scenes of mountebanks performing on the public square was of weak constitution, a restless and unhappy spirit in perennial search of the new. Baptized at Valenciennes in 1684, Watteau moved to Paris around the age of eighteen and began to produce small votive paintings in series to make ends meet. From around 1705 he collaborated with Claude Gillot, a painter of theatrical scenery, and then in 1708 started to work for the curator of the Luxembourg Palace, a decorator specializing in arabesques. During this period he copied Rubens's scenes from the *Life of Marie de Médicis* in the Luxembourg Palace, assimilating their spirit and even reproducing parts of them in subsequent paintings. In 1709 he entered the competition for the Prix de Rome of the Académie Royale of painting and sculpture, a prize that would have earned him a royal scholarship to study art in Rome, but only came second. He tried again in 1712, after having achieved some success with paintings of military subjects, in the hope that he would at last be able to go to Italy to see his beloved Venetian painting firsthand. He did not win, but made a favorable impression on the academicians, who agreed to accept him as a member: "My friend [...] you are unaware of your talent, and distrustful of your powers; believe me, you know better than us, that we consider you capable of honoring our Academy; take the necessary steps, we consider you one of us." The necessary steps consisted in the execution of the *morceau de réception* to be submitted to the Académie, but five years were to pass before the presentation of the *Embarkation for the Island of Cythera*, the painting with which Watteau was admitted to the academy with the unprecedented title of painter of *fêtes galantes*. In the meantime he continued to devote himself to scenes inspired by the opera and the *commedia dell'arte* and painted the famous *Gilles*. In 1719 he went to London, probably to be examined by a famous doctor. On his return to Paris in 1720 he produced another fundamental work, the *Gersaint Signboard*: this was not so much a shop sign for his friend and art dealer Gersaint as a way of letting Paris know he was back and ready to paint. In 1721 Watteau died with the faithful Gersaint at his bedside. The 18th century is reflected in his paintings and in the wide range of sentiments that he represented, before neoclassicism replaced the grace and fantasy of the rococo with new ideals.

Gilles
oil on canvas, 184.5x149.5 cm
Louvre, Paris

With the *commedia dell'arte* were created the masks, the fixed roles in which actors specialized: Pantaloon, Harlequin, Columbine. After the expulsion of the Italian players from Paris in 1697, for having ridiculed Madame de Maintenon, the characters were kept alive at fairs. In the hands of the actor

Dominique the mask of Pierrot, introduced into French comedy by Molière, was transformed into what Harlequin had originally been: a shy and foolish valet, frustrated in love. Pierrot had a double called Gilles, dressed in the same costume but with a different role: Pierrot appeared on the stage, whereas Gilles was the protagonist of the *Parades*, short comedies without rules that were used to attract people to the show proper. Thomas-Simon Gueullette had given a new respectability to the character, performing the part of Gilles and writing a series of *Parades* for him. In one set of four *Parades*, Gilles receives a legacy that allows him to aspire to the hand of the beautiful Isabelle, but only on condition that he first learn good manners, grammar, history and how to dance. Gilles's attempts are doomed to failure, and he ends up without the girl and without his money. The four stories that describe the fiasco are grouped under the title *Washing the Head of an Ass You Lose the Soap*: it is Gilles the ass, and a real ass, with a livelier gaze than the protagonist, that appears in Watteau's painting. With this interpretation it is easy to identify the other figures: Isabelle, her father and her suitor Leander, recognizable by his headgear in the form of a cockscomb. The fifth figure, next to the ass, is the teacher who seeks in vain to instruct Gilles. The remarkable size of the painting, datable to around 1717, has led to the suggestion that it was intended to serve as an advertising poster or the signboard of a theater, or as a decoration for the café owned by the actor Belloni.

Embarkation for the Island of Cythera
oil on canvas, 129x194 cm
Louvre, Paris

With this work of 1717 Watteau made his entry into the Académie Royale de Peinture in Paris with the title of painter of *fêtes galantes*. The pairs of lovers are ready to set sail for Cythera, the island of love, in a progression that was already known to the ancients: persuasion, represented by the lady on the right with her eyes lowered and a cupid tugging at her skirt; consent, by the lady in the middle accepting the helping hand of her escort to rise; amorous agreement, by the couple embracing and moving away. Scholars have pointed out various theatrical sources on which the artist may have drawn, from Dancourt's *Les Trois Cousines* to *La Vénitienne* by de la Motte and La Barre, while some of the ideas may have come from the exclusive circles of the regency, whose members used to meet to cultivate poetic and erotic pleasures, or from the boats that took couples along the Seine from Paris to the park of Saint Cloud for amorous trysts. A completely different light is thrown on the painting if we take into consideration two other works, *The Triumph of the Arts* of 1700 and *Les Amours déguisés* (*The Disguised Loves*) of 1713, in which the island sacred to Venus represents a political utopia and a challenge to the absolutism of Louis XIV. Since the 17th century, in fact, Cythera had been the symbol of a new, free and peaceful society, guided by love, and nautical images had been associated with France from the time of the Renaissance at least: thus the boat for Cythera may represent the aspiration to a new State. At the beginning of the 18th century the name of Cythera was synonymous with subversion, a significance that has been lost over the years.

Associated with an image of frivolity, decadence and aristocratic privilege, the painting in the Louvre would be pelted with balls of paper by the pupils of David, and would have to be hidden in a storeroom during the French Revolution to prevent its destruction. (E.F.)

Chardin

Jean-Baptiste-Siméon Chardin was born in Paris on November 2, 1699. His training at the Académie Royale was oriented principally toward the painting of still lifes and animals (his first paintings with figures date from after 1733). His reputation as a genre painter began to spread after his success at the Salon of 1737, and was closely linked to the circulation of engravings after his works throughout Europe. By the early 1740s he was already a famous painter, presented at court, a councilor of the academy and the subject of eulogistic articles in the *Mercure de France* written by Chevalier Antoine de La Rogue, a friend of Watteau's. In 1755 he was entrusted with the organization of the Salon (although the prestigious post would not be bestowed on him officially until 1761). His ties with the marquis de Marigny, the brother of Madame de Pompadour, allowed him to obtain, in 1757, an apartment at the Louvre and an adequate annuity. He died in Paris on December 6, 1779. Denis Diderot, a great admirer of Chardin, said of the works on show at the Salon of 1765 that the "magic [of his pictures] defies understanding" and explained the reason for his wonder: "Approach the painting, and everything comes together in a jumble, flattens out and vanishes; move away, and everything creates itself and reappears."

The realism of Chardin's still lifes is not based on a minute depiction of the objects represented, polished in its details, but on his capacity to capture the relations of light and color through a pictorial simplification. It is no accident that his work would be highly esteemed by Cézanne and by van Gogh, who wrote: "I am increasingly convinced that true painters do not 'finish' their works, in the sense in which 'finished' is too often understood; in other words worked so accurately that you could stick your nose into them. From very close up the best paintings, and precisely those that from a technical point of view are the most complete, are done with brushstrokes of color set side by side; they only have their full effect from a certain distance. Rembrandt insisted on this, even though he suffered as a result (the good burghers preferred van der Helst, because they could admire his works from very close-up). From this point of view Chardin is as good as Rembrandt." For his contemporaries and probably for the artist himself, the still life, considered a minor genre with respect to history painting, constituted a limitation (even Diderot wrote: "I am aware that Chardin's models, those inanimate entities that he imitates, do not change their position, color or form [...] the genre of painting that Chardin practices is the easiest"), and yet the choice of the inanimate subject, and the absence of any moral, philosophical or religious significance, is part of the reason for Chardin's high reputation today. Gide said that he loved Chardin because it was possible to just admire the painting in his works, and Proust declared: "Now if all this is beautiful to the eye, it is because Chardin has found it beautiful to paint; and he found it beautiful to paint because he considered it beautiful to the eye."

Smoker's Case
oil on canvas, 32.5x40 cm
Louvre, Paris

The painting is signed at bottom left, on the edge of the table. The objects represented, a pipe, some crockery and a few other things, belonged to the painter,

as can be deduced from the inventory drawn up on the death of his first wife in 1737. The work, one of the finest examples of 18th-century still life, was much appreciated by Cézanne: Chardin's ability to render the truth of things, through a process of simplification of form that has been compared to Corot's

treatment of the landscape, could not fail to arouse the interest of a painter who was conducting research along very similar lines, however different the means that he used. In this work as in others, Chardin shows that he is not a realistic painter in the proper sense of the term. His art is not strictly representational:

what the porous and never pure shades of white, the thick and lumpy paint, seek to capture on the canvas, with that magic that seemed inexplicable to Diderot, is the reaction of the material to the light, in compositions that are always carefully calculated and effective. Note for example the play of diagonals that stir the still life

into movement, avoiding any sense of stasis: the perspective of the wooden case that gives depth to the painting, the line of light marked by the pipe, the oblique shadows on the table top.

Back From the Market
(*La Pourvoyeuse*)
oil on canvas, 47x38 cm
Louvre, Paris

Three versions of this subject exist: the one reproduced here, now in the Louvre, is probably the picture shown at the Salon of 1739, the other two, in Berlin and Ottawa, date from 1738. It is the most famous of Chardin's genre paintings and depicts a woman just back from the market, where she has been buying food. As is always the case in the French artist's work, the composition is perfectly studied, with the sequence of doors left half-open or ajar that alternatively immerse the details in shadow or inundate them with light. The handling of the paint, as the critics have pointed out, with the brushstrokes laid on side by side, gives the picture the appearance of *gros point* embroidery. Speaking of this work, Malraux pointed out that Chardin, far from being a minor master of the 18th century dependent on the still life of the Flemish baroque and susceptible to the decorative taste of his time, was in reality, like Corot, a graceful and imperious simplifier. In effect Chardin set out to represent the colors and forms of reality, but without getting bogged down in detailed description: it is for this reason that the modernity of his painting aroused such admiration in Cézanne and the Cubist painters.

Self-Portrait at the Easel
Pastel, 46x38 cm
Département des Arts Graphiques, Louvre, Paris

In the last years of his activity Chardin tackled the theme of the self-portrait several times, always in the medium of pastel. This technique was used by the artist increasingly often from the beginning of the 1770s onward and came to replace that of oil almost completely. The reasons for this choice lie not so much in the course of Chardin's stylistic development as in his failing health, which meant that he could no longer tolerate the fumes given off by the paint, which tended to burn his eyes. The

painter who had dedicated his artistic career to the still life and the genre scene demonstrates here, in a work of wholly private character, not intended either for a client or for the market, his skill in the representation of the human figure and an uncommon depth of psychological penetration. An ideal model must have been, of course, the numerous self-portraits of Rembrandt, against which Chardin seems to have measured himself directly in several studies of heads from these years.

The work illustrated here has, in common with other celebrated pastels in which the painter portrayed himself, a taste for the bizarre, especially in the strange headgear, a feature which struck acute observers like Proust. He rightly pointed out, in *Contre Saint-Beuve*, that the "scruffiness" and "comic strangeness of his dress" were masterfully combined with "the noble hierarchy of colors" and "the order of the laws of beauty." According to the great French writer, in his self-portrait, as in so many still lifes, the artist was seeking the pictorial "truth" of the object represented, i.e. harmony of

light and color, but this was accompanied by a study of the expression and the attitude worthy of a great portraitist. Compared with the other pictures he painted of himself, Chardin here looks much thinner, markedly older and in pain: it is likely that it was one of the artist's last works, perhaps dating from 1779, the year of his death. (S.G.C.)

Hogarth

William Hogarth, born in London in 1697 and of modest social origin, served his apprenticeship in the workshop of the silversmith Ellis Gamble. In 1720 he enrolled in a private drawing school on St. Martin's Lane, but abandoned his studies before he had completed them to devote himself to engraving on copper and painting.

The work with which he made his name was *Masquerade and Operas*, a print published in 1724 that ridiculed the classical and Neo-Palladian circle of Richard Boyle, third earl of Burlington. The following year he married Jane Thornhill, daughter of Sir James Thornhill, the greatest English painter of historical subjects in the 1720s.

During the early 1830s Hogarth found himself clients in elegant society by painting individual and group portraits of small size, a simple formula that was very popular at the time in London. The works with which he obtained an even greater success were series illustrating ruinous or ill-fated lives, a genre inaugurated in 1732 with *A Harlot's Progress*, a group of six engravings that display significant similarities to a series of Venetian prints from around 1655-58, *Lo specchio al fin de la putana*. Hogarth's cycles of prints can be considered the pictorial equivalent of the bourgeois literature of the thirties and forties, and one of the most expressive writers of the day, Henry Fielding, made his links with the works of Hogarth explicit in the introduction to *Tom Jones*, his most famous novel. The affinity between the painter and the writer lay in the ironic picture they presented of the English society of their time, described with pitiless frankness and at times fierce indignation, but without abandoning their comic and occasionally even indulgent vision. Both represented daily life in all its antiheroic splendor, with a completely new realism and a style that spurned the then predominant models of classicism.

Hogarth was also attentive to the suggestions of theatrical performances. He conceived his series of engravings as acts in a play, which allowed him to infuse his works with dynamism and dramatic force, as well as a great liveliness of observation and a remarkable capacity for psychological insight.

In 1732 he started to work on the series entitled *Rake's Progress*. Here too parallels have been found with a series of Venetian engravings, *La vita del lascivo* (1660-75).

Around 1733 he published his first writing, *The Case of Designers, Engravers [. . .] Stated in a Letter to a Member of Parliament*. This polemic in defense of copyright made a decisive contribution to the political campaign that was to lead to the Engravers' Copyright Act of 1735, which came to be known as the Hogarth Act.

The Graham Children
National Gallery, London

In 1745 he produced one of his most celebrated series of engravings, the *Marriage à la Mode*, and in 1753 published a treatise on aesthetics, *The Analysis of Beauty*. He also devoted himself to religious painting with the triptych (1755-56) for the church of St. Mary Radcliffe in Bristol. Appointed court painter (1757), he spent the last years of his life writing his *Autobiographical Notes* and died in London in 1764.

The Graham Children
oil on canvas, 160.5x181 cm
National Gallery, London

The painting of 1742 is animated by a surprising vivacity: it looks as if the children have posed for just a moment, before returning to their play. Moreover, the cat ogling the canary in the cage really looks as if it can't wait to leap on its prey. The impression of vitality is also conveyed by the composition, which lacks a central focal point, so that our attention shifts continually, following the studied exchange of glances between one figure and another, and even directed out of the painting at us.
The lively subjects of the painting are the children of the pharmacist of Chelsea Hospital, and the eldest of them was to take his father's place. The painting shows affinities with van Dyck's portrait of *The Children of Charles I* (Royal Collection, Windsor) where a more tranquil atmosphere holds sway, but one that is completely different from the stiffness of other contemporary portraits of the children of the royal family.

The Marriage à la Mode: Breakfast Scene (Shortly after the Marriage)
oil on canvas, 69.8x90.8 cm
National Gallery, London

The *Marriage à la Mode* series, to which this painting belongs, illustrates the dramatic course of a marriage made out of interest in a satirical tone. In this scene we see the husband and wife in the drawing room of their home, perhaps inspired by the London residence of Horace Walpole, beginning a new day. The husband is slumped on a chair after a night of carousal, while the wife is stretching her limbs on the other side of the table. The representation is rich in details that describe the scene with precision: the steward leaving the room with the household account book under his arm is clutching a pile of bills, only one of which has been paid. As is often the case in Hogarth's work, the gestures are studied with attention, in a manner that he may have assimilated from theatrical performances. Nor does the artist let slip the chance to make fun of the over elaborate style of decoration then in vogue, by placing a clock dripping with fish in the right-hand corner of the picture.

The sale of the paintings in this series is a telling example of how the art market functioned in 18th-century England. The following advertisement appeared in the *London Daily Post and Advertiser* on April 2, 1743: "Mr. Hogarth intends to publish by subscription, six prints from copper-plates [...] after his own paintings [...] representing a variety of modern occurrences in high-life and called *Marriage a-la-Mode* [...]." On April 19, 1745, the same newspaper carried the information that the six paintings were visible at the painter's house and could be purchased as soon as the engravings were ready, which they would be by the end of the year. Other series of engravings were published by the artist and sold to the public by subscription through advertisements in newspapers, and the success of these ventures shows just how bourgeois British society had become with respect to the rest of Europe. It can be explained by the existence of a larger middle class than elsewhere, already accustomed to the caricatures, cartoons and satirical scenes carried by publications like *The Tatler* or *The Spectator*. (A.F.)

Gainsborough

Thomas Gainsborough was born at Sudbury, Suffolk, in 1727. He displayed a very precocious talent and at the beginning of the 1740s was already enrolled in the St. Martin's Lane Academy in London. It may have been here that he came across the work of Francis Hayman, which influenced the style of his early paintings.

Gainsborough's first dated picture is the study of the bull terrier *Bumper* of 1745 (private collection). The artist made his name in the artistic circles of the capital with *The Charterhouse*, acquired in 1748 by the Foundling Hospital of London, but in the same year, following the death of his father, he was obliged to return to the town of his birth. In that period he executed one of his most famous works, *Mr. and Mrs. Andrews* (National Gallery, London), which combines a remarkable capacity for psychological penetration, typical of all his portraits, with a surprising feeling for the representation of the English countryside. This is a good example of Gainsborough's real vocation for landscape painting, which he began to practice after seeing the works of the Dutch painter van Ruisdael. In numerous paintings and drawings he depicted the woods and meadows of Southern England, in landscapes veined with a subtle melancholy, an impression conveyed in part by the cunning use of warm and soft light.

His first major commission was for two views for the duke of Bedford, but portrait painting proved a more profitable activity, and the artist devoted himself to it from 1758. In 1759 he arrived in Bath, a spa town frequented by the elegant society of the time. His portraits proved an immediate success, and he stayed in Bath until 1773. During this period he did not neglect his contacts with London, and in 1761 he exhibited at the Society of Arts. In 1768 he was invited to be one of the founding members of the Royal Academy and a few years later he moved to the capital, where he remained until his death in 1788.

In London he modified the style of his portraits, and in *Mrs. Graham* of 1777 (National Gallery, Edinburgh) he sought to achieve a grander effect by introducing architectural elements. Even the style of his landscapes changed, influenced by the emerging Romantic current from 1783 onward. The following year he broke with the Royal Academy, but the quarrel had no effect on his official prestige and after his death Joshua Reynolds, the most famous English painter of the day and president of the Royal Academy, observed that if it were ever possible to speak of an English school of painting, Gainsborough would certainly be considered one of its greatest exponents.

Lady and Gentleman in Landscape
oil on canvas, 73x68 cm
Louvre, Paris

In all probability the picture represents the artist and his wife. It is believed to have been painted at the time of their marriage, in 1746, and is therefore an early work.
The subject recalls the conversation pieces, small groups of people in a landscape that had been made very popular in 1728 by Philip Mercier, a French artist who had been appointed principal painter to the British court. He probably saw these models in the studio of Hayman, who had already painted a conversation piece around 1730, *The Wagg Family of Windsor*. It is also likely that Gainsborough had painted landscape backdrops for Hayman's portraits in the 1740s. In any case, the influence was mutual, and Hayman altered his own style following his collaboration with the young painter.
The choice of iconography shows French and Dutch influences, but the characteristic and original trait of Gainsborough's work is the greater importance he bestows on the landscape.

Portrait of a Lady in Blue
oil on canvas, 73x68 cm
Hermitage, St. Petersburg

The painting, dating from between 1770 and 1780, entered the Hermitage in 1912, when it was catalogued as a portrait of the duchess of Beaufort. But there is no documentary evidence for this identification, perhaps suggested by the fact that Gainsborough's wife, Margaret Burr was the illegitimate daughter of the duke of Beaufort. However, the canvas does present similarities with a portrait of the artist's wife, at half length, painted at around the same time (1778, Courtauld Institute Galleries, London). The use of color, laid on in long and light brushstrokes, is extremely refined, with evanescent hues that frame the woman's eyes and mouth, creating a surprising effect of sfumato. Generally Gainsborough's portraits reveal a great capacity for psychological insight that derived from an attentive observation of reality, a characteristic that renders his work very modern. (A.F.)

Goya

Francisco de Goya y Lucientes was born at Fuendetodos in 1746 and received his training in Saragossa from a local painter, José Luzán. In 1771, on his return from a journey to Italy, he obtained his first important commission, the decoration of a ceiling in the church of Nuestra Señora del Pilar in Saragossa.

Through his brother-in-law, the painter Francisco Bayeu, he received another major commission to produce cartoons for the royal tapestry factory of Santa Barbara in Madrid. The sixty-three cartoons he painted between 1774 and 1791 and now in the Prado depict scenes of popular life full of grace and lively pictorial effects: among the most famous are *The Parasol* (1777) and *Blind Man's Buff* (1788-89). In 1778 King Charles III of Spain opened the royal collections and Goya seized the opportunity to broaden his knowledge of Spanish painting by studying the works of Velázquez, which made a deep impression on him. In the meanwhile his reputation continued to grow in Madrilenian circles. In 1780 he was elected to the Royal Academy of Madrid and some years later the king appointed him *pintor de cámara*. In 1792 a grave illness left him seriously weakened and completely deaf. His career does not appear to have suffered, and in 1798 he painted the frescoes in the dome of San Antonio de la Florida in Madrid. More celebrated are the etchings of the *Los caprichos* series, published the following year, which reflect the change in his sensibility. The cheerful and carefree tones of his early work slowly gave way to an art that was at once fantastic and realistic, taking on the character of a fierce critique of society and expressing an uncompromising condemnation of all types of superstition, brutality and oppression.

His standing with the high society of Madrid was very great in those years, and this is also attested by his friendship with the duchess of Alba. He painted numerous portraits of her, and one of them (1797, Hispanic Society of America, New York) is considered a masterpiece.

In October 1808 the painter was summoned to Saragossa to document the resistance of the city's inhabitants to Napoleon's invading troops. The drawings and small paintings he executed at that time were utilized for the series of *Los desastres de la guerra* (*The Disasters of War*), begun in 1810 and finished in 1820. In those ten years Goya moved from what was almost a work of journalism, intended to record the conflict between the Spanish and the French invaders, to an intense reflection on that experience which found expression in a harsh condemnation of any form of violence.

In 1814, with the restoration of Ferdinand VII, Goya painted two pictures illustrating the executions of May 2 and 3, 1808, which had followed the insurrections against the French troops. Two years later he produced one of his most famous series of engravings, *La tauromaquia*, dedicated to the art of bullfighting. In 1819 he fell ill again and retired to his house in the country, the "Quinta del Sordo" on the outskirts of Madrid. The approval of the constitution, which Ferdinand VII was forced to accept in 1820, may have permitted the great freedom in the choice of the subjects with which the walls of the Quinta del Sordo were painted between 1820 and 1823, by removing the threat of the Inquisition: these "black paintings" present an almost dreamlike, nocturnal and irrational world that seems to anticipate Expressionist and Surrealist painting. Among the works, which have been transferred onto canvas and are now in the Prado, it is worth singling out *Saturn*, *The Witches' Sabbath* and the *Holy Office of the Inquisition*. In 1823, with Ferdinand's reactionary shift in policy and the reconstitution of the tribunal of the Inquisition, Goya decided to leave the country and in 1824 moved to Bordeaux, where he died four years later.

Blind Man's Buff
cartoon, 269x350 cm
Prado, Madrid

One of the themes of the tapestries commissioned from Goya and intended to embellish the Camera of the Princes in the royal palace of El Pardo was the game of *Blind Man's Buff*. The artist made the drawing for it in 1788 and the same year,

or perhaps the following one, painted the cartoon that was to be used as a model for the weaving of the tapestry. The painting was part of a series of rustic scenes, including *The Swing* and *The Greasy Pole*, in which Goya was able to underline the light-hearted character of the subjects through a style of great fluency. This characteristic is evident in other cartoons for tapestries, such as the

Flower Girls and *Spring* of 1886-87, which display the same freshness of color. According to some historians the joyful atmosphere of these works is a reflection of one of the most serene periods in the artist's life, which would be brought to an end in 1792 with the grave illness that left him deaf.

La Maja desnuda
(*The Naked Maja*)
oil on canvas, 97x190 cm
Prado, Madrid

The mysterious painting is the companion
to another picture, also in the Prado,
which portrays the same woman in the
same setting, but clothed (*La Maja
vestida*). The woman has not yet been
identified, and the hypothesis that she
may have been the duchess of Alba,

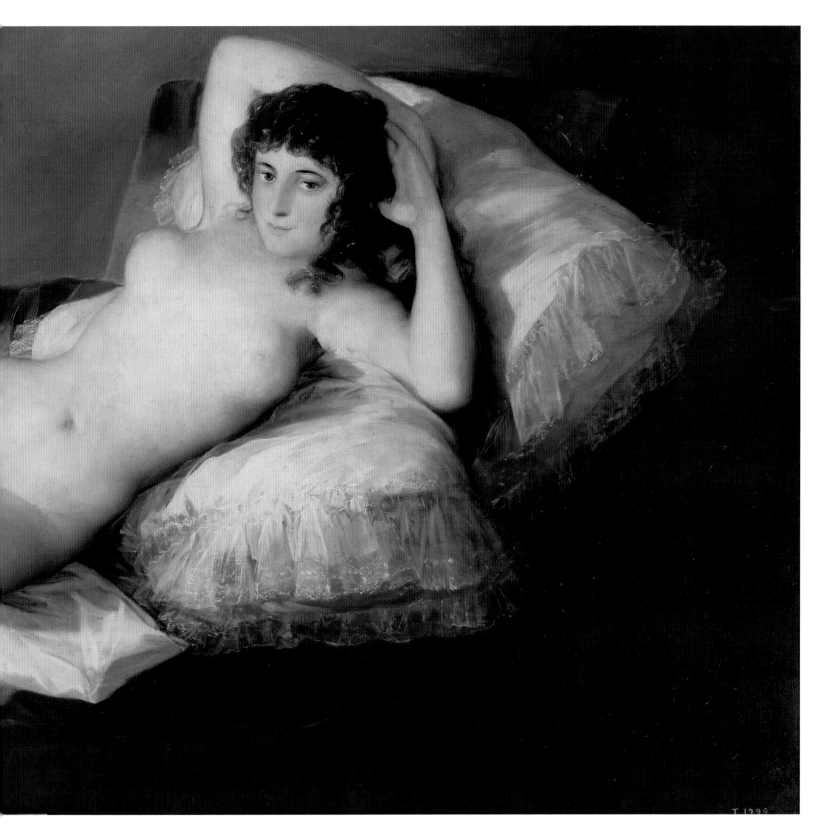

stemming perhaps from the fact that she showed an interest in the canvas, is belied by the lack of resemblance to portraits of the noblewoman. The picture must have been painted by the year 1800, when the engraver Pedro González de Sepúlveda saw it in the collection of the minister Manuel de Godoy along with other "Venuses," although he judged it to lack good drawing and refinement of coloring. Godoy is the first known owner of the *Maja vestida*, which suggests that it was

painted for him. This hypothesis is supported by the fact that in those years he had favored Goya over any other painter, and that if the request had not come to him from such a powerful man it is likely that the artist would never have risked tackling such an explicitly erotic theme, in open conflict with the cultural and religious ethos of the day. On March 16, 1815, even though the painting was not displayed in a public place, the *Cámara Secreta de la Inquisición de*

Madrid ordered that the painter be brought in for interrogation about the two paintings of *Las Majas*, to find out whether he admitted to being their author and for whom he had executed them. The reaction of the Inquisition, even after a lapse of fifteen years since the execution of the painting, should not surprise us: in the Spain of the time such a realistic nude was quite exceptional, and had a sole precedent in a mythological representation by Velázquez, *Venus and*

Cupid (National Gallery, London). But the *Maja desnuda* caused far more scandal than the depiction of a figure from myth, as it was the first time a real woman, even if her identity was unknown, had been portrayed with such realism and sensuality. Goya's composition is extremely refined, and the model's opulent forms and penetrating gaze are enhanced by the light that is reflected from her perfect, nacreous flesh.

The Family of King Charles IV
oil on canvas, 280x336 cm
Prado, Madrid

From the correspondence of Queen Mary Louise with Godoy, the collector who was Goya's main client in those years, we learn that the king had expressed the desire to be portrayed with his family in April 1800. Shortly afterward Goya moved to Aranjuez, where he started to make preparatory studies of the members of the family that were to be included in the painting, in which he also found room for himself, in semidarkness in the background next to a large canvas. The picture represents, from the left, Don Charles Mary Isidore with his arm around his elder brother, Ferdinand prince of Asturias and the future

Ferdinand VII; behind them stand the king's sister, Mary Josephine, while Queen Mary Louise, who was considered the true mastermind of the court, is the most brightly illuminated figure and occupies a central position with her youngest children, Mary Isabelle and Francis. Next to his consort stands the king, Charles IV; behind him we glimpse his brother, Anthony Pascal, and to his left the members of the family of the princes of Parma, Louis of Bourbon and Mary Louise with their son, the king's cousin, Louis. The formality of the portrait required the men and women to wear the honors awarded by the two rulers: the women have the sash of the order of Mary Louise, the men that of Charles IV; those who have the right to do so also wear the emblem

of the Golden Fleece. Two figures have not been identified with certainty, the woman next to Ferdinand and the one on the other side, in profile, who may be Charlotte Joachine, daughter of the royal couple and queen of Portugal.
Goya is successful in his aim of producing an official portrait of the family, managing brilliantly to avoid the risk of producing the usual array of figures on parade. The fact that he included himself suggests that the painter wished to allude to Velázquez's *Las Meninas*, which was considered a family portrait and of which he had made both a copy in sanguine and an engraving in 1778. In fact there are three elements in common with that work: the painter portrays himself along with the royal family, standing next to a canvas; the

room of a palace decorated with paintings; and the central position of the queen, which recalls that of Margaret of Austria. The influence of Velázquez is always present in the artist's portraits: it is revealed in the handling of light and space and in the paint laid on in spots, a tendency that grew ever more pronounced in Goya over time, so that the portraits painted after 1800 seem to anticipate the technique of the Impressionists. Goya's portraits, direct, psychological and realistic, renewed the genre and cleared the way for the diverse artistic currents of the 19th century.

FRANCISCO DE GOYA

May 3, 1808
oil on canvas, 266x345 cm
Prado, Madrid

On May 2, 1808, there had been an uprising against the French in Madrid, in which Spanish troops had also taken part. The reaction of the French army of occupation led to the execution of the rebels by firing squad, which went on until the afternoon of the following day. In 1814, on the return of the deposed king Ferdinand VII, Goya himself proposed to the government that he should depict the most important episodes of the resistance, and as a result painted this picture and another dedicated to the events of May 2. The scene represented is the moment just before the execution. The firing squad is set diagonally and looms over the condemned men. The figure in the white shirt, although located to one side, is the focal point of the painting and seems to be drawing all the squad's fire on himself. The violence depicted goes beyond the representation of a single episode, and gives Goya the opportunity to demonstrate the folly of all wars. The drama that unfolds here has been described by Giulio Carlo Argan in the following words: "The soldiers have no face, they are puppets in uniform, symbols of an order that is actually violence and death […]. There is no heroism in the patriots who are dying, at least not in the classical sense of David, but fanaticism and terror. History as slaughter, as disaster (the etchings of the *Los desastres de la guerra* date from this time). The carnage take place in the yellow glow of an enormous square lantern – here is 'the light of reason' – while all around is the darkness of a night like any other and in the background lies the sleeping city." (A.F.)

19TH CENTURY

David

J acques-Louis David was born in Paris on August 30, 1748. Following the death of his father in a duel, he was raised by his uncles François Buron (1731-1818) and Jacques-François Desmaisons (*c.* 1720-89), both architects, who encouraged the young man to develop his artistic talents. David received his first training, from 1766 to 1774, in the studio of the painter Joseph-Marie Vien (1716-1809), who taught at the Académie Royale. In 1774 he won the Prix de Rome, which allowed him to go to Italy for five years, until 1780. Here he had the opportunity to study classical art, and on his return to Paris he devoted himself entirely to the painting of historical and mythological subjects. He became an associate member of the academy in 1781, thanks to *Belisarius Asking Alms*, a picture that aroused great admiration, and a full member two years later with *Andromache Mourning Hector*. Around 1784 he painted one of his masterpieces, the *Oath of the Horatii*, to a commission from Louis XVI. In 1789 David lent his enthusiastic support to the Revolution, and in 1791 was elected to the National Convention, later becoming a member of the Committee of Public Safety. His involvement in politics was intense, and the artist backed Robespierre and voted for the execution of the king. After the *coup d'état* of 9 Thermidor 1794 (July 27), in which Robespierre was overthrown, David withdrew from public life and began to concentrate on painting again: *The Intervention of the Sabine Women* dates from the second half of the nineties. In 1797 he met Napoleon, for whom he was to paint numerous works over the following years, including the large canvas representing the *Coronation of the Emperor*. In December 1803 he was made a Chevalier of the Légion d'Honneur. With the Restoration the painter was forced into exile, and spent the last ten years of his life in Brussels, devoting himself principally to mythological subjects and portraits. He died in Brussels on December 29, 1825. David is considered one of the initiators of neoclassicism, and there can be no doubt that works like the *Oath of*

the Horatii or *The Sabines* had an enormous impact and determined a shift in the artistic taste of the period. Starting out from the French classical tradition, stretching back to Poussin, David, in an attempt to recover the original qualities of Greek and Roman art, created a new pictorial language focused on clarity of gesture and cleanness and sharpness of form, in opposition to the rococo's emphasis on decoration. Numerous painters were his pupils, including Gros, Gérard and Ingres, but his cultural influence went beyond his teaching activities: David was one of the earliest intellectual artists in the modern sense, if not the first, playing a direct part in the political events of his day, and his engagement in civil life was clearly reflected in his creative activity.

The Oath of the Horatii
oil on canvas, 330x425 cm
Louvre, Paris

The picture was painted between 1784 and 1785 and represents the three Horatii brothers swearing to defend their country in the celebrated duel with the Curiatii. The solemn pledge is made before their father, who is holding in one hand the three swords that the brothers will use in the fight; on the right we see a group of weeping women. The choice of a subject linked to republican Rome is indicative of the cultural climate of those years, on the eve of the French Revolution. Even more significant, as Jean Starobinski pointed out in a famous essay, is the theme of the swearing of an oath, the act by which several different wills freely commit themselves to a higher goal: in revolutionary ideology, which is already lurking in this work, it is a fundamental act of civil engagement. A celebrated picture by the great Swiss artist Füssli, painted just a few years earlier, represents the *Oath of the Confederates* and reflects the same cultural and political mood. David has created a composition in which the greatest emphasis is given to the meaning of the gestures, a work that we could define as eloquent, based on a rhetoric of the image that spurns any embellishment and pomposity in favor of a clear and straightforward language. The center of the composition is the father's hand grasping the weapons, toward which the brothers' extend their arms as they make their vow. Note the highly effective device of the correspondence between the hands of the Horatii, two of them close together and one set slightly apart, and the tips of the swords, underlining the identification of the young men with the commitment to fight which binds them. The entire painting is skillfully constructed with geometrical rigor around a pattern of diagonals and triangles (the legs of the brothers and their father, the pike on the left, the arms and the swords, the bodies of the women) that contrasts with the imposing rhythm of the colonnade in the background, intensifying the sense of action. For these formal characteristics and for the effort made to be faithful, in the costumes and architecture, to classical models, deliberately chosen from those of the republican era, the painting can be regarded as one of the works that marked the advent of neoclassicism in France and Europe.

Marat Assassinated
oil on canvas, 165x128.3 cm
Musées Royaux des Beaux-Arts, Brussels

Painted shortly after the murder of Marat, the picture bears the dedication (*À MARAT*), the signature (DAVID) and the date (*L'AN DEUX*, or 1793) engraved on the wooden box that serves as a makeshift desk, in the foreground. Marat, one of the fathers of the Revolution, was stabbed by Charlotte Corday on July 13: he was taking a bath, something he did frequently because of a skin disease, and the assassin had succeeded in getting herself admitted on the pretext of handing him a petition. In David's picture Marat is still holding the petition given to him by Corday, and the text is clearly legible: "July 13, 1793. To the citizen Marat. My great unhappiness gives me a right to your kindness." On the box, alongside the inkwell and quill, is set his response "you will give this assignat to your mother [...]," a mark of the humanity of the Jacobin politician. Note the disparity between Corday's use of the pre-Revolutionary dating system and the "*an deux*" (year two) inscribed by David in classical lettering: the murderer's mendacity is contrasted by the painter's votive dedication, celebrating Marat in a heroic image that would forever be associated with the new, republican era. It is the ideological core of the work, expressed by David not just through the texts, even though these perform a function of unusual importance, but above all through the composition and the language of painting. The character of the picture and its aesthetic and cultural implications were clearly grasped by Baudelaire, who wrote: "The drama is here, vivid in its pitiful horror. This painting is David's masterpiece and one of the great curiosities of modern art because, by a strange feat, it has nothing trivial or vile. What is most surprising in this very unusual visual poem is that it was painted very quickly. When one thinks of the beauty of the lines, this quickness is bewildering. [...] Now Marat can challenge Apollo. He has been kissed by the loving lips of Death and he rests in the peace of his metamorphosis. This work contains something both poignant and tender; a soul is flying in the cold air of this room, on these cold walls, around this cold funerary tub." In this case David's classicism is based not on ancient Greek or Roman sources, but Renaissance ones: Marat's lifeless arm is taken from Michelangelo's *Pietà* in St. Peter's. The citation of a prestigious model is united with an unprecedented identification of Marat, martyr of the Revolution, with Christ, further reinforcing the ideal and moral message of the painting.

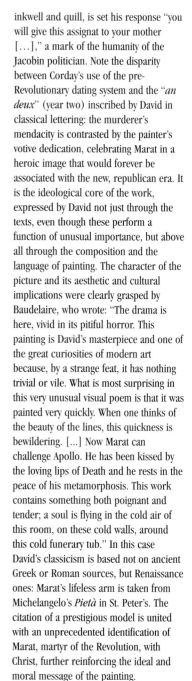

Du 13. Juillet, 1793.
Marie anne Charlotte
Corday au citoyen
Marat.
il suffit que je sois
bien Malheureuse
pour avoir Droit
a votre bienveillance.

À MARAT,

DAVID.

Napoleon's Coronation as Emperor of the French
oil on canvas, 621x979 cm
Louvre, Paris

Napoleon was crowned emperor of the French in Notre-Dame on December 2, 1804. The ritual had been carefully prepared on the instructions of Bonaparte himself: the grand master of ceremonies

Louis-Philippe de Ségur and the lord chamberlain de Rémusat were entrusted with the organization and ceremonial, the architects Percier and Fontaine with the temporary decorations and Jean-Baptiste Isabey with the design of the clothing worn by the participants. David was given the task of recording the event for posterity. The solemn ritual got under way with the arrival of twelve processions of

delegates from all the cities of France, the army, the legislative assemblies and the magistracy. Then the pontifical procession arrived at the cathedral from the Tuileries, and finally Napoleon with his family. The coronation proper took place in three phases: first Pius VII blessed the scepter and crowns and replaced them on the altar, then Napoleon took the crown and set it on his own head, and lastly he crowned his wife Josephine empress. This is the moment represented by David, the concluding act of the ceremony. The figure of the pope, whose presence was desired by Napoleon to lend an aura of legitimacy to the reestablishment of a monarchy, is kept to one side, as was required by the ceremonial. At the center is Napoleon, already crowned with the laurel wreath and invested, by his own hand, as emperor of the French: the crowning of his wife becomes the first act

of imperial sovereignty. The work also has the function of celebrating the new ruling class, and the large canvas contains a huge series of portraits: a multiplicity that contrasts with the characteristics of David's works of just a few years earlier, which were always constructed around a few focal elements presented with emphasis and clarity. The only precedent lay in the *Oath of the Tennis Court*, a celebratory work that performed, in a republican context, a function similar to that of the large canvas painted for the emperor Napoleon. (S.G.C.)

Friedrich

Caspar David Friedrich was born at Greifswald, Pomerania, in 1774 and first studied under the architect Johann Friedrich Quistorp. In 1794 he enrolled in the academy at Copenhagen, and in 1798 moved to Dresden, where he spent the rest of his life. Here he came into contact with people like Goethe, Schlegel, Schelling and Novalis and frequented the writers of the Phöbus group: Heinrich von Kleist, Theodor Körner and Amadeus G. Müllner. In 1808 he painted *The Cross on the Mountain* (Gemäldegalerie, Dresden). His art was strongly influenced by the aesthetics of Schelling (and in particular his *Discourse on the Figurative Arts and on Nature*, published in 1807) and the ideas of Schleiermacher, who saw the contemplation of nature as a means of spiritual elevation (Friedrich himself declared: "the only true wellspring of art is our heart"). The works of Philipp Otto Runge (*The Color-Sphere*, 1810) and Goethe (*Theory of Colors*, 1810) were also of great importance to the painter. In the same year Johanna Schopenhauer wrote in the *Journal des Luxus und der Moden*: "And now, my friend, I would like to take you to the landscapist Friedrich. You are well aware how many different views there are about his works, as a new phenomenon in the field of art. I am ready to admit the need to determine rules, sacred for the artist as well as for the judge of matters of art, as without them everything would subside once more into a messy and aimless progress by trial and error. They are necessary, like every straight road toward the goal. But if an individual, prompted by his genius, abandons this road and heads off down a new path, however dangerous, I believe that one can watch him go about his enterprise, without wishing to hinder him by throwing stones, and wait to see if he does not eventually reach his goal. [...] Friedrich's works differ markedly from those of other landscape painters above all in the choice of subjects. In the majority of his paintings the air, which he is able to handle in a truly masterful manner, takes up more than half the space and often the middle distances and backgrounds are wholly absent, for he chooses subjects in which it is not necessary to represent them. He delights in painting boundless expanses. Faithful to reality down to the smallest detail, he has also arrived at a very high degree of perfection as far as his artistic technique is concerned, in his oil paintings as well as in his sepia drawings. His landscapes have a melancholic and mysterious religiosity. They speak to the spirit rather than to the eye."

From the second decade of the 19th century onward the artist enjoyed a good reputation, and Frederick William III of Prussia himself bought two of his paintings at the Academic Exhibition in Berlin. In 1817 he became a member of the Dresden Academy, and in 1818 married Caroline Bommer. In those years he got to know the Norwegian painter Johan Christian Clausen Dahl, with whom he went to live in 1820, and the German philosopher Karl Gustav Carus, the author of *Nine Letters on Landscape Painting*, who was his pupil. They formed the nucleus of what would come to be known as the "Dresden School." In 1824 Friedrich fell ill, and the persecution complex from which he suffered led to his progressive isolation and the almost complete interruption of his artistic activity up until 1827. Paralyzed in 1835 by a brain hemorrhage, Caspar David Friedrich died at Dresden in 1840.

The Cross in the Mountains
(*Tetschen Altarpiece*)
oil on canvas, 115x110.5 cm
Gemäldegalerie, Dresden

The canvas, commissioned in 1807 by Count Franz Anton von Thun und Hohenstein for the private chapel of the castle of Tetschen in northern Bohemia, was finished in December 1808. The idea of using landscape for an altarpiece stirred fierce controversy, set off by the critic Friedrich Wilhelm Basilius von Ramdhor, who considered it bizarre. The choice of landscape as a religious allegory can probably be traced back to the poet and theologian Gotthard Ludwig Theobul Kosegarten, who had commissioned a sacred work from Friedrich in 1806, and was in keeping with a Romantic sensibility of which Friedrich was the principal exponent in painting and that was increasingly popular with the younger generations. The painter himself

responded to von Ramdhor's criticisms, giving his own interpretation of the *Tetschen Altarpiece* in a letter to the Dresden-based writer Friedrich August Schulz published in the *Journal des Luxus und der Moden*: "Jesus Christ, nailed to the tree, is turned here towards the sinking sun, the image of the eternal life-giving father. With Jesus's teaching an old world dies – that time when God the Father moved directly on the earth. This sun sank and the earth was not able to grasp the departing light any longer. There shines forth in the gold of the evening light the purest, noblest metal of the Savior's figure on the cross, which thus reflects on earth in a softened glow. The cross stands erected on a rock, unshakably firm like our faith in Jesus Christ. The firs stand around the cross, evergreen, enduring through all ages, like the hopes of man in Him, the crucified." The frame, which is an integral part of the work, was carved to Friedrich's own design by the sculptor Karl Gottlob Kühn.

The Sea of Ice (Arctic Shipwreck)
oil on canvas, 96.7x126.9 cm
Kunsthalle, Hamburg

The idea for the painting came from the polar expeditions of the ships *Hecla* and *Griper*, in 1819-20 and 1824, which received extensive coverage in the press of the time and inspired the work of several landscapists. The slabs of ice breaking and sliding one over the other had been studied by the artist in a series of oils painted in the winter of 1820-21 while observing the frozen river Elba. In Friedrich's work the representation of nature always has a religious significance. His statement "the divine is everywhere, even in a grain of sand; once I depicted it in a canebrake" is famous: a sort of

Romantic pantheism that found its most fitting expression in the genre of the "sublime" landscape, with the representation of endless spaces, of the sometimes terrible power of nature, capable of crushing human beings. The elements of the landscape take on a precise significance, in a sort of symbolic code that can be deduced from the artist's own writings and figurative works: thus the ice represents eternity and the wrecked ship, the mortality of human life.

The Tree of Crows
canvas, 59x74 cm
Louvre, Paris

In the distance, on the left, we see Arkona, the site of an ancient temple on the island of Rügen; on the back of the picture is written *Hünengrab* ("Hun tomb"), indicating that the mound must once have been a grave. The bare oak tree, associated with the grave, alludes to the finality of death in the pagan world. The theme of the tomb is a very common one in Friedrich's work: in 1803 he had written the lines: "Why, I've often asked

myself, / do you so often choose as subject of your painting / death, transience and the tomb? Because to live in eternity / often means surrendering to death." Here too, as in the majority of Friedrich's pictures, the landscape takes on a religious connotation. The painting, which from the stylistic viewpoint centers on the silhouette of the complicated tangle of branches against the twilit sky, constitutes an effective application of the Goethean theory of colors: the cold tones on the very low horizon behind the mound create the impression of an almost infinite depth (a feature of Friedrich's painting that made a great impact on his contemporaries, and in particular on Goethe himself), while the reddening of the clouds, which seem to be moving toward us, makes the funereal outlines of the tree and the flight of crows stand out. (S.G.C.)

Turner

"Before him, there was no London fog," the Irish writer Oscar Wilde would say of Turner: in his landscapes, in fact, it is not so much the elements of nature that stand out as the atmosphere through which we see them. As his great admirer Ruskin would write: "He saw also that the finish and specific grandeur of nature had been given, but her fulness, space and mistery never [...]. For the conventional color he substituted a pure straightforward rendering of fact, as far as was in his power; and that not of such fact as had been before even suggested, but of all that is *most* brilliant, beautiful, and inimitable; he went to the cataract for its iris, to the conflagration for its flames, asked of the sea its intensest azure, of the sky its clearest gold."

Joseph Mallord William Turner was born in London in 1775 and enrolled at a very early age in the Royal Academy schools in London. He began his career by working mainly as a topographical watercolorist, an activity that led him to travel extensively in England and Wales, and in the rest of Europe. In fact journeys were to be a constant feature of his life, made for reasons of work but above all to find new places from which to draw inspiration. In 1779 he became an associate member of the Royal Academy and in 1802 a full member: this was also the year of his first trip abroad, which took him across France and to Switzerland. On his way back he stopped in Paris to visit the Louvre. In the meantime he pursued his career within the Academy and was appointed professor of perspective in 1807. That year saw the publication of the first volume of his *Liber Studiorum*, a collection of engravings taken from his principal landscapes and divided into distinct categories: historical, architectural, mountainous, pastoral, and marine, with architectural elements. He made journeys to Belgium and the Netherlands and along the Rhine, and went to Italy for the first time in 1819. He returned to France to visit Normandy, the Loire Valley and Brittany, and in 1828 was in Italy again, going to Florence and Rome. Then he made more journeys to France, the German cities and Italy, went back to Belgium and, in 1840, Italy, spending time in Venice. In 1844 he paid his last visit to Switzerland, whose landscape exercised a particularly powerful attraction on 19th-century artists. Before the 18th century, the country was generally regarded as an inaccessible and inhospitable place that had to be traversed in order to reach Italy: the journey was dangerous, the mountains difficult to cross, the nature wild. With the advance of the Industrial Revolution, Switzerland acquired a new image, that of an unspoiled and natural land in which the lost origins of humanity could be found. His last trip abroad was to France, in 1845. Returning to England, he died in London in 1851.

Turner made his love for the painting of landscape and for the landscapists who had preceded him or were his contemporaries the center of his life. In the first draft of his will, drawn up in 1829, he left the National Gallery two of his paintings on condition they be hung alongside two companion pieces by Claude Lorrain, an artist who provided him with an inexhaustible source of motifs and reflections on color. He also left money to fund a chair of landscape painting at the Royal Academy, a Turner gold medal to be awarded to a landscapist and the foundation of a charity for "decayed artists." Over the following years he added codicils to prevent his works from being separated, and in 1846, asked to be buried in Saint Paul's Cathedral among "his brothers in art."

Snowstorm: Hannibal and His Army Crossing the Alps
oil on canvas,145x236.5 cm
Tate Gallery, London

Turner had crossed the Alps for the first time in 1802. Two years earlier, Napoleon had invaded Italy with his troops through the St. Bernard Pass, evoking Hannibal's exploit of 218 BC: Rome's war with Carthage was compared with Great Britain's war against France. With this picture Turner introduced the landscape into history painting: the vortex of the storm sweeps over the men, tiny figures at the mercy of the elements. The sources for this painting of 1812 were two books present in the painter's library, the English

translation of the Latin writer Livy's histories of Rome and Oliver Goldsmith's *Roman History*, while a lost painting by Cozens and a pair of ceramic medallions representing a similar subject may have provided him with further ideas. In 1810, moreover, the artist had witnessed a spectacular storm while staying at the Yorkshire home of his friend Walter Fawkes, a reformist parliamentarian and amateur historian who had probably pointed out the connection between the historical event and the weather. In the catalogue of the Royal Academy in 1812, the work was accompanied by verses written by Turner himself, taken from his collection of poems entitled *The Fallacies of Hope*, in the conviction that

painting and poetry were closely related. The landscape disintegrates into the blurred vision of a blind struggle: to make observers feel as if they were caught up in the storm, Turner would have the picture hung at a lower height than was usual for a canvas of such size. It is a vision that inspires fear, the aesthetic experience of the sublime in contrast to the soothing harmony of the beautiful, the "delectable horror" stirred by tempests, vast spaces, silence, the power of natural phenomena and the infinite, a sense of dismay that does not threaten observers, but allows them to feel, according to the theories of the time, the strongest emotion that the mind is capable of experiencing.

Rain, Steam and Speed – the Great Western Railway
oil on canvas, 91x122 cm
National Gallery, London

Watching trains go by was a common pastime for grownups in the early Victorian age. The year in which the painting was executed and shown at the Royal Academy, 1844, the Great Western Railway was extending the line from Bristol to Exeter and this may have stimulated Turner's imagination. The railroad was transforming the landscape and its perception: glorified as an inevitable mark of progress, it was also fiercely opposed by those who feared the effects of industrialization and the speed

of trains on the rhythms of life. Ruskin, for once in disagreement with Turner, argued that beauty required peace and quiet, inconceivable in a station: "There was always more in the world than men could see, walked they ever so slowly: they will see it no better for going fast." A train is steaming over the bridge at Maidenhead, the only point at which the London-Bristol line crossed the Thames. The bridge was an act of technological daring on the part of I.K. Brunel, with flat brick spans that it was feared would not withstand the weight of the first train. The directors of the Great Western Railway ordered Brunel not to remove the timbering used during its construction. The engineer agreed, but then secretly

WILLIAM TURNER

Landscape with River and Bay
oil on canvas, 94x123 cm
Louvre, Paris

"Pictures of nothing and very like," was how a contemporary critic described Turner's paintings. In fact vagueness was one of the charges laid against the painter, in addition to the opposite one of assigning too much importance to the content, by inserting pointless historical references into the representation of nature. The artist's last works are characterized by a dissolution of form, in which the confines between land, air and water are broken down. Nature is immersed in a dazzling and undefined glare, a pure realm of color, and the fluidity of the watercolor is transferred to the oil painting. In *À la recherche du temps perdu*, Marcel Proust, taking his inspiration from Turner, describes a painter who "had been able to accustom his eyes not to recognize fixed boundaries, of absolute demarcation, between the land and the ocean." In the aesthetics of the infinite, even indeterminacy is a source of the sublime. This canvas painted around 1835-40 is connected with the engravings of the *Liber Studiorum* from many years earlier and was probably intended to represent the artist's late style in his bequest to the nation. It is not known exactly how it left the painter's studio, but it is presumed that it was among the unframed or rolled up canvases that were stolen after his death.
It was to defend the artist from the accusations of the critics that Ruskin had undertaken his colossal work on *Modern Painters*. "For the limited space and defined forms of elder landscape, he substituted the quantity and the mistery of the vastest scenes of earth." Turner had rescued landscape painting from the realm of the minor genres. (E.F.)

reduced the supporting structure slightly: the arches looked as if they were underpinned, but in reality were suspended in the void. On the left a small boat with fishermen, on the right cultivated fields and a man plowing, perhaps in reference to the play on words provided by the name of a traditional folkdance, *Speed the Plow*. Rain, the steam of the locomotive and speed, three elements that render the vision indistinct and blurred. The Impressionists could not fail to be struck by the painter's interest in natural phenomena and the representation of light: Pissarro wrote to his son in London suggesting he go to see the picture, while Monet recognized that Turner had known how to paint "with his eyes open."
The train is coming toward the observer and, as in the first experiments with cinematography, seems about to burst out of the canvas and into the room. But it is not the speed of the train that we notice. In front of Turner's locomotive streaks a tiny hare: we do not know whether it is driven by fear or by a sense of mockery.

Ingres

S on of the painter and sculptor Jean-Marie-Joseph Ingres, Jean-Auguste-Dominique Ingres was born in Montauban, in the Tarn-et-Garonne region of France, on August 29, 1780. His early artistic training took place at the Toulouse Academy, where he distinguished himself for his drawing from antiquity, winning several prizes. In the 1790s he also frequented the studio of the landscape painter Briant. In 1797 he moved to Paris and entered David's studio, where he came into contact with the Penseurs or Primitifs, who championed a classical art harking back to the Greece of Phidias, and the Muscardins, fascinated by the French art of the Middle Ages: without adhering to either current, he came under the influence of both. Quickly attracting the attention of the Parisian *haute bourgeoisie* by his talent, in 1803 he received the commission for a portrait of *Bonaparte as First Consul*. The following year he showed *Napoleon Enthroned* at the Salon, although David himself was unhappy with the work. He then left for Rome, stopping over in Florence: the time he spent in Italy proved fundamental to Ingres's artistic development, giving him the opportunity to make a thorough study of the masterpieces of the Italian Renaissance, from Masaccio to Raphael. His annual *envois* to the Académie (*The Valpinçon Bather* and the *Oedipus*) were highly criticized. In Rome he worked for the French officials present in the city, and in Naples for the king Joachim Murat. The fall of the empire obliged Ingres to return to Paris, but he went back to Italy in 1820, following the flop of the *Grande Odalisque* at the Salon. It was only in 1824, back in Paris again, that he achieved the official recognition he had long sought with *The Vow of Louis XIII*, and the following year Charles X awarded him the Légion d'Honneur. From 1834 to 1841 he was director of the Académie de France in Rome. Now a lodestar for French painting, he fought in 1848, as a member of the commission for the Fine Arts, for the admission of artists to the Salon independently of the judgment of the jury. Baudelaire wrote that Ingres "followed the slightest undulations of the lines, like a thrall of love," and the painter himself declared that "drawing is the probity of art." In this sense Ingres, in many ways an eclectic where the themes he tackled and stylistic choices he made were concerned, contrasted markedly with the artists of the next generation, such as Géricault or Delacroix, for whom he had no liking. Ingres died in Paris in 1867, and in the same year an exhibition with over five hundred of the artist's works was staged at the École des Beaux-Arts.

Portrait of Mademoiselle Rivière
oil on canvas, 100x70 cm
Louvre, Paris

Commissioned in 1804 along with portraits of her father Philibert Rivière, a functionary of the empire, and her mother Marie-Françoise Beauregard, the picture shows us the young Caroline at the age of just fifteen, destined to die only a few months after the completion of the work, in 1805. Shown with the other two portraits of the family at the 1806 Salon, it got a negative reception. Ingres had first established his reputation as a portrait painter and in this work, although inevitably measuring himself against the example of his master David, he already displayed the originality of his artistic research. The representation of the dress, gloves and fur is of an almost virtuoso naturalism, but the face of the subject reflects a desire for simplification and formal balance that led Ingres's contemporaries to accuse him of "Gothicism." In reality the painter, on the eve of his Italian journey, was already holding a dialogue with Renaissance painting, and the landscape that extends behind the girl is an intelligent and original reworking of the scheme of the 15th-century portrait.

JEAN-AUGUSTE-DOMINIQUE INGRES

JEAN-AUGUSTE-DOMINIQUE INGRES

La Grande Odalisque
oil on canvas, 91x162 cm
Louvre, Paris

The painting, commissioned in 1813 by
Caroline Murat, queen of Naples, as a
companion piece to the so-called
Dormeuse de Naples (a work now lost
and known to us only through copies),
was never delivered owing to the fall of
Napoleon's empire. The choice of the
subject responded to the taste for the
exotic and Oriental that was all the rage in
those years, but at the same time the work
reflects the artistic interests of Ingres,
representing a modern version of the
Renaissance theme of the reclining Venus.
Shown at the Salon of 1819, it was
criticized for a presumed weakness of the
anatomical drawing (the back looked too
long and the right elbow was not clearly
delineated): in reality the flaws pointed
out by the critics of the day were
introduced deliberately by the artist, to
increase the fluidity of the scheme of
composition. The laying on of the paint in
large areas of color, typical of Ingres's
painting in those years, lends an Oriental
character to the work (already noted at
the time of its first showing by more
perceptive connoisseurs, such as Amoury-
Duval), and almost seems to anticipate
the European discovery of Japanese
painting by half a century. Critics have
underlined the derivation from David's
famous *Madame Récamier*, a work on
which Ingres himself had collaborated in
his youth: here, however, in the elongated
and elegant proportions of the figures, we
can discern the profound influence of his
study of the Tuscan Mannerists. It has also
been pointed out that the headgear of the
Odalisque is a reference to Raphael's *La
Fornarina*, one of Ingres's favorite works.

The Turkish Bath
canvas transferred onto panel,
diam. 108 cm
Louvre, Paris

The Turkish Bath, a canvas transferred
onto panel, is a work from Ingres's old
age, a fact that, when dating it in 1862, he
proudly underlined by adding "*aetatis
LXXXII*" ("aged eighty-two"). It was
painted for Prince Napoleon in 1859, but
rejected by his wife on the grounds that it

contained too many nudes. Ingres then
changed the rectangular format of the
work into a tondo, and seems to have
gone on working on it up until 1863.
Comparison with a photograph taken in
1858 reveals the alterations made by the
painter, who added the woman on the
edge of the pool, on the left, and
eliminated a figure in the foreground on
the right; the choice of the round format
allowed the artist to achieve a balance of
composition that was absent in the initial
version.
In this work Ingres seems almost to be
taking stock of many years of meditations
on his beloved theme of the female nude,
once again presented in an exotic setting.
The figure at the center, for example, is an
almost exact reproduction of the
celebrated *Valpinçon Bather* (1808, see
picture on the left), and the woman on
the right, lying back with her arms raised
above her head, echoes a portrait of the
artist's first wife, Madeleine Chapelle,
painted in 1814. (S.G.C.)

Géricault

Jean-Louis-Théodore Géricault was born in Rouen on September 26, 1791. In 1796 the family moved to Paris, where Théodore commenced his studies. He got his early training from Carle Vernet, a painter of genre scenes and sporting subjects, especially horses, and then under Pierre Guérin, a classicist strongly influenced by David. Very soon, however, Géricault abandoned his academic education and continued, between 1811 and 1815, his studies independently, copying the great masterpieces of Rubens, van Dyck, Caravaggio and Salvator Rosa in the recently established Musée Napoléon. At the age of only twenty-one, and essentially self-taught, he presented *The Charging Chasseur* (now in the Louvre) at the Salon of 1812. This attracted the attention of the critics by the originality of its composition and the quality of its execution, which showed the influence the example of Rubens had exercised on the young artist. At the 1814 Salon he showed the *Wounded Cuirassier Leaving the Battlefield*, a work that did not get as favorable a reception as *The Charging Chasseur* but demonstrated the progress the painter had made in his effort to render his figures monumental. Joining the Musketeers, he played a part in Louis XVIII's flight to Belgium. His short and wholly negative experience of military service led him to abandon the martial subjects that had so fascinated him previously. Indeed for some time he attempted to change his style, embracing the manner and above all the themes of neoclassical painting, which he had learned years before in Guérin's studio. In 1816 he went to Rome, stopping on the way to visit Florence, where he was impressed by the art of Michelangelo. In 1817 he started to paint contemporary subjects again, with the execution of the *Race of the Barbary Horses* in Rome; in the fall of the same year he returned to Paris. He now sought out themes based on events of his own time, but with the force and exemplarity of classical subjects: the *Raft of the "Medusa,"* which attracted a great deal of criticism on its presentation at the Salon of 1819, represents the highest expression of this phase of his art. Between 1820 and 1821 Géricault was in England, convalescing after a nervous breakdown linked to the controversy over the *Raft*. His health failing, he gave up working on a large scale on his return to Paris and painted for Dr. Georget the series of ten portraits of the insane, which can be considered the masterpiece of his later period. Géricault died in Paris on January 26, 1824.

The Raft of the "Medusa"
oil on canvas, 491x716 cm
Louvre, Paris

The work was shown at the Salon of 1819 with the title *Scene of Shipwreck*. It was not necessary, for the public of the time, to specify the shipwreck to which it referred. The tragedy of the frigate *La Méduse* had shaken France and caused a serious scandal for the government, dominating political debate for some time: the ship, which was carrying the governor of Senegal and numerous officials of that

colony, some five hundred people in all, had foundered on the shoal of Arguin on July 5, 1816. After five days of vain attempts to free her, a raft had been built and launched with a hundred and forty-nine people aboard. The lifeboats that were supposed to tow the raft soon cut

the cables, and for two weeks the castaways were left to drift in the ocean, while hunger, thirst and desperation set one against the other. When the raft was finally rescued there were only fifteen survivors, all of them at death's door. The government had sought in vain to hush up

the whole story, for which the French navy bore grave responsibilities. Struck by the tragedy like many of his fellow countrymen, Géricault decided to devote a large picture to the subject, in which he saw, quite apart from its political implications (although these were not

irrelevant), an exceptional opportunity for a study of anatomy and psychology. While working on the picture the painter paid regular visits to the hospital of Beaujou to observe and draw the dying, and arranged with doctors and nurses to be supplied with anatomical parts and cadavers to paint (some of these studies, reutilized in the final work, have survived). At first Géricault had considered representing the mutiny of the sailors against their officers, and then the moment of the raft's rescue or a scene of cannibalism. Eventually the choice fell on an episode of greater dramatic force: the sighting of a vessel to which the castaways tried in vain to signal their presence. The reaction to the *Raft of the "Medusa"* at the Salon of 1819 was generally negative, for political reasons (the painter himself complained: "I have been accused of having defamed the entire Ministry of the Navy with the expression of one head") as well as stylistic ones. In a climate where neoclassicism held sway the painting was bound to cause perplexity for the daring nature of its composition (Landon, the critic of the *Annales du Musée*, wondered: "Where is the center?"). But it was above all the way the paint was handled, the bold use of chiaroscuro, which made the picture look almost as if it were stained, that did not meet with the approval of the critics. And Géricault himself, even though he had sought such luministic effects through such technical means as the extensive use of bitumen, asked the painter Lehoux, who had made a copy of the work: "Is my picture really so splattered with black and white?" But he then went on to say: "If I were to paint the picture over again I would change none of this."

Woman with Gambling Mania
oil on canvas, 77x64.5 cm
Louvre, Paris

The painting is one of a series of ten portraits of the insane that were probably painted between 1820 and 1824. Géricault had gone to Dr. Étienne-Jean Georget to cure the depression into which he had fallen following the controversy over the *Raft of the "Medusa,"* and offered the ten studies to the physician, perhaps for use as teaching material in his lectures on pathology, as a mark of his gratitude. Each of the pictures portrays a person suffering from a particular mental problem (it is likely that they were patients at the Salpêtrière Hospital, where

Georget practiced). The work reproduced here, the most famous of the series, depicts an elderly woman with a mania for gambling. Critics have pointed out similarities with a painting by the Scottish artist David Wilkie, *Chelsea Pensioners Reading the Gazette of the Battle of Waterloo* (which we know to have been admired by Géricault during his stay in England), especially in the representation of the alienated expression. In fact the realism of this painting, devoid of any hint of rhetoric or pathos, does reflect the influence of contemporary British art. On the other hand the work constitutes, in its almost clinical detachment from the subject portrayed, one of the earliest examples of the study of the physiognomy

of the insane or, in particular, of criminals, a branch of medical science that was to arouse great interest over the course of the 19th century. From a technical point of view the ten studies, carried out in the same spirit in which he had reproduced parts of the anatomy in the preparatory studies for the *Raft of the "Medusa"* some years earlier, represent one of Géricault's finest achievements. (S.G.C.)

Delacroix

Ferdinand-Victor-Eugène Delacroix was born on April 26, 1798, at Charenton-Saint-Maurice. His father had been foreign minister at the time of the Directory, and then became a prefect of the empire, under Napoleon, in Marseilles and Bordeaux. Rumor has it, however, that his real father was the famous statesman Talleyrand, who in fact gave his patronage to the artist in the early part of his career. After an initial training under the neoclassical painter Pierre Guérin, a follower of David, Delacroix came into contact with Géricault, posing for the *Raft of the "Medusa"* in 1817. The young painter, who started to work independently in 1818, seems to have been influenced by the examples of Michelangelo and Rubens, and in those same years threw himself into a passionate study of Dante and Petrarch. He took part in the Salon d'Automne for the first time in 1822 with the picture *The Barque of Dante* (Louvre, Paris), fruit of his literary leanings and in a typically Romantic mold. Two years later he painted the canvas *The Massacre at Chios* (Louvre, Paris), illustrating an episode of the Greek war of liberation from the Turks. Out of personal preference, and following the example of Géricault, whom he greatly admired and who died that same year, Delacroix turned his attention to events of contemporary history. Stylistically the work was programmatically opposed to the classicism of Ingres and the disciples of David. In the twenties Delacroix got to know Victor Hugo (collaborating with him on several stage productions) and in 1825 made a journey to England. While there he encountered the work of Constable, which was to exercise a profound influence on him. In 1827 he showed eleven canvases at the Salon, including the *Death of Sardanapalus*. In 1830 he finished his best-known work, *Liberty Leading the People*, and in the same period commenced his activity as an essayist and art critic.

In 1831 he was awarded the Légion d'Honneur and was invited to accompany the delegation of the French government to the sultan of Morocco. The African experience of 1832 influenced his work, particularly in his choice of exotic subjects, which were to encounter considerable success. Over the following years, thanks to shrewd exploitation of his social contacts, he obtained numerous official commissions from the government, especially during the reign of Louis-Philippe. The presence of as many as forty-two of his paintings at the Universal Exposition of 1855 was a sort of official consecration for Delacroix, whose genius was extolled by Baudelaire. In an article for *Le Pays* that year he wrote: "How will posterity view Delacroix? [...] They will say that he was a unique concord of the most astonishing qualities; that he had, like Rembrandt, a sense of intimacy and of inner magic, a spirit of combination and decoration like Rubens and Le Brun and the color of Veronese." Eugène Delacroix died in Paris on August 13, 1863.

Henry de Fantin-Latour
Homage to Delacroix
Musée d'Orsay, Paris

EUGÈNE DELACROIX

Death of Sardanapalus
oil on canvas, 395x495 cm
Louvre, Paris

The work, shown at the Salon of 1827, was described in the exhibition catalogue as follows: "The rebels are besieging the palace. Lying on a splendid bed, at the top of a huge pyre, Sardanapalus orders the eunuchs and functionaries of the palace to cut the throats of his women, his pages, even his horses and favorite dog: nothing that had served his pleasure was to survive him." The theme is not taken, as has sometimes been claimed, from Lord Byron's *Sardanapalus*, written in 1821, although the English poet's work may have exercised some influence, if only on the popularity of the subject. The canvas was greeted with almost unanimous rejection: the critics pointed out oversights and errors, but above all a sense of confusion. The work is deliberately anti-classical, based entirely on a swirl of colors, in a manner based on the study of Rembrandt (a source that was looked down on by his contemporaries), on the Romantic emphasis of the gestures and on an intentionally asymmetrical and overblown composition.

July 28th: Liberty Leading the People (*Liberty on the Barricades*)
oil on canvas, 260x325 cm
Louvre, Paris

The picture was painted in 1830, just after the insurrection against the Bourbon monarchy in which Delacroix had taken part, although very much in the background, as a member of the National Guard. The painter portrays himself in the figure with the rifle and the stovepipe hat on Liberty's right.
It is his best-known painting, destined for lasting fame. The work, openly political, combines a realism derived from the lesson of Géricault with a symbolic representation, in the personification of Liberty holding the French tricolor. The attempt to create a modern political symbolism, set in the reality of contemporary events, produces an ambivalent result, but one that is certainly innovative with regard to the cultural and aesthetic conventions of the time. Unlike in his earlier works, Delacroix here tries to construct a calmer and more balanced composition and deliberately lowers the tone of his palette, relying on the use of a more marked chiaroscuro, which brings out and gives emphasis to the three figures on which the allegory is centered: Liberty, the figure with the top hat and the urchin brandishing the pistols. The background cloaked in smoke owes

something to his familiarity with the work of Constable. The picture was well received at the Salon, and bought by Louis-Philippe for the sum of 3000 francs to be hung in the Luxembourg Palace. In the end, however, it was considered too inflammatory to be exhibited.

Women of Algiers in Their Apartment
oil on canvas, 395x495 cm
Louvre, Paris

Exotic themes, and in particular those depicting the harems of the Orient, were extremely popular in the French painting of the 19th century. Delacroix had had the opportunity to visit a harem on his journey to Africa in 1832 and had been greatly impressed. He wrote in his diary: "It is beautiful! It is as it was in Homer's time! Woman in the gynaeceum looking after children, weaving wool or embroidering marvelous textiles. This is woman as I understand her!" The work was shown at the 1834 Salon and bought by Louis-Philippe, a great admirer of the painter. The same subject is represented in various works by Delacroix's great adversary, Ingres, but the approach is totally different. Delacroix's interest is focused chiefly on the brilliant colors, rendered with brushstrokes loaded with paint and an insistent chiaroscuro that investigates the movements of the light: look at the figure in the middle, with her body fully illuminated and the head in semidarkness, or the gleam of the objects in the background and behind the half-closed door. The composition is asymmetrical, with the oblique perspective of the rear wall and the door bordered in bright red, and the contrast between the black woman standing on the right and the reclining female figure on the left (traditionally identified as a Parisian woman called Élise Boulanger). Baudelaire wrote of the painting: "This little poem guides us toward the edges shrouded in sadness." The success of the composition lasted right up to the 20th century, and Picasso painted fifteen variations of it. (S.G.C.)

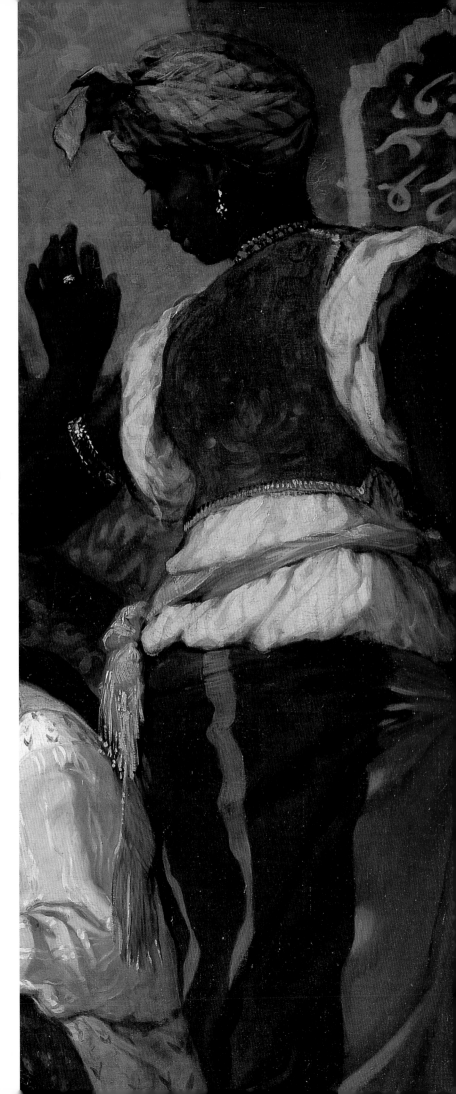

Corot

J ean-Baptiste-Camille Corot was born in Paris on July 16, 1796. He received his training from the landscapist Victor Bertin, from whom he learned the principles of classical composition. Between 1825 and 1828 he made a journey to Italy that was to have a decisive influence on his artistic evolution: in that period, in fact, he started to make the studies of landscape in oil that would characterize his production, and that were among the earliest landscapes painted from life in French art, comparable to those of the Barbizon School. They were works executed by the artist for himself, which broke with the conventions of the classical landscape that had dominated French taste since the time of Poussin and were not intended, at least at the outset, for sale or for major exhibitions in Paris. For years, in fact, Corot led a double life, devoting himself in the winter months to painting large canvases of historical or biblical subjects in an academic style in his studio and spending the summer traveling around Europe, making sketches *en plein air* of the places he visited. In 1834 he was back in Italy, staying for the most part in Tuscany, with visits to the lakes and Venice. His made his last journey to the peninsula in 1843, when he worked for some time in the environs of Rome. Around 1845 Corot's private vein of painting was discovered and appreciated by the critics, and the painter began to sell his landscapes. The style of the paintings of that period, which has been justifiably defined as proto-Impressionist, is characterized by silvery tones and soft brushwork. In 1846 he was awarded the Cross of the Legion of Honor, mark of a growing fame. From the fifties onward, Corot became a point of reference for numerous artists in Paris, toward whom he often displayed great generosity, as when he bought a house in 1873 for the painter Daumier, who had lost his eyesight and was living in poverty. In the last years of his life he also experimented with new techniques in the field of engraving. He died in Paris on February 22, 1875.

*The Ponte d'Augusto at Narni
(The Bridge at Narni)*
oil on paper glued onto canvas, 34x48 cm
Louvre, Paris

The picture represents the Ponte
d'Augusto on the Nera River at Narni, near
Terni, and was painted by Corot during
his visit to Italy in 1826. The artist
presented another version of the same
subject at the Salon of 1827, the first
landscape that he showed in public (now
in the National Gallery of Canada,
Ottawa). A comparison of the two pictures
helps us to understand the contribution
made by the artist to the history of the
landscape. The work intended for
exhibition presents the characteristics of

the classical landscape: a wing of trees is set on the left, the road describes an elegant curve as it approaches the foreground, several figures are present and everything is perfectly finished, although in Corot's typical style of painting. The picture in the Louvre, on the other hand, is a study from life that concedes nothing to classical canons. The brushwork is rapid, with broad strokes, and focuses on the relations of color and light between the constituent elements of the view. The light is the low, slanting rays of the morning, entering from the right of the painting: the time of day appears to have been important for the artist, allowing him to capture the play of shadows that accentuates the reliefs of the landscape. Here Corot, as in his other "Italian" works, practiced a highly personal style, with an extreme simplification of form, that showed the way for the development of French painting over the following decades. Not without reason, *The Ponte d'Augusto at Narni* has been defined as a "pre-Impressionist" picture, and the description seems to apply, even more than to the technique adopted, to the very conception of the landscape painting and its function.

Woman with a Pearl
oil on canvas, 70x55 cm
Louvre, Paris

The portrait, signed "Corot" at bottom right, is considered one of the artist's best figure studies. The model has been identified, although not with certainty, as Berthe Goldschmidt, who may have posed for the painting between 1868 and 1870: according to one of the first owners of the painting, Jean Dollfus, she was the daughter of a dealer in antique fabrics and was sixteen or seventeen at the time. Notwithstanding the picture's traditional title, the object on the girl's forehead is not a pearl, but a leaf that has detached itself from her headdress. Note the perfect formal balance and framing of the portrait, with the face turned slightly with respect to the bust to look toward us, and the folded arms that close the composition: it is evident that here Corot

has chosen to draw on the models of Renaissance portraiture, from Leonardo to Raphael. However, the point of reference closest in time is Ingres; even the handling of the paint appears less simplified and sketchy than in his earlier studies and in many pictures from the same period. It almost seems as if in a work of his maturity Corot wanted to return to the classical manner that he had learned in his youth, following, once again, two different paths in the evolution of his style. (S.G.C.)

Courbet

To satisfy the aspirations of his father, the young Gustave Courbet left Ornans, the town in the Franche-Comté where he was born in 1819, to attend law school in Paris. He soon abandoned his studies, however, and set about teaching himself to paint by analyzing the masterpieces in the Louvre. Around 1840 he enrolled in the Académie Suisse, and went on to frequent the studios of the academic painters Steuben and Hesse. The subjects of the artist's early paintings were the landscape of his birthplace, the Franche-Comté, stories from the Bible like *Lot and His Daughters* (1841, private collection, Paris) and themes taken from literary sources such as *Walpurgis Night* (1841, no longer in existence). In 1844 one of his pictures, a self-portrait (*Courbet with a Black Dog*, 1842, Petit Palais, Paris), was accepted for the first time at the Salon. It was this official exhibition of art – held in Paris every year – that determined the relations between the artist and the authorities and between the artist and the public. At that time the jury responsible for selection enjoyed the highest esteem of the general public, and its judgments affected the price of paintings.

The year 1846 marked a turning point for Courbet, who abandoned the Romantic current to join the emerging Realist movement. He started to get an ever colder reception in academic circles, and from 1847 onward several of his paintings, including the celebrated *Man with a Pipe* (1846, Musée Fabre, Montpellier), were rejected by the Salon. Influenced by socialist ideas, the artist took part in the revolution of 1848. That same year the jury of the Salon was done away with, and Courbet was free to show numerous paintings. In 1850 he exhibited the *Burial at Ornans* at the Salon, and it was this work that established his reputation despite the harsh reaction of the critics. In the same period he met the collector Alfred Bruyas at Montpellier. Bruyas became his friend and patron and the moment of their meeting was to be immortalized in a famous painting, *Bonjour, Monsieur Courbet!* (1854, Musée Fabre, Montpellier).

Louis Napoleon's *coup d'état* in 1851 ushered in the Second Empire and created a political situation unfavorable to Courbet, who was obliged to leave Paris. In 1853 he presented *The Bathers* (Montpellier, Musée Fabre) at the Salon, but the realism of its nudes was considered indecent and upset the emperor. In 1855 the Universal Exhibition was to be held in Paris, and the artist executed *The Artist's Studio* with the intention of showing it on that occasion, but the painting was rejected by the jury. So Courbet decided to put on an independent show at the Pavillon du Réalisme, a temporary structure that the artist himself had erected on the Champs-Élysées, just a short distance from the Palais de l'Industrie, venue of the official exhibition. The painter used the catalogue to expound some of his principles, declaring that his aim was to produce "living art," and the exhibition confirmed his position as leader of the Realist movement. From that moment on Courbet enjoyed considerable success, but this was brought to an end in 1870, the year war broke out and the Commune of Paris was established. After the crushing of the Commune, he was accused of complicity with the insurgents who had demolished the column in the Place Vendôme, tried and condemned to six months in prison. Sued for damages, he was forced to flee to Switzerland in 1873 and died at La Tour-de-Peilz in 1877.

Burial at Ornans
oil on canvas, 315x668 cm
Musée d'Orsay, Paris

The painting was executed in 1849 and shown at the Salon of 1850. The decision to represent ordinary people in a picture of large dimensions prompted much criticism: at the time it was thought that the common people could only be the subject of descriptive paintings of small size, which either oozed a sense of superiority on the part of their authors or were satirical in their intent. The choice of the dimensions and format of the history painting, considered the highest of the genres, to depict the people attending this funeral is in itself sufficient to demonstrate the importance Courbet assigned to them.
In a letter to Jules Champfleury, the writer and art critic who was to draw up the manifesto of the new literary current of Realism in 1857, the painter wrote:

"Among those who have already posed are the mayor, who weighs a hundred kilos, the curate, the commissar, the cross-bearer, the notary, councilor Marlet, my friends, my father, the altar boys, the gravedigger, two old men of the 1793 revolution wearing the clothes of that time, a dog, a dead man and his bearers, the sextons (one of them has a nose like a cherry but of large proportions and five inches long), my sisters, other women, etc. I thought I could do without two choristers of the parish, but there was no getting round it; they came to tell me that they were offended because they were the only ones in the parish not to have been portrayed. They complained bitterly, saying that they had never done me any ill and did not deserve such an affront."
When the painting was exhibited Champfleury declared: "From now on the critics will have to decide whether they are for or against realism."

The Artist's Studio
oil on canvas, 361x598 cm
Musée d'Orsay, Paris

Courbet painted the picture between 1854 and 1855 with the intention of showing it at the Salon of 1855. The Salon that year was of particular importance as it was connected with the second Universal Exhibition: the first had been held in London in 1851 and had proved an enormous success. The painting was rejected and Courbet told his collector friend from Montpellier, Bruyas (one of the people in the picture), that the jury had turned it down because they thought it necessary to curb a tendency that would be disastrous for French art.
So the artist organized a one-man show with admission by ticket at the Pavillon du Réalisme, and exhibited forty of his canvases. However, the reaction of the public was no different from that of the Salon's jury and very few people came to

the exhibition: Delacroix wrote that when he went to see the works, which he considered genuine masterpieces but vulgar, he found himself completely alone for an hour.
The painting, which is highly symbolic in content, depicts a large studio with Courbet at the center, working on a landscape under the attentive eyes of a child. Behind him stands a model, or perhaps his inspiring muse, Reality, devoid of any clothing. The studio is filled with a large number of figures and some critics recognize in them the representation of two distinct realities; on the left of the painter we see a varied cross section of humanity including a poacher, a cloth merchant and a rabbi; on the right are the intellectuals, Baudelaire, reading a book, Proudhon and Champfleury. Perhaps the fact that Courbet is painting a landscape indicates the direction in which his interests were moving: from that time on, in fact, he was

increasingly to concentrate on the genres of still life and landscape, and his landscapes and seascapes were to have a great influence on the Impressionist painters.

Les Dormeuses (*Sleeping Women*)
oil on canvas, 135x200 cm
Petit Palais, Paris

The picture, painted in 1866, had been commissioned by Khalil Bey, a Turkish diplomat who had assembled an important collection, including paintings by Delacroix, Chassériau, Corot and Ingres. In this collection, dispersed in 1868 after Bey was declared bankrupt, particular emphasis was given to erotic themes: it was to the same Turkish diplomat that Ingres had sold the *Turkish Bath*, returned to him by Prince Napoleon and transformed into a tondo.
We can place the *Sleeping Women* in the category that the writer and art critic Champfleury defined as "elegant nudity," a type of production that had surfaced in the 1860s and to which Courbet occasionally devoted himself in just that decade. The picture originally had a companion piece, *The Awakening* (1866, Petit Palais, Paris); together, the paintings represented the love of women for women, at least as it was understood by men who painted for other men.
The sensuality and physicality of the figures transform the academic nude into a frankly erotic subject that is fully in keeping with the work of an artist who was accustomed to controversy over his choice of subjects. At the time, in fact, nudes were often disguised as mythological scenes and met with the favor of the critics as well as the public. In 1863 Alexandre Cabanel had exhibited his *Birth of Venus* (Musée d'Orsay, Paris, 1863) at the Salon, and this roguishly idealized nude was appreciated by Napoleon III, who bought the painting and made its author a knight of the Legion of Honor. (A.F.)

Manet

He was born in Paris in 1832, into a well-to-do middle-class family. In 1850, overcoming the opposition of his father, he decided to devote himself to painting and entered the studio of the painter Thomas Couture, where he remained for six years, making journeys to Italy, Germany and the Netherlands. However, he soon came into conflict with his master, who favored the study of posed models, while his young pupil was fascinated by more natural subjects and compositions, taken from real life. The rupture between the two came in 1858, when Manet painted *The Absinthe Drinker* (now in Ny Carlsberg Glyptothek, Copenhagen), in open opposition, even in the choice of theme, with the conventions dear to Couture and the figurative culture of the time. It is possible to discern here the influence, destined to become mutual and lasting, of Charles Baudelaire, who was one of Manet's earliest admirers and never tired of defending the artist against the often fierce criticism that was to dog him throughout his career. In 1863 he painted the *Déjeuner sur l'herbe*, perhaps the work that caused the greatest scandal: rejected by the official Salon, it was shown at the first Salon des Refusés; on this occasion Manet came into contact with the circle of painters and artists who frequented the Café Guerbois, including Monet, De Nittis and Nadar. This was also the year of the *Olympia* which, although later accepted at the Salon, stirred a great deal of controversy. In 1865 he made a journey to Spain, where he was able to study the work of Goya. His works were rejected at the Universal Exhibition of 1867, provoking a passionate defense from Émile Zola. In 1874 he was invited to take part in the celebrated exhibition of the Impressionists at Nadar's studio, but did not do so. The same year Mallarmé wrote an article praising his painting. From 1878 onward Manet, already suffering from the ataxia that would lead to his death, chose to give up sending his works to the Salon and showed them exclusively in his own studio. In 1881 he was awarded, through the good offices of his friend Antonin Proust, the Legion of Honor, the only official recognition for his art that he received in his lifetime. He died in Paris on April 30, 1883.

Le Déjeuner sur l'herbe
oil on canvas, 206x264 cm
Musée d'Orsay, Paris

Among the paintings turned down by the jury of the 1863 Salon, the work was exhibited, along with those of other rejected artists (including Courbet and Doré) at the Salon-Annexe, created on the orders of Emperor Napoleon III to calm the controversy that had sprung up following numerous protests from the painters. Manet had been studying the

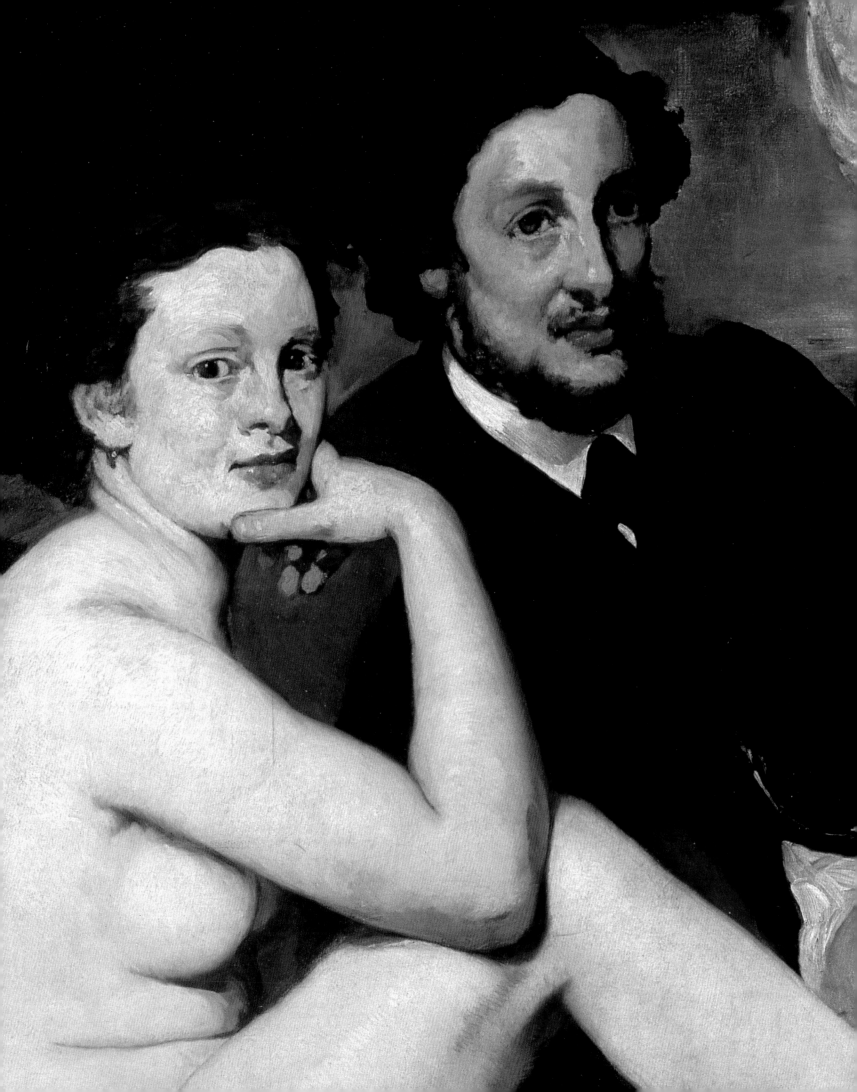

composition, inspired by Renaissance pictures, for some time: in particular the pose of the three figures at the center derives from a print made by Marcantonio Raimondi after Raphael, the *Judgment of Paris*, and it is possible to identify the strong influence of Titian's *Concert Champêtre*. The artist knew that the painting would be seen by his contemporaries as a provocation and an offense against public decency ("they are going to maul me," he had confided to a friend), and yet hoped to make a name for himself with this work. The theme in itself was not particularly scandalous: a group of figures against a natural backdrop, a female nude. But it was the contrast between the avowedly classical composition and the contemporary setting, between the bourgeois dress of the men and the nakedness of the woman, that shocked. Even more disconcerting for contemporaries was Manet's manner of painting, as the elderly Delacroix understood at once: "The strident tint cuts into the eyes like a steel saw; the figures stand out with a force and crudity that are not softened by any compromise. It has all the acerbity of those fruit that never ripen." Manet proposed a painting in flat areas of color, based on sharp contrasts and influenced by his study of Goya and Velázquez, as well as by Japanese prints, especially those of Utamaro. At the same time he constantly sought a balance of composition and experimented with soft harmonies of color, in subdued tones: an art, as Zola would put it, based on simplifications of form created "by the artist's clear and judicious eye […] delightful in their grace and real in their asperity." With the *Déjeuner sur l'herbe*, Manet placed himself at the head of the young painters who no longer accepted the academic conventions of the time: though he did not himself take the route that was to lead to Impressionism, he did, with the masterpieces of these years, sow its intellectual and artistic seeds.

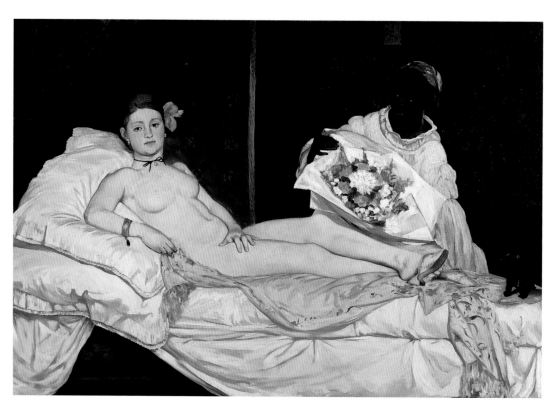

Olympia
oil on canvas, 130x190 cm
Musée d'Orsay, Paris

Shown at the Salon of 1865, the *Olympia* caused a scandal. The public was shocked by the work and the judgment of the critics was even harsher than it had been two years earlier with the *Déjeuner*: "The corrupt Olympia," wrote the newspapers, was an "odalisque with a yellow belly, a disreputable model unearthed who knows where" and Manet was "the buffoon of the Exhibition." Once again the artist had deliberately set out to create a sensation, and had declared: "the Salon is the real battlefield; it is there we have to fight." But Manet's work was not just a provocation aimed at the bourgeois morality of the public and the aesthetic conventions of the Salon. It was also a dialogue with his beloved Renaissance and Spanish models, with Titian's *Venus of Urbino* and Goya's *Maya*. Certainly the non-classical, even ungainly nude, the contemporary elements inserted, as in the *Déjeuner*, in a traditional composition (such as the slippers), were features that disconcerted the public, as did the cat

arching its back, which took the place of Titian's little dog and had a deliberately mocking flavor. But from the formal viewpoint Manet's research is extremely rigorous: the composition is very well thought-out, with a perfect equilibrium created by the contrasting poses of the two women, where the converging diagonals of the busts are balanced by the vertical line of the hanging in the background. The powerful chiaroscuro, almost erasing the forms of the body, makes the handling of colors stand out even more strongly: this is based not just on the evident contrast between light and dark tones, but on a vast range of shades of white, from the brilliance of the sheets and the wrapping of the flowers to the warmer tints of Olympia's body, the bedcover or the servant's dress, which are matched by the variety of blacks and browns in the background. The work was immediately regarded as Manet's masterpiece, and the artist proudly reproduced a photograph of it, between a print by Utamaro and an engraving of Velázquez's *Borrachos*, in the portrait he painted of Émile Zola (Musée d'Orsay, Paris).

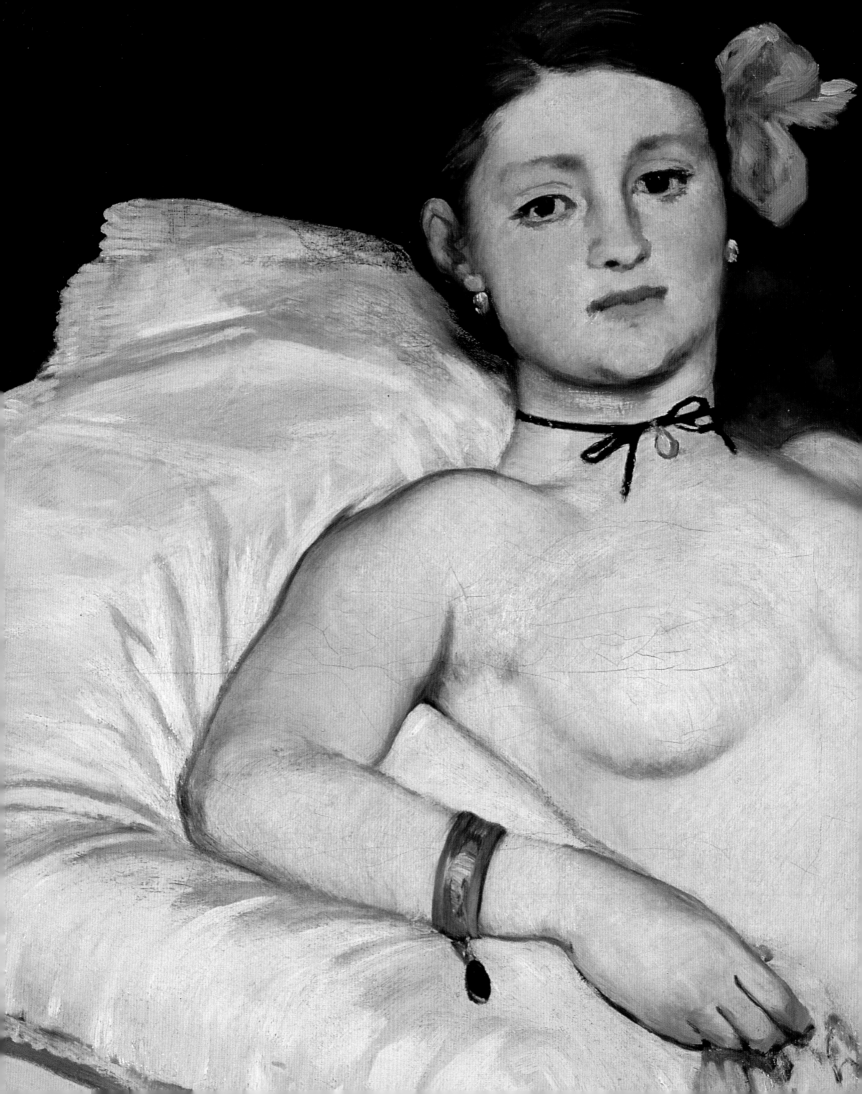

The Balcony
oil on canvas, 169x125 cm
Musée d'Orsay, Paris

Painted between 1868 and 1869, it is
based on a work by Goya, *The Majas on
the Balcony*, from around 1808-12 (now
in a private collection). Manet measured
himself against the painting of the great
Spanish artist several times, reworking
some of his celebrated compositions, as
in the case of the *Olympia*, which recalls
the *Maya desnuda*, or the *Execution of
the Emperor Maximilian*, derived from
May 3, 1808. The comparison with the
art of Goya was not limited to an updating
of the subjects, although this must have
been one of the aspects that most struck
the public of the time, but was in the first
place an investigation of his style and his
conception of painting. At first sight the
composition is more rigid, less flowing
than the Spanish model. But Manet is
aiming at a more rigorous balance of
color and form, to which the apparently
frozen gestures of the figures, which
hostile critics often accused of looking
like manikins, also contribute: here the
pattern formed by the hands leads the
observer's gaze from the man in the
background to the young woman putting
on her gloves and then to the woman
leaning on the railing, in a movement
underscored by the converging lines of
the fan and parasol. And then, as always,
the paint itself lies at the center of the
artist's interest, with the large expanses of
color, in line with a tendency to simply
the image. This is combined, however,
with a great chromatic sensitivity, revealed
here, as in the *Olympia*, in the tonal
variations of white.

ÉDOUARD MANET

A Bar at the Folies-Bergère
oil on canvas, 96x130 cm
Courtauld Institute Galleries, London

The picture is one of the last painted by
the artist, whose lower limbs were already
almost completely paralyzed, between
1881 and 1882. It was accepted at the
Salon of 1882 and was one of the very few
works by Manet to meet with public
approval. It depicts the bar of the
celebrated Parisian nightclub Les Folies-
Bergère. The use of the mirror to extend
the space depicted in the picture is taken
from *Las Meninas* by Velázquez, a painter
much admired by Manet. Here, however,
as critics immediately pointed out, the
perspective of the reflected image is not
correct, but shifted to the side: the mirror
is set parallel to the bar, but we see the
girl's back on the right of the
composition, along with the customer
facing her. The effect is disconcerting: we
find ourselves face to face with the
barmaid, and therefore in the position of
the bearded man, but the reflection
disrupts the perspective and underlines
our distance from the work:
contemporary accounts speak of "people
crowded in front of the painting,
exchanging bewildered comments on the
mirage of this canvas." The work is
considered one of the closest, from the
stylistic viewpoint, to those of the
Impressionists, and it is true that in the
painting, as in others from these years, we
find brushwork that in some ways
resembles Monet's (especially in the
crowd or the large chandelier reflected in
the mirror). But the difference from the
Impressionists remains profound, both
technically, with Manet's fondness for the
use of black as a color, and in the very
conception of the work, whose carefully
planned composition is not taken from
life, but worked out, including the effect
of the reflected lights, in the artist's
studio. (S.G.C.)

Monet

Claude Monet was born in Paris in 1840 but grew up in Le Havre, where his family moved when he was still a small child. At a very early age he attracted the attention of the landscape artist Eugène Boudin, who took him to paint in the open air and passed on to him his fondness for the Dutch tradition of landscape painting. Monet then moved to Paris, where he enrolled in the Académie Suisse and met Camille Pissarro. The pair frequented Baudelaire, as well as Courbet and other Realist painters. Their evening discussions inspired and encouraged them to develop a style remote from the schemes of academic painting. On his return from military service in Algeria, the artist went back to Le Havre, where he started to paint from life again with Boudin and the Dutchman Johan Barthold Jongkind. In 1862 he went to live in Paris again, where he frequented the studio of the academician Charles Gleyre and made friends with Renoir and Sisley.

His early works broke with the academic tradition but still showed the influence of his favorite painters: while the *Pavé de Chailly* echoes the manner of Corot, in the *Mouth of the Seine at Honfleur* Monet reveals that he had assimilated Boudin's lesson, and in *Camille Doncieux* (*Lady in Green*) (Kunsthalle, Bremen), shown with success at the Salon of 1866, he pays homage to Édouard Manet.

In 1870 war broke out and Monet, who did not want to take part, joined Pissarro in London. Here he saw the works of the English landscapists and became a friend of Paul Durand-Ruel, the gallery owner who was to become his most important agent. His stay inspired some splendid foggy landscapes like *The Thames and the Houses of Parliament* (1871, National Gallery, London).

On his return to France (1871) he settled at Argenteuil. In those years he assumed an increasingly important role within a group of anti-academic artists close to the Realist current, known as the Batignolles group after their habitual meeting place, the Café Guerbois on rue de Batignolles in Paris. In 1873, under the direction of Monet, they founded the "Societé Anonyme," whose members included Degas, Pissarro, Renoir and Sisley. In 1874 the society held an exhibition in the studio of the photographer Nadar, and on that occasion Monet showed a view of the harbor of Le Havre whose title, *Impression, soleil levant* (*Impression, Sunrise*, 1872, Musée Marmottan, Paris), would inspire the name given to the group. A journalist sent to review the exhibition took his cue from the painting and sarcastically described the painters as "impressionists," deriding them as the authors of evanescent and incomplete pictures, based on first impressions.

Monet took part in the joint exhibitions of the Impressionists up until 1879, when he decided no longer to show his work at them, and in 1883 his first one-man show was organized by Durand-Ruel. In that same year he moved to the house at Giverny, whose garden was to inspire the famous series of the *Water Lilies* (Musée de l'Orangerie, Paris), to which he would devote himself from 1908 until his death in 1926.

The paintings are studies of the same subject under different conditions of atmospheric light and almost turn into exercises of abstract painting, so great is the emphasis on color and scant the concern for a "photographic" representation of the pool with its flowers. But the artist had already shown his interest in the execution of a series of works depicting the same subject at different times of day and varying conditions of light. In 1892-94 he painted perhaps the most celebrated of these series, devoted to the facade of Rouen Cathedral.

Women in the Garden
Musée d'Orsay, Paris

Women in the Garden
oil on canvas, 255x205 cm
Musée d'Orsay, Paris

This picture, executed between 1866 and 1867, marked the beginning of a fundamental period in Impressionism, that of painting *en plein air*, in the open air. Between 1865 and 1866 Monet worked on a *Dejeuner sur l'herbe* inspired by Manet's famous work of 1863 (Musée d'Orsay), and sought to develop a personal relationship with nature by painting as much as possible from life. All that survives of the *Dejeuner sur l'herbe* (known as *The Picnic* in English) are three preparatory studies and the central parts of the picture, as the artist never finished it: he had retouched it on the basis of comments made by Courbet but afterwards regretted the changes he had made, and rolled up the canvas and left it in the house at Chailly, which he had to abandon as he was unable to pay the rent. He gave the painting to his landlord in lien, and when he reclaimed it, several years later, found it moldy and damaged by the damp in several places. Later he decided to work on a similar subject exclusively *en plein air*, without preparatory studies: *Women in the*

Garden. This was a picture of considerable size and Monet himself said of it: "I really painted this canvas on the spot, looking directly at nature, something that was not done at the time. I had made a hole in the ground, a sort of pit, and gradually lowered my canvas into it, when it came to painting the upper part. I was working at Ville d'Avray, where I had sometimes been advised by Courbet, who came to see me." There is another anecdote about Courbet, who found the painter idle when he paid him a visit: when he asked why, he was told that he was waiting for the sun. Courbet replied that he could be painting the background in the meantime, but Monet did not accept the advice, arguing that he wanted to obtain a complete uniformity of light. This response is particularly significant, in that it underlines what was new about the Impressionist technique: it required in fact that every phase in the realization of the work be done outdoors, doing away with any intervention in the studio.
In the painting reproduced here all the attention is focused on the light and the shadow of the trees, and the presence of the female figures is subordinate to the importance given to the natural setting. The artist is not interested in painting

portraits in a landscape, or in explaining the reasons for the women's meeting, creating dynamics that would bring the stiffly posed figures to life and reveal their psychological attitudes, and so we should not be surprised at the lack of expression on their faces.
These artistic choices were very different from the values appreciated by the teachers of the Academy, and it is no wonder that the canvas was rejected by the Jury of the 1867 Salon.

Poppies
oil on canvas, 50x65 cm
Musée d'Orsay, Paris

Monet painted the canvas in 1873, *en plein air* in the countryside around Argenteuil. The painter was by now a

strong believer in working outdoors, and had persuaded Sisley, Pissarro and Renoir to do the same. Renoir often went to see him in Argenteuil, and the two artists painted together, immersed in nature. A picture by Renoir, *Path through the Long Grass* (Musée d'Orsay, Paris), also bears witness to the work they did side by side, representing a landscape similar to the one reproduced here.
The painting, shown at the first Impressionist exhibition of 1874, depicts an expanse of meadows and fields lit up by the bright red of the poppies. In his pictures Monet gave no more importance to the figures than to the natural setting, and the ones represented here, two women each accompanied by a child, are not brought into any greater focus than the rest of the painting: blurred and indistinct, they blend into the patches of color and are treated like details of the landscape. The figures in the foreground, who are in fact the artist's wife Camille and his son Jean, are easier to make out, while the others, silhouetted against the trees at the edge of the meadow, are visible only on closer examination.

Claude Monet
73

Saint-Lazare Station
oil on canvas, 75.5x104 cm
Musée d'Orsay, Paris

Monet rarely turned his attention to the
city, but in 1877 he decided to paint the
station of Saint-Lazare, which both Manet
and Caillebotte had chosen as a subject
before him. The artist painted two views,
and with these concluded the series of
works devoted to city life to concentrate
on the representation of landscapes. He
was fascinated by the effects that steam
created in this space with its linear
structures, and captured the atmosphere
with thick and bold brushstrokes,
dissolving the architecture of the station
and the buildings in the background into
the smoke, steam and shafts of light.
Monet's enthusiasm for stations is also
reflected by the words he addressed to
Auguste Renoir, and which son Jean
Renoir quoted in the memoirs devoted to
his father: "At the moment of departure
the smoke of the locomotive is so dense
that nothing can be seen. It is a marvel,
real magic." The painter was not
interested in depicting people in the
midst of chaotic city life, and it should
come as no surprise that one of the most
favorable comments came from Émile
Zola, who on the occasion of the
presentation of seven of the twelve
pictures he painted at the third
Impressionist exhibition, in 1877,
compared stations to the classical

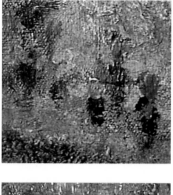

elements of the landscape and wrote:
"This year, Monet exhibited some superb
station interiors. You can hear the
rumbling of the trains as the station
engulfs them. You can see the smoke
billowing out beneath the vast hangars.
[...] Our artists have to find poetry in
train stations, the way their fathers found
poetry in forests and rivers." The
painting was bought by Gustave
Caillebotte in 1878.

Rouen Cathedral

oil on canvas
Musée d'Orsay, Paris

The paintings illustrated here belong to a group of works depicting the facade of Rouen Cathedral that Monet commenced in 1892, when he went to the city for family reasons, and concluded in 1894. Each picture is dedicated to a specific moment of the day, so each day the painter must have worked on several canvases in parallel, going back to them the next day at roughly the same time. This is confirmed by the annotations, such as "late afternoon, around six," that are found on some of the paintings. So each work is different from the next as a result of variations in the lighting conditions, but forms part of a whole that can be divided into other groups: pictures painted by the light of morning, in full sunlight or around sunset.

The *Rouen Cathedral* series is made up of about fifty paintings that study the variations in light at different times of day on a single, unchanging subject, the facade of the famous Gothic church. Catching the light with its white and highly reflective marble surface, complicated decorations and strongly splayed portals, this creates constantly shifting patterns of light and shade. So there are canvases in which the pale blues of dawn predominate, or the white tones of the morning light, and while the facade takes on golden reflections at noon, in the afternoon it is tinged with shades of red and orange.

During the execution of these pictures Monet went through different states of mind, as his letters reflect; at times he seems to have been overcome by despondency, as in one he wrote on March 30, 1893 to Paul Durand-Ruel: "My stay here goes ahead: this does not mean that I am close to finishing my cathedrals. Alas, I can only repeat: the more I see, the worse I get at rendering what I feel; and I tell myself that anyone who says he has finished a canvas is tremendously arrogant. Finished, meaning complete, perfect; and I work at full stretch without getting anywhere, seeking, groping, without achieving much, but to the point of exhaustion."

In 1895 the painter showed twenty or so of the roughly fifty pictures he had painted at Durand-Ruel's gallery. Not everyone appreciated the paintings and the reasons for the discordant views can be sought in part in what the painter Camille Pissarro wrote to his son Lucien: "It is the unhurried work of a strong will, which pursues the tiniest nuances of effect and which I have not seen done by any other artist. There are those who deny the need for such research when is taken to this point." (A.F.)

Degas

T he young Edgar Degas, born in Paris in 1834 to an upper middle-class family, soon abandoned his studies at university to devote himself to painting. In 1853 he began to frequent the Louvre, where he made copies of the works of the great masters. Two years later he entered the studio of Louis Lamothe, a pupil of Ingres, and acquired there a sound technical training, inheriting from his teacher a passion for drawing that was to remain a constant feature of his art.

Between 1856 and 1859 the artist paid several visits to Italy, and in particular to Florence, where he stayed with some relatives of his, the Bellelli family. In fact one of the most interesting paintings of those years is his portrait of that family (Musée d'Orsay, Paris). In Italy he also met Diego Martelli, an outstanding exponent of the Macchiaioli current. The pictures of the early 1860s represent subjects linked to ancient history, such as *Spartan Girls Challenging Boys* (National Gallery, London), but he also painted the first of a long series dedicated to horseracing, *At the Races: the Start* (1860-62, Fogg Art Museum, Cambridge, Mass.).

The attraction he felt for the atmosphere of Realism led him to associate with a number of painters around the middle of the sixties, including Monet, Manet and Pissarro, who around ten years later would acquire the label of Impressionists but were then just known as the Batignolles group, after the name of the street on which their meeting place, the Café Guerbois, was situated.

In that decade Degas became a regular visitor to the Opéra, which inspired such pictures as the *Orchestra* or the *Dance Foyer at the Opéra* (both in the Musée d'Orsay, Paris), inaugurating the long series of paintings and sculptures devoted to dancers. He portrayed them throughout his life, in an infinity of poses, at the theater, practicing and in the dressing rooms, capturing their customary gestures and expressions. Over the years his quest for realism and attentive studies of movement gave way to a taste for invention, with more fragmentary visions and brighter, more swirling colors. He painted every kind of female figure, noblewomen, singers, laundresses and milliners, analyzing their psychological aspects through the immediacy of a gesture and modeling their bodies with extraordinary plays of light. In 1872-73 he went to New Orleans to visit his mother's family, and depicted them at work in the *Portraits in a Cotton Office* (Musée des Beaux-Arts, Pau).

On his return to Paris he linked up with the painters of the Batignolles group again, and in 1873 participated in the foundation of the society of painters that the critics were to dub "Impressionists," giving the term a negative and ironic connotation. Degas differed from Monet and the other painters of the group not just in his choice of subjects (he preferred the life of the city to landscapes), but above all in his refusal to paint from life.

In the second half of the seventies he started to make more frequent use of pastel, while in the eighties he turned his attention to sculpture, an activity to which he devoted himself almost exclusively as his eyesight began to fade. From the middle of the nineties he took an interest in photography and made use of it for his sculptures too. In the last years of his life he curtailed his relations with the Impressionists, progressively withdrawing into isolation. He died in Paris in 1917.

The Bellelli Family
Musée d'Orsay, Paris

The Bellelli Family
oil on canvas, 200x250 cm
Musée d'Orsay, Paris

Degas started to work on the painting around 1857, during the time he was a guest of the family of his father's sister, Baroness Bellelli, in Florence, and did not finish it until 1859. The artist wanted to portray the figures in a familiar attitude, maintaining poses that were comfortable for them. For this reason the group is not drawn up "on parade": the uncle is seated in an armchair with his back to us and all we see is his face in profile, while one daughter is sitting on the edge of a chair and her folded leg is completely hidden under her skirt. The desire to place his subjects in natural attitudes should not lead us to believe that the painting is the equivalent of a snapshot: the artist arrived at it after numerous studies and sketches, modifying the composition several times and allowing his stylistic choices to reflect the psychology of the personages as well. The work shows how the painter has maintained intact the taste for drawing that had come down to him from Ingres. Unlike the latter, however, he did not focus his attention on the human face, but took the same care over it as he devoted to the other parts of the body, an approach that brought him into line with Realism.

The Absinthe Drinker (L'Absinthe)
oil on canvas, 92x68 cm
Musée d'Orsay, Paris

The picture, painted between 1875 and 1876, represents the actress Ellen Andrée and the engraver Marcellin Desboutin sitting in the Café de la Nouvelle-Athènes, the place where the Impressionists had begun to meet after the early period of the Café Guerbois. The American actress was a friend of Manet, who also portrayed her in a painting of 1878 (Oskar Reinhart Collection, Winterthur), as he did Desboutin (1875, Museu de São Paulo). According to the actress's own account, the two of them actually posed in front of a glass of absinthe, a drink that was viewed with particular disfavor by the right-minded of the time, who held it responsible for alcoholism in the working class.

The scene is supposed to represent a prostitute and her pimp, perhaps at dawn after a night of drinking, in an atmosphere that is not very different from that of Zola's novels. It certainly lays bare the lack of communication between the two figures, who are not looking at one another but remain isolated in separate worlds.

The composition is carefully studied and unusual: looking at the picture we get the impression we are standing next to the tables. It is not just the adoption of a viewpoint at close range and to one side that draws us into the scene, but also the attitude of the man who is located at the

edge of the canvas and staring out of it, thereby involving us directly in the representation.

The picture was painted in 1876 and may have been shown at the second Impressionist exhibition, held the same year, and at the exhibition in London in 1893, where it was heavily criticized for glorifying the more negative aspects of the artist's life, the so-called *vie bohémienne*.

The Orchestra
oil on canvas, 56.5x46.2 cm
Musée d'Orsay, Paris

The idea for the painting, executed between 1868 and 1869, arose in part out of a desire to portray his friend Désiré Dihau, the bassoonist in the foreground. It can even be considered a group portrait, given that the face of the composer Emmanuel Chabrier is also visible, although barely, in the box. This was the first painting Degas devoted to the orchestra, but also the first to depict dancers, a subject in which he was to show increasing interest.

As in *L'Absinthe*, Degas uses an unconventional framing, which makes it look as if the group of musicians continues outside the picture, but what is most striking about this composition is the contrast between the members of the orchestra, illuminated by a light from above that contributes to the definition of their figures, and the ballerinas on the stage, caught in the strong source of light underneath, which renders them evanescent. (A.F.)

Renoir

" *A* picture should be something that is pleasant, joyful and pretty; there are already enough unpleasant things in life to dissuade us from producing still others": here we find the idea of the painting as fun, as joy, as vitality, a concept that stretches from Renoir all the way back to Rubens.

Renoir was born at Limoges in 1841 and around the age of thirteen went to work as a decorator in a porcelain factory in Paris, while attending a school of drawing in the evenings. When the company failed as a result of competition from the new industrial system of mechanically printed decorations, he took up painting fans and waterproof cloth panels for missionaries in Indochina and decorating Parisian bars and cafés. In the meantime he frequented the Louvre to study the works of such masters as Rubens, Watteau, Fragonard and Boucher.

Then he enrolled in the painting courses held by Charles Gleyre, where he met other young artists like Sisley and Monet. Following the example of the Barbizon School, the group of friends made trips to the forest of Fontainebleau to paint from life. These were years of economic hardship, in which the artist sometimes did not even have enough money to buy paints and often had to stay with friends, years in which his paintings were more often rejected than accepted at the Salon, but in which his enthusiasm never failed him, as his lively discussions with the circle of young painters who gathered around Manet at the Café Guerbois demonstrate. Impatient with excessively rigid theories, Renoir, a great admirer of Corot and Delacroix, also opposed their criticism of the study of the old masters. In 1865 he met Lise Tréhot, who was to remain his favorite model for years, and in 1868 his *Lise with Umbrella* was accepted by the Salon, the annual public exhibition for which works were selected by a board of members of the Académie Royale. The realistic treatment and concreteness of the works of this period clearly reflects the lesson of Courbet, but the study of variations in the effects of light captured with rapid brushstrokes that was to characterize the artist's later paintings is already beginning to emerge. In 1869 Renoir often went with Monet to work on the banks of the Seine, and both painted La Grenouillère, a floating cabaret on the islet of Croissy: a representation of contemporary life, of the fleeting moment, of the atmosphere that changes as the lights and reflections on the water change.

In 1873 he met the young art dealer Durand-Ruel, who was courageously supporting the new tendencies in painting. In 1874, rejected by the Salon again, he organized the Societé Anonyme Cooperative with other artists and exhibited several paintings, including *The Box*, in the studio of the photographer Nadar: it was on this occasion that the name Impressionists was coined from the derogatory comments of a critic. Around 1880 the Impressionist movement entered a phase of profound disorientation. Renoir felt that he had exploited its possibilities to the full: "I had wrung Impressionism dry, and I finally came to the conclusion that I knew neither how to paint nor how to draw. In a word, Impressionism was a blind alley, as far as I was concerned." In 1881 he made two journeys. "In Algiers I discovered white," he would write. Then he set off for Italy with Aline Charigot, his model and future wife, prompted by the need to look at the pictures under the skies that had housed their authors. In Venice he admired Titian, at Pompeii the sense of the timeless character of everyday life that emerges from antiquity, in Rome Raphael. Renoir was now in search of classical solidity. His outlines grew sharper, his brushwork smoother: "I am not satisfied and erase, go on erasing. I hope this mania will pass." Next he went to Spain, to see the work of Velázquez, and then to London, Dresden and the Netherlands, in the footsteps of the masters of the past. Meanwhile his second son Jean, who would go on to become a famous film director, was born in 1894. In 1897 he broke his arm in a fall from a bicycle: the strong rheumatic pains that resulted from this injury would degenerate into rheumatoid arthritis and confine him, from 1911 onwards, to a wheelchair. His desire to paint stayed with him to the end. His arm was sound and his eyesight keen, but his skin was delicate and could be injured by the slightest contact: to overcome the problem he had a thin piece of canvas placed in the palm of his hand and grasped the brush with his numb fingers. In Paris, in 1919, the Louvre was opened specially so that he could visit it by himself. Renoir moved slowly through the rooms on his "litter," and asked his bearers to stop in front of Veronese's *Marriage at Cana*. He died the same year. His last words were "I think I am beginning to understand something about it."

Woman Reading
Musée d'Orsay, Paris

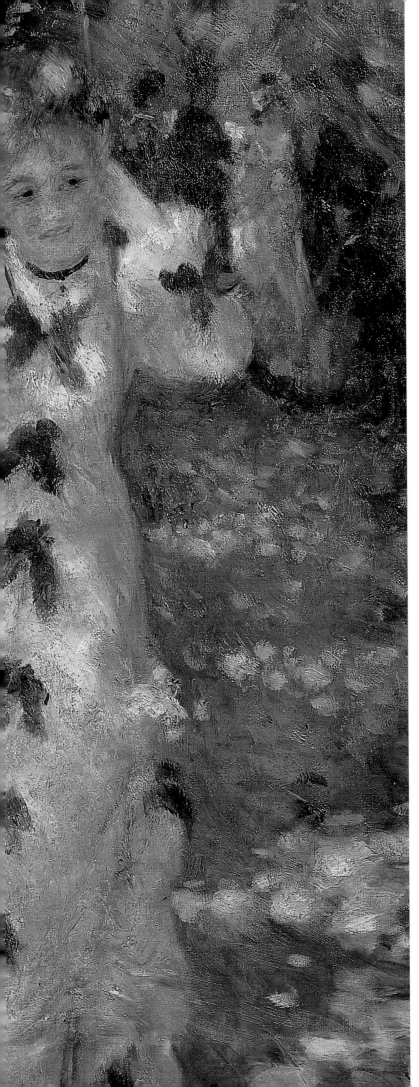

Woman Reading

oil on canvas, 46.5x38.5 cm
Musée d'Orsay, Paris

"I like pictures that make me want to walk around inside them, if they are landscapes, or to caress them, if they are of women": for Renoir painting was not just a pleasure for the eyes, but for the touch as well. In this picture dating from 1874-76 Renoir treated the image of a woman reading, which for other painters of the second half of the 19th century symbolized female emancipation, as an opportunity to play with the effects of the sunshine on the girl's hair, to model the forms with light. "What I like is skin, the rosy skin of a girl that hints at the good circulation of her blood. And what I love above all is serenity." What pleased Renoir in women was their capacity to live in the present moment, their ability to "make life bearable." "I like women. They have no doubts about anything. With them the world becomes very simple. They give everything the right value and know very well that their washing is just as important as the constitution of the German empire. When you are with them you feel reassured!" But he also liked women who "don't know how to read and who clean their own baby's bottom." And he loved children, whose curiosity and capacity for wonder he shared. Loath to display his feelings, Renoir used his brush to caress the dimples of their cheeks, the folds in their wrists, and in this way, as his son Jean would recall, declared his paternal love to the world.

The Swing

oil on canvas, 92x73 cm
Louvre, Paris

With the proceeds from the sale of some pictures, Renoir had rented a neglected garden on via Cortot in Montmartre and set up a swing in it. His picture of this swing, painted in 1876, was shown at the third Impressionist exhibition along with

the *Moulin de la Galette*. Both pictures were bought by the artist Gustave Caillebotte, who had always helped out his fellow painters materially and who, in his will of 1876, made a bequest of Impressionist paintings to the State on condition that they be exhibited "neither in a barn nor in a provincial museum, but at the Luxembourg and later the Louvre," a clause that encountered fierce opposition from academic circles. The painting is structured around the *tache*, or "blot," a brushstroke separate from all the others and not blended into the ground. Initially used to represent the fragmentation of reflections on water, the *tache* was then used for the whole work. At the exhibition in 1877 a critic attacked this approach on the grounds that the effects of the light made it look as if the clothing were covered with grease stains. But the idea made an impression on a great writer, Émile Zola, who took the inspiration for some of the images in his novel *Page d'amour* from this painting, where the little girl watches with amusement as the sunlight moves slowly toward her, creating dancing round spots, and the older girl stands on the seat of the swing, holding onto the ropes with her arms braced and waiting for a push.

PIERRE-AUGUSTE RENOIR

Dance at the Moulin de la Galette
oil on canvas, 131x175 cm
Louvre, Paris

"What freedom! Not having to worry about a story anymore, as it has been told hundreds of times. This is what is important: getting away from the subject, avoiding literature and so choosing something that everyone is familiar with." In the quarter of Montmartre, a shed built around two disused windmills had become the haunt of seamstresses and sales clerks from the clothes stores in the northern districts of Paris, who went there to dance on Saturdays and Sundays. Renoir painted the modern life of the city, its pastimes and its meeting places, recording the scene with immediacy and working, as he liked to put it, like a "cork that bobs on the surface and is carried along by the current" or like a "workman of painting." Seamstresses and their friends modeled for the painting, on which Renoir often worked in the garden on via Cortot, getting his companions to help him move the large canvas. During his Impressionist period – this work dates from 1876 – his palette was very simple: white lead, three shades of yellow, two of green and two of blue, raw Sienna, vermilion and madder lake, without the black that, after his trip to Italy, he was to call "the king of colors." And the *tache* was still predominant.

Despite making sketches in the open air, in the manner typical of the Impressionists, Renoir did not disdain finishing his canvases in the studio. Besides, as he explained after the criticism he received at the first Impressionist exhibition, "a picture is made to be seen inside a beautiful house, with windows that often give a false light. So it is necessary to add, to the work painted from life, a bit of work in the studio; you have to be able to get away from the exhilaration of true light and digest your impressions in the grayness of an apartment. Then you go back to get a bit of sun. You come, you go, and in the end you get something!"

"I arrange my subject as I want it, then I go ahead and paint it like a child. I want a red to be sonorous, to sound like a bell; if it doesn't turn out that way, I put in more reds or other colors till I get it. I am no cleverer than that. I have no rules and no methods [...]. Nowadays they want to explain everything. But if they could explain a picture, it wouldn't be art. Shall I tell you what I think are the two qualities of art? It must be indescribable and it must be inimitable [...]. The work of art must seize upon you, wrap you up in itself, carry you away. It is the means by which the artist conveys his passions; it is the current which he puts forth which sweeps you along in his passion." (E.F.)

Cézanne

Paul Cézanne was born at Aix-en-Provence on January 19, 1839. In 1852 he entered the Collège Bourbon, where he made friends with Émile Zola: this marked the beginning of a relationship of mutual esteem and artistic influence that was to last for over thirty years. In 1858 he won a prize for drawing at the École in Aix and decided to devote himself to painting, although he still enrolled in the law school of the university to satisfy the wishes of his father. In 1861 he persuaded his father to let him go to Paris to study art: he met Pissarro, made regular visits to the Louvre and went to the Salon but, turned down by the Ecole des Beaux-Arts, returned to Aix the same year, where he was taken on by the bank founded by his father. The following year he was back in the capital, where he frequented Renoir, Monet and Sisley as well as Pissarro. In 1863 he visited the celebrated Salon des Refusés with Zola, and had words of admiration for Manet and, above all, Courbet and Delacroix. Returning to Aix, he began to alternate, as he was to do for the rest of his life, stays in Paris and in the city of his birth. In 1865 Zola dedicated the *Confession de Claude* to him. His paintings did not have much success, and although Manet, to whom he was introduced in 1866, appreciated his still lifes, the works he submitted regularly to the Salon were always rejected. In 1872 he moved with his family to Auvers-sur-Oise, where he lived for two years with Dr. Gachet, who collected the works of young French painters and was able to fully understand Cézanne's art. At Auvers he also met van Gogh. In 1874, at Pissarro's insistence, he showed *The House of the Hanged Man* and the *Modern Olympia* at the first exhibition of the Impressionists, held in the studio of the photographer Nadar, but they did not get a positive reception: in 1876, he refused to take part in the second exhibition. In 1882 he was accepted for the first time at the Salon, through the intercession of the painter Guillemet, who presented him as his pupil. Over the course of the eighties he had the opportunity to paint with Renoir and Monet. The publication of Zola's *L'Œuvre* in 1886 brought their long friendship to an end: Cézanne recognized the protagonist, Claude Lantier, a painter driven to suicide by his inability to realize his artistic ideal, as a portrait of himself. In 1889 he showed *The House of the Hanged Man* again at the Universal Exhibition in Paris, and in the same years took part in exhibitions of the Les Vingt group in Brussels. In 1894 he visited Monet at his home in Giverny, but Cézanne's emotional instability led them to quarrel. Although his first one-man show, the following year, was not a success with the public and critics, it did arouse the admiration of his colleagues and old friends. While continuing to lead a very solitary life, almost always at Aix, he did take part in the Salon des Indépendants and the Salon d'Automne several times in the last years of his life: young artists and admirers often went to see him, recognizing him as a master. Cézanne died at Aix-en-Provence on October 15, 1906, as a result of a chill that he had caught a few days earlier, while painting in the countryside.

The Bridge at Maincy
oil on canvas, 58.5x72.5 cm
Musée d'Orsay, Paris

The picture, one of Cézanne's best-known landscapes, dates from the years 1879-80, when Cézanne was living at Melun, near Maincy. It represents the bridge over the Almond River, linked with the mills on the opposite bank, and is one of the earliest examples of the artist's so-called "constructive" period, which followed his participation in the Impressionist

exhibition of 1877 and the negative reaction to his works. In the paintings of these years the artist's research was wholly focused, as Venturi has pointed out, on "reaching the essence of things by means of simplification," i.e. the reduction of the description of nature to geometric forms (the artist himself would say, in 1904, that it was necessary to "treat nature by means of the cylinder, the sphere, the cone, everything brought into proper perspective"). The shift away from Impressionist poetics is evident: the objective is not to capture the fleeting appearance of things, as in Monet's painting, but their internal, and timeless, structure. The material (the bridge, the water, the trees, the atmosphere itself) is represented with a multitude of brushstrokes set one alongside the other like pieces in a mosaic, and in each touch we perceive the effort to analyze the luministic and chromatic values of the object. This is apparent in the theme, so dear to the Impressionists, of reflection on water, which here concedes nothing to the depiction of the movement of the river and the continual variations of light: on the contrary, it becomes an opportunity to carry on with the incessant examination of the plants, the wooden structures of the bridge or the stone arches.

Woman with Coffeepot
oil on canvas, 130x97 cm
Musée d'Orsay, Paris

This is the portrait of a servant, painted between 1890 and 1894. It was a period in which Cézanne used models for his works with greater frequency. But he is only marginally interested in producing a physical or psychological likeness: he himself claimed that he painted a coffeepot or the face of a woman in the same way, almost certainly in reference to this work. The painting turns on an analysis of the relations between the masses of the objects represented (the woman's dress, the coffeepot, the cup), and their reaction to light. The choice of a very restricted palette, with cold colors for the dress and the small still life on the right, and browns in the background, simplifies Cézanne's study of light and

form. Note how the blue fades almost to white where it catches the light, and how this permits a breakdown of the cloth and its folds into simple geometric shapes. The shift toward a more subtle coloring, allowing the painter to make progress in his incessant artistic research, was favored in these years by his exploration of watercolor as a medium.

The Card Players
oil on canvas, 45x57 cm
Musée d'Orsay, Paris

This is a subject the painter tackled several times between 1890 and 1892, when he was living in his hometown of Aix-en-Provence. There are three versions of the picture under examination here, perhaps the last in the series. He chose local people as models: the figure on the left is recognizable as a gardener called "Père Alexandre," portrayed by Cézanne several times in those years. The paintings of card players were preceded by careful studies of the figures' features, reflecting an interest in psychological and social factors that almost parallels the literary work of Émile Zola, for many years the painter's close friend. In the version in the Louvre, even more than in the one

reproduced here or the one in New York's Metropolitan Museum of Art, the players, with their monumental presence occupying the whole of the canvas and the simplification of their individual features, take on the universal character of human types. But Cézanne's main interest is pictorial. As he declared: "Painting is not only to copy the object, it is to seize a harmony between numerous relations,"

where by relations he meant those of color, light, volume and composition. Look, for example, at the analysis of the players' jackets, or their hats, with numerous passages of tone and color and turning on a warm symphony of browns and yellows, contrasting with the landscape in the background, barely sketched in shades of blue, gray and white.

PAUL CÉZANNE

Mont Sainte-Victoire Seen from Gardanne

oil on canvas, 63.5x83 cm
Kunsthaus, Zurich

The Provençal mountain, already present in some of the works of his youth, became the main object of Cézanne's analysis in the last years of his life. At least eighteen variations on this theme are known. We can almost feel the effort made by the aging painter as he attempts, with extreme rigor, to go just a little deeper in his investigation of the chromatic relations, of which every single brushstroke has to take account. The mountain is depicted from different points of view and at different times of day, in a quest, inevitably never fulfilled, for a representation of nature that attains to the truth of the object, that is faithful to the vision of what has been defined as the artist's "inner eye." Cézanne sets himself a goal he knows to be extremely difficult to reach and that will inescapably lead to the discarding of the conventions that held good before him. In 1903 he wrote to Ambroise Vollard: "I work tenaciously, I see the promised land before me. Will my fate be that of the great leader of the Jews, or shall I be able to enter? […] I have made some progress. Why so late and with such difficulty? Could it be that Art is in reality a priesthood that demands of the pure that they belong to it entirely?" And, two years later, to Émile Bernard: "Yet since I am now old – almost seventy – the color impressions conveyed by the light are in my case the cause of abstractions which neither permit me to cover my canvas entirely nor to pursue the delimitations of objects when their points of contact are fine and delicate; the result is that my image or painting is incomplete. On the other hand the planes are placed one on top of the other." The version of the *Mont Sainte-Victoire* in Zurich, reproduced here, is one of the last (painted between 1904 and 1906), and illustrates the painter's words perfectly. The classical space of perspective has ceased to exist, distance seems to have been canceled out, and the green of the fields has the same value, from the viewpoint of the painting, as the color used to represent the clouds. The rendering of the atmosphere itself, according to Cézanne's pictorial principles, requires a chromatic and volumetric analysis no less thorough than that of the mountain. Some parts of the canvas left unpainted take on a luministic function and at the same time contribute to that sense of inevitable incompleteness and lack of limitation of the forms that characterizes the artist's late work. (S.G.C.)

Gauguin

" I am a great artist and I know it. It is precisely because I am that I have put up with so much suffering: to follow my calling in life. If not I would consider myself an outlaw." Gauguin wrote these words to his wife in March 1892. In fact it was the consciousness of the originality of his art that gave him the strength to continue in spite of all the difficulties, after abandoning everything, family, work, friends and a good economic and social position, and having to make ends meet by posting bills in Paris and selling tarpaulins in Copenhagen, or by working on the construction of the Panama Canal.

Born in Paris in 1848, he joined the stockbroking firm of Bertin, married a well-to-do Danish woman and started to collect works of art (Cézanne, Pissarro, Sisley) and to paint, taking part in some of the exhibitions of the Impressionists. In 1883 he lost his job as a consequence of the stock market crash in France and convinced himself that he could make a living from painting.

Leaving his family in Denmark, he went back to France and in 1888 moved to Pont-Aven in Brittany. Here his technique began to take shape, partly through contact with the young Émile Bernard, who was developing a style of painting based on bold forms surrounded by dark lines. It was a manner borrowed from Japanese prints, stained glass and cloisonné enamels, a technique in which the enamel is poured into small cells (cloisons) arranged in a precise pattern. Thus Gauguin renounced shading, modeling and realistic color, giving greater importance to the surface and preferring two-dimensional images, with arbitrary colors: results that he attained in part by painting from the reflection of the model in a mirror, which served to flatten the dimensions. The cardinal work of the period was *The Vision After the Sermon*, which he offered to donate to a church, but the gift was turned down.

From October to December Gauguin went to live with van Gogh in Arles, but the experience came to a dramatic conclusion and Gauguin returned to Paris, where he frequented the circles of the Symbolist poets, seeking the truth hidden in appearances. Determined to find an uncorrupted environment that would provide him with more vital inspiration, Gauguin held an auction of his paintings in 1891 and, after a grand banquet with his friends at which the Symbolist poet Mallarmé presided, set off for the tropics, heading for the island of Tahiti. He wanted to get away from more colonized and Westernized places. Entering into an arranged marriage with a young native woman called Tehamana, he studied the religion of the islanders, based on worship of the forces of nature. But he also brought with him "a little world of friends [...] in the form of photographs and drawings that will speak to me every day": they were reproductions of works of art, testimonies to his vast figurative culture which ranged from contemporary artists to Egyptian art, pre-Colombian sculpture and the reliefs of the Parthenon and the Buddhist temple of Borobudur.

In 1893, penniless, Gauguin went back to France and prepared his canvases for an exhibition at the gallery of Durand-Ruel, the dealer who had supported the Impressionists. So the publication of *Noa Noa*, the journal written by Gauguin in collaboration with Charles Morice, should probably be seen as a move to promote his Polynesian paintings.

The exhibition was not a success and he returned to Pont-Aven, but further problems led him to leave France forever and go back to Tahiti in 1895, where his already precarious state of health worsened. In 1897 he painted *Where Do We Come From? What Are We? Where Are We Going?*, a picture that is considered the artist's pictorial last testament. Gauguin tried to commit suicide, but recovered and went back to work. His last years were marked by his efforts to protect the indigenous population against exploitation by the French colonial authorities: as a result he was forced to leave Tahiti and move to the Marquesas Islands, where he died in 1903.

In July 1886, discouraged by the constant lack of money, he had written to his wife from Pont-Aven: "So let us resign ourselves and let come what may: perhaps one day, when all will have opened their eyes to my art, an enthusiast will raise me from the mud."

La Belle Angèle (*Portrait of Madame Satre*)
Musée d'Orsay, Paris

LA BELLE ANGÈLE

Gauguin 89

PAUL GAUGUIN

La Belle Angèle (Portrait of Madame Satre)
oil on canvas, 92x73 cm
Musée d'Orsay, Paris

"It is a portrait put down on the canvas like the big heads in the Japanese crêpons; there is the bust-portrait and its outlines and then the background. [...] The woman is somewhat like a young cow, but there is something so fresh in it and, again, countrified, that it is very pleasant to see": this is how Theo van Gogh described the painting in a letter to his brother Vincent. The woman represented in this portrait of 1889 is Marie-Angélique Satre, wife of the future mayor of Pont-Aven, who turned down the picture when Gauguin offered to give it to him. Degas, on the other hand, so appreciated the canvas that he bought it at the auction held in 1891. Using a procedure typical of Japanese prints, from which he also took the idea of locating the main subject off center, Gauguin isolates the portrait in a circle, against a richly decorated background. The device was one utilized by the illustrators of magazines of the time, like *L'Illustration*, but Gauguin may also have been inspired by the headed letter-paper of Villa Giulia, the hotel near the pension where he was staying, on which the bust of a Breton woman with a bonnet was inscribed in a circular medallion.

Tahitian Women on the Beach
oil on canvas, 69x91 cm
Musée d'Orsay, Paris

In this work of 1891, the two monumental figures, represented from very close up, occupy the whole surface of the canvas, leaving no room for the setting, which is usually identified as a beach. The woman wearing a mission dress is plaiting strips of palm leaves, probably to make a hat. In reality the two female figures appear to be portraits of the same person and this might be explained by Gauguin's habit of using drawings as a base for his paintings, even after his first stay in Tahiti: in this case the same woman must have posed as a model for two preparatory drawings that the painter then combined in a single composition. Given the impossibility of traveling back in time to find an uncontaminated world, there was a growing passion for exoticism, for journeys to distant lands. The image of woman painted by Gauguin and described in *Noa Noa* did not adhere to European aesthetic canons, but was still beautiful: "the mouth had been modeled by a sculptor who spoke all the languages of thought and of the kiss, of joy and of suffering. And I read in her the fear of the unknown, sadness and bitterness mixed with pleasure, and that gift of passivity that apparently yields and then, in the end, remains dominant."

P A U L   G A U G U I N

Nave Nave Moe (*Sacred Spring*)
oil on canvas, 73x98 cm
Hermitage, St. Petersburg

Painted in France in 1894 after his first stay in Tahiti, the title in the Tahitian language was written directly on the canvas by Gauguin. The stages of human life are represented symbolically, with one young girl drowsing, her state of purity accentuated by the presence of the halo, another about to bite into a fruit and two women engaged in conversation, in a procedure analogous to that of *Where Do We Come From? What Are We? Where Are We Going?* in which images of humanity in its various stages, from childhood to old age, succeed one another from right to left, evoking the incomprehensible mystery of our origin and our future. In the background a group of Tahitian women are dancing around gigantic idols, perhaps representing Hina, goddess of the moon that is about to rise and associated with the fear of the spirits of death. The lily reinforces the idea of the purity of the uncontaminated island, a promised land in which everything seems to obey the laws of nature.

"Art is an abstraction, take it from nature by dreaming before her and think rather of the creation that will result; it is the only means of ascending to God, by doing as our Divine Master does, creating." (E.F.)

Van Gogh

" I must warn you that everyone will think that I work too fast. Don't you believe a word of it. Is it not emotion, the sincerity of one's feeling for nature, that draws us, and if the emotions are sometimes so strong that one works without knowing one works, when sometimes the strokes come with a continuity and a coherence like words in a speech or a letter, then one must remember that it has not always been so, and that in time to come there will again be hard days, empty of inspiration." So Vincent van Gogh described the meaning of his painting and his life to his brother Theo in July 1888: a life marked by intense work, incomprehension, debts, breakdowns, spells in psychiatric hospital, recoveries and new breakdowns, but always sustained by an irresistible vocation for painting.

Born in 1853 at Groot Zundert in the Netherlands, in 1869 he was apprenticed to the branch of the art dealers Goupil and Co. in The Hague, later moving to the branches in London and then Paris. From 1876 onward a powerful religious bent, sometimes verging on fanaticism, was to guide his choices. He was sent to work as a lay preacher in the coalmining district of the Borinage in Belgium. The dreadful living conditions of the miners had a deep effect on Vincent, who chose to share their extreme poverty, an attitude that met with the disapproval of his superiors in the Church and led to his dismissal from the post. After documenting the life of the miners in drawings, he moved to Brussels to pursue his study of painting, with the financial assistance of his younger brother Theodorus (Theo), an art dealer who was his principal confidant and ally, as the extensive correspondence between them demonstrates.

He then returned to the Netherlands, where he was to remain until 1885, amid disappointments in love and family crises, devoting himself to painting in oil and seeking new subjects and new sources of inspiration. This was the period of his sketches and paintings of peasants, culminating in the celebrated *Potato Eaters*. In the second half of the 19th century, with the changes that were taking place in society as a consequence of industrialization, pictures of peasants and fishermen, representing a vanishing style of life, were in great demand among the middle class. Painters had even got into the habit of collecting tools and costumes in which to dress their models. Van Gogh was undoubtedly aware of these trends on the art market, but his interest in the world of the poor, stimulated by his admiration for the painter Jean-François Millet, was genuine. As he wrote to Theo, a picture of peasants should smack of lard, smoke, the steam of cooking potatoes, a stall of dung, a field of ripe grain, potatoes or manure, and he complained that the peasants always wanted to pose "in their Sunday clothes."

After a few months in Antwerp, where he was particularly impressed by the paintings of Rubens, he moved to Paris in 1886 and, coming into contact with the Impressionists, abandoned the dark colors of the Dutch period. He also developed an interest in Japanese prints, which were to have a great influence on the art of that time, adopting their unbridled use of color and of black, a shade shunned by the Impressionists, and dreaming of setting up a community of artists along Japanese lines, in harmonious union with nature.

Following the call of the sun and the south, Vincent moved in 1888 to Arles, in Provence, where he rented the famous "yellow house" and where, in October, he was joined by Paul Gauguin. Using a rich palette of colors, Vincent painted the house, his room, sunflowers and the landscape of Arles. The two artists did not get on and in December, at the height of an argument, Vincent threatened Gauguin with a razor and then cut off the lobe of one of his own ears. He was admitted to hospital, where he was to return in February 1889 after a new nervous breakdown. When he was discharged, the people of Arles, alarmed by the painter's behavior, got up a petition asking for him to be committed again. The yellow house was closed. In May Vincent decided to have himself admitted to the psychiatric hospital of Saint-Rémy. There he painted what he could see from the window, self-portraits or copies of the prints Theo sent him. In June he painted the *Starry Night* in energetic, swirling brushstrokes.

After a brief visit to Paris, to meet the nephew for whom he had painted *The Blossoming Almond Branches* and the sister-in-law who was to transcribe the brothers' letters with devotion, the painter set off for his last home, Auvers-sur-Oise. On July 27, 1890, Vincent shot himself, dying two days later in the company of his brother Theo, who would only survive him by six months. In the pocket of his jacket was his last letter to his brother, in which he had written: "we can only make our pictures speak." The violent charge of energy and emotion that poured from his brushes was to open the way to the new painting, to the Expressionists and the Fauves.

Self-Portrait
Musée d'Orsay, Paris

Self-Portrait
oil on canvas, 65x54 cm
Musée d'Orsay, Paris

In the Saint-Rémy hospital, in the absence of other models, van Gogh painted several self-portraits. As he wrote to Theo: "they say [...] that it is difficult to know oneself, but it isn't easy to paint oneself either [...]." What the artist attempted to produce in these portraits was not so much a physical likeness (these were the years of heated debate over the role of the emerging medium of photography) as an expression of emotions through color. This picture was painted in September 1889, when he was starting to feel better: "my face is much calmer, although it seems to me that my look is vaguer than before." The red of the beard contrasts with the other colors, even though the jacket ought to be a bright lilac, a shade that has often faded in the painter's canvases. Perfectly conscious of his mental illness, he wrote to Theo that many other artists had suffered and this did not represent an obstacle to painting. And to his mother: "I still look like a peasant from Zundert [...] I plow my canvases as if they were fields."

The Artist's Room in Arles
oil on canvas, 56.5x74 cm
Musée d'Orsay, Paris

There are three versions in oil of the painter's room in the yellow house. This one was painted in September 1889 at the hospital in Saint-Rémy for his mother and sister, to whom he wanted to send small copies of his best works. As he wrote to his brother, his intention was to utilize the color, laid on without shading as in Japanese prints, to convey the idea of repose and sleep: "the picture should relax the brain, or rather the imagination," in contrast to the *Night Café*, where he sought to put across the idea that "the café is a place where you can ruin yourself, go mad, commit crimes," entrusting red and green with the task of expressing violent passions. In this version, the walls are also hung with a self-portrait and a completely blank mirror, which has the function of resting the eye according to a widespread precept of the time: the use of white was supposed to lighten the preponderant effect of the violent colors. The sense of imbalance created by the impression that the objects are falling toward the observer stems both from the renunciation of conventional perspective and from the shape of the room itself, with its sloping outer wall.

The Starry Night
oil on canvas, 73.7x92.1 cm
Museum of Modern Art, New York

Van Gogh had already painted at night, outdoors, by the light of candles set on the brim of his hat and around the canvas. In this picture of June 1889, he wanted to depict a starry night to prove that the imagination could give greater value to painting. Over the centuries, painting had conquered the night: from the sky dotted with stars of medieval art, but with the foreground still illuminated by daylight, to the experiments of Caravaggio in which the painting lost its characteristic of total visibility, admitting zones of darkness. Here the night sky is a theater of light, the exaggerated movement of the heavenly bodies is rendered with broad and thick brushstrokes. A cypress, another of van Gogh's favorite subjects, links sky and earth. Some scholars have seen the presence of the moon and eleven stars as a recollection of van Gogh's biblical studies, referring to the account of Joseph's dream in Genesis: "I have dreamed a dream more; and behold: the sun and the moon and the eleven stars made obeisance to me." But the painter had already spoken clearly of his interest in the night in a letter to Theo: "For my own part, I declare I know nothing whatever about it. But to look at the stars always makes me dream, as simply as I dream over the black dots of a map representing towns and villages. Why, I ask myself, should the shining dots of the sky not be as accessible as the black dots on the map of France? If we take the train to get to Tarascon or Rouen, we take death to reach a star. One thing undoubtedly true in this reasoning is this: that while we are alive we cannot get to a star, any more than when we are dead we can take the train."

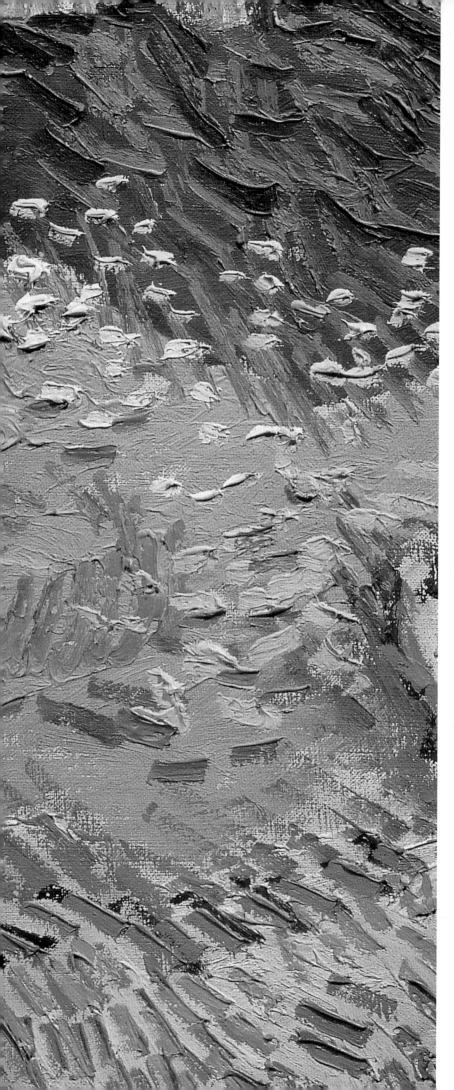

The Church at Auvers
oil on canvas, 94x74 cm
Musée d'Orsay, Paris

In the May of 1890 van Gogh went to stay at Auvers-sur-Oise, under the supervision of Dr. Paul Gachet, a collector and friend of artists: he took an immediate liking to the doctor, but also had the impression that he was mentally unstable, like himself. He went to see him frequently, stopping to paint in his garden or studying his collection of Impressionists. Vincent alternated moments of serenity with moments of despair: happy over a visit by his nephew, to whom he showed all the animals on a farm, he sought to express in his paintings "the health and restorative forces" that he felt in the countryside, but was also weighed down by sadness and an extreme loneliness. He worked unceasingly, and it was in this period that he painted the *Portrait of Doctor Gachet*, *Wheat Field with Crows* and *Church at Auvers*.

Van Gogh described the painting in a letter to his sister: "the building appears to be violet-hued against a sky of a simple deep blue color, pure cobalt; the stained-glass windows appear as ultramarine blotches, the roof is violet and partly orange. In the foreground some green plants in bloom, and sand with the pink glow of sunshine on it." This was in the June of 1890. One month later van Gogh would take his own life. (E.F.)

GEORGES SEURAT

Seurat

" Little young chemists who pile on little dots," was how Gauguin had described the group of the Neoimpressionists in 1892. Headed by Georges Seurat, they were engaged in a search for a scientific foundation to the process of vision that could be applied to painting, a logical method to be used instead of the spontaneous and irregular brushwork of the Impressionists.

Seurat was born in Paris in 1859 and in 1878 enrolled in the École des Beaux-Arts, where he studied the old masters and admired, in the school's chapel, the copies of Piero della Francesca's frescoes in the church of San Francesco at Arezzo. He was fascinated by Delacroix and his method and read scientific treatises on the laws of optics and color. From the textbook written by Charles Blanc and the ideas of the chemist Michel-Eugène Chevreul he took the theories on the optical mixture of colors, which held that their luminosity was enhanced if they were not mixed on the palette, but set side by side on the canvas in separate, small touches of pure color. In addition, according to the law of simultaneous contrast, colors depend on relationships and the brilliance of a color is affected by the ones next to it. There are three primary colors, blue, yellow, red, which are combined in pairs to form the secondary colors. The primary color that does not participate in the creation of a secondary one is its complementary color. The juxtaposition of complementary colors enhances them: thus placing a green (combination of yellow and blue) next to a red (the primary color left out of the mixture) will make both more brilliant.

The sensation aroused by the Impressionist exhibition of 1879 convinced Seurat and his friends to leave the Ecole des Beaux-Arts and follow their own road. The new style of painting and his reading, two years later, of Ogden Rood's treatise *Modern Chromatics*, gave a new impetus to the artist's development. It was in this period that he started to paint on small panels of wood, which he called *croquetons*, sketching landscapes and the life of ordinary people in the open air. In 1884, rejected by the official Salon, he showed *Une Baignade, Asnières* (*Bathers at Asnières*) at the exhibition of Independent Artists, a voluntary grouping that rejected the principle of works being selected by a panel of judges. Here he met the artists who were to join him in his research, above all Paul Signac. The same year he started work on his seminal painting *Sunday Afternoon on the Island of La Grande Jatte*, executed with the new technique of *pointillisme*, or Divisionism as he preferred to call it. It would be shown in Paris in 1886, at both the exhibition of the Impressionists and that of the Independents. The critic Félix Fénéon, favorably struck by the painting, used the term Neoimpressionism for the first time. The following year, the picture was shown in Brussels at the annual exhibition of "Les Vingt." Seurat and Signac were present at the inauguration: "a great success for us: Seurat's canvas was invisible, impossible to get near so great was the crowd." Seurat then started to work on *The Models*, while spending the summer, as was his custom, on the coast of the English Channel, where he painted interesting seascapes. Then it was the turn of *The Circus*, in which the painter applied his new technique to the representation of artificial lighting in an outdoor setting, and of *Le Chahut*, a dance that was in vogue in Montmartre. In 1891, before he had even finished it, Seurat presented *The Circus* at the Salon des Indépendants. Unappreciated by contemporary critics, the picture would be ignored by the painter Puvis de Chavannes when he visited the exhibition, to Seurat's great disappointment. Just a few days later, he died of diphtheria. His mother took possession of the painting, which would be bought by his friend Signac.

The myth of Seurat the artist-scientist has long led people to believe that his paintings were the result of careful calculation, of the application of a sterile recipe. But no pseudoscientific theory required the paint to be laid on in little dots, in points (*pointillisme*): this technique was born out of the artist's experimentation and inventiveness. The first decade of the new century concluded with the emergence of the historical avant-garde movements: their research found an important precedent in Seurat.

*Sunday Afternoon on the Island
of La Grande Jatte*
oil on canvas, 207.6x308 cm
Art Institute, Chicago

Shown at the eighth and last Impressionist
exhibition, the canvas had made an
immediate impact on the critics with its
dimensions, its technique and the rigidity
of its figures. It was executed over the
space of about two years, from 1884 to
1886, and we know of twenty-seven small
studies in oil, an equal number of
drawings and three canvases relating to
different parts of the large painting. The
use of dots of pure color to form the
images confers an ordered and rational
appearance on the composition: the
moment of life caught as it unfolds by the
Impressionists is transformed into a
suspended and abstract instant, outside
time. The "primitivism" of the painting
suggests parallels with Egyptian art, and
with the Italian painting of the 15th
century. But his sources of inspiration
should also be sought in the popular
print, in posters and in fashion. *La
Grande Jatte* was the island in the Seine
where the middle classes of Paris used to
go on their day of rest, Sunday, whereas
the free day for workers was Monday. The
women in the picture, as stiff as
manikins, are wearing the fashionable
dress of the early 1880s, plumped out by
a wickerwork cage or a cushion. The way
that figures are cut off at the edges
creates the impression that the scene
continues beyond the canvas and the
painted frame, added later, serves to
strengthen the chromatic contrasts. But
amidst all this regularity there are
anomalies: the figures are represented on
notably different scales and the woman
fishing, although located on the same
plane as the one in the middle with the
little girl, barely reaches to her shoulder.
Seurat's work was long undervalued. In
the 1920s *La Grande Jatte* was allowed to
leave France without much opposition.

The Circus

oil on canvas, 186.2x151 cm
Musée d'Orsay, Paris

The artist's last work, datable to 1890-91 and shown while still unfinished at the Salon des Indépendants, *The Circus* disconcerted the critics. Not even his friends had expressed their opinions. The spectacle of the circus fascinated artists and writers. Particularly famous in the Paris of that time, the Cirque Fernando (later to become the Medrano) was near

Seurat's studio and a favorite of many painters. The picture constituted a new stage in the artist's research, in which he simplified his palette in an investigation of the expressive symbolism of color and focused his attention on the rhythm of the composition and the dynamism of the lines. In fact, according to the principles of Humbert de Superville, taken up by Charles Henry, lines are associated with particular emotions: upward slanting lines convey gaiety and pleasure, and this is the case with the horsewoman; horizontal

lines express calm and stability, as in the case of the audience; descending lines convey sadness. The wide painted border bestows greater luminosity on the colors. The scene is almost a snapshot that freezes the actions of the figures, the horse suspended above the ground, the rider off balance, the whip snaking through the air, the acrobat tumbling. Seurat was convinced that it was possible to study movement by means of photography and showed a keen interest in Marey's experiments with a

"photographic gun," the forerunner of the motion-picture camera. The results are particularly clear in *Chahut*, which recalls Marey's chronophotographs and anticipates the Futurists. Unacknowledged in Seurat's own time, *The Circus* entered the Louvre in 1924. This "luminous apparition," this "dream of colors," as Signac described it, had already left a deep mark on the art of the 20th century. (E.F.)

Toulouse-Lautrec

Henri de Toulouse-Lautrec was born at Albi in the South of France in 1864, to a family of the old nobility. His youth was marred by two disastrous falls from horses that prevented his lower limbs from developing normally and excluded him from the sporting and leisure activities typical of his social sphere. Since childhood, however, he had shown an interest in drawing, and in 1882 began to study art with the local painter René Princeteau. Later he moved to Paris, studying at the ateliers of Léon Bonnat and then Fernand Cormon, where in 1886 he met van Gogh. He remained in touch with van Gogh until 1888, painting a portrait of him (1887, Stedelijk Museum, Amsterdam). In 1887 he left Cormon's studio and went with another painter, René Grenier, to live in the building in which Edgar Degas had set up his atelier. Toulouse-Lautrec was influenced by the work of the older artist and tackled many of the same themes, with apparently minimal but often decisive variations of accent. He also fell under the spell of *Japonisme*, the current vogue for Japanese woodcuts and art objects, and drew on the Impressionist and Neoimpressionist movements, developing an original style which he used to represent scenes of real life in the quarter in which he lived, Montmartre. Here he turned the spotlight on the spectacle of a shadowy world, made up of anonymous figures with humble trades or bohemian and promiscuous circles, moving away from academic models in his themes and modes of representation. In 1888 his participation in an exhibition in Brussels organized by Les Vingt, then an important international association of avant-garde artists, allowed him to establish a reputation as one of the most modern painters of his time.

In the same year he produced his first masterpiece, *Equestrienne (At the Circus Fernando)* (1888, Chicago Art Institute), deploying an original style in which, taking his cue from Japanese prints, he represented movement with a few, essential lines and colors, already displaying what were to become the distinctive traits of his painting. The cafés-concerts of Paris also exercised a strong attraction on him: one of the first pictures devoted to this milieu was the *Dance at the Moulin Rouge* (McIlhenny Collection, Philadelphia). In the last decade of the century he painted his most celebrated pictures, such as *Jane Avril Dancing* (1892, Musée d'Orsay, Paris), *At the Moulin-Rouge* (1892, Chicago Art Institute) and *Cha-U-Kao at the Moulin-Rouge* (Reinhardt Collection, Winterthur), and devoted himself with great success to lithography. He designed numerous posters for the artistes and the places where they performed: among the most important are the *Moulin Rouge-La Goulue*, *Ambassadeurs: Aristide Bruant*, *Divan Japonais* (portraying Jane Avril) and *Jane Avril-Jardin de Paris*.

His graphic work was also published in the periodical *La Revue Blanche*, founded in 1891. His collaboration with the magazine also brought him into contact with a group of Symbolist painters, the Nabis, with whom he realized the scenery for Alfred Jarry's *Ubu roi* (1896). There was no letup in his artistic research and one of his last paintings, *An Examination at the Faculty of Medicine* (Musée Toulouse-Lautrec, Albi), shows a continual evolution in his style. The artist died at Malromé, near Bordeaux, in 1901.

La Toilette (*Seated Redhead*)
oil on cardboard, 67x54 cm
Musée d'Orsay, Paris

The painting is inspired by the works in Degas's "Series of nudes of women bathing, washing, drying, rubbing down, combing their hair or having it combed," which were shown at the last Impressionist exhibition of 1886, prompting a scandalized reaction from the right-minded.

Toulouse-Lautrec portrays the young woman, perhaps a dancer, by adopting an unusual view from above, which emphasizes her supple back. Significant is the choice to show her carrying out everyday acts and in attitudes to which she is accustomed, as if she has been stealthily caught in moments of intimacy. In his portraits the artist sought to capture the truth of the attitudes and the social milieu of the subjects he represented, displaying a great gift for psychological insight.

The picture must have been painted by 1896, as it was shown in February of that year at the Brussels exhibition of Les Vingt, a Belgian group formed in 1884 that included artists like James Ensor and Theo van Rysselberghe. Its members had undertaken to find room in their exhibitions for an equal number of artists, including foreign ones, who represented the most modern tendencies, and in 1886 had also invited Monet, Renoir and Redon to take part.

Jane Avril Dancing
oil on cardboard, 85x45 cm
Musée d'Orsay, Paris

The dancer does not convey a sense of harmony or grace, but one of strenuous vitality as she performs one of the breathless, whirlwind dances typical of the café-concert: the almost disjointed movements reflect the frenzied and vigorous rhythm of the dancing of Jane Avril, whose incredible energy had earned her the nickname of 'Mélinite,' an explosive similar to dynamite. The cafés-concerts were the painter's favorite haunts, and he would remain seated at a table for hours, making drawings and sketches. This painting of 1892 inspired one of the his most famous posters, *Jane Avril au Jardin de Paris, Café-Concert*. The dancer was perhaps the artist's closest friend in the world of the cafés-chantants, and Toulouse-Lautrec devoted many works to her, including one executed that same year which portrayed her entering the Moulin Rouge (Courtauld Institute Galleries, London). Avril was no ordinary person: she was unusually cultivated for someone of her background, knew the writers Verlaine and Huysmans and eventually abandoned the cafés-concerts to become an actress in the theater, where she appeared in Ibsen's *Peer Gynt*. (A.F.)

Bibliography

The aim of the bibliographic notes that follow is to suggest a number of monographic works that may help in the understanding of individual artists and in setting them in the perspective of the historical period and cultural climate in which they operated. Consequently, the list makes no pretense to be complete but is intended solely as a guide.

14TH CENTURY

E. Borsook, *Ambrogio Lorenzetti*, Florence 1966.

G. Previtali, *Giotto e la sua bottega*, Milan 1967.

J. White, *Duccio - Tuscan Art and Medieval Workshop*, London 1979.

F. Deuchler, *Duccio*, Milan 1984.

L. Bellosi, *La pecora di Giotto*, Turin 1985.

C. Frugoni, *Pietro e Ambrogio Lorenzetti*, Antella (Florence) 1988. Eng. trans, *Pietro and Ambrogio Lorenzetti*, Antella (Florence) 1988.

G. Ragionieri, *Duccio*, Florence 1989.

C. Volpe, *Pietro Lorenzetti*, ed. by M. Lucco, Milan 1989.

Ambrogio Lorenzetti: il Buongoverno, ed. by E. Castelnuovo, Milan 1995.

B. Zanardi, *Il cantiere di Giotto*, Milan 1996.

Giotto, catalogue of the exhibition (Florence 2000), ed. by A. Tartuferi, Florence 2000.

S. Romano, *La basilica di Assisi*, Rome 2001.

La Basilica di San Francesco in Assisi, ed. by G. Bonsanti, Modena 2002.

15TH CENTURY

C. de Tolnay, *Hieronymus Bosch*, Baden-Baden 1965.

M. Cinotti, *L'opera completa di Bosch*, Milan 1966.

G.T. Faggin, *L'opera completa di Van Eyck*, Milan 1968. Eng trans., *The Complete Paintings of the Van Eycks*, Harmondsworth 1987

M. Davies, *Rogier van der Weyden: An Essay, with a Critical Catalogue of Paintings Assigned to Him and to Robert Campin*, London 1972.

Antonello da Messina, catalogue of the exhibition (Catania 1982), Rome 1981.

C. Ginzburg, *Indagini su Piero*, Turin 1981.

E. Marino O.P., *Beato Angelico: Umanesimo e Teologia*, Rome 1984.

R. Lightbown, *Mantegna. With a Complete Catalogue of the Paintings, Drawings, and Prints*, Berkeley-Los Angeles 1986.

F. Sricchia Santoro, *Antonello da Messina e l'Europa*, Milan 1986.

Antonio Paolucci, *Piero della Francesca. Complete Catalogue*, Florence 1990

C. Bertelli, *Piero della Francesca*, Milan 1991.

M.L. Testi Cristiani, *Botticelli*, Milan 1992.

V. Alce O.P., *Vita, opere e teologia del Beato Angelico*, Bologna 1993.

L. Arbace, *Antonello da Messina*, Florence 1993.

A. De Nicolò Salmazo, *Il soggiorno padovano di Andrea Mantegna*, Padua 1993.

P. Joannides, *Masaccio and Masolino. A Complete Catalogue*, London 1993.

D. de Vos, *Hans Memling: The Complete Works*, New York 1994.

R. Goffen, *Giovanni Bellini*, New Haven-London 1995.

W. Hood, *Fra Angelico at San Marco*, New York 1995.

P. Morachiello, *Beato Angelico. Gli affreschi di San Marco*, with an essay by G. Bonsanti, Milan 1995.

J.T. Spike, *Masaccio*, New York 1996.

G. Bonsanti, *Beato Angelico. Catalogo completo*, Florence 1998.

R. Freemantle, *Masaccio*, Florence 1998.

C. Spantigati, *Van Eyck*, Florence 1998.

C.B. Strehlke, *Angelico*, Milan 1998.

D. de Vos, *Rogier van der Weyden*, Munich 1999. Eng. trans. *Rogier van der Weyden*, Amsterdam 2001.

A. Tempestini, *Giovanni Bellini*, Milan 2000.

C. Acidini Luchinat, *Botticelli. Allegorie mitologiche*, Milan 2001.

16TH CENTURY

E. Panofsky, *La vita e le opere di Albrecht Dürer*, Milan 1967.

Grünewald. L'opera completa, ed. by P. Bianconi, Milan 1972.

M. Rosci, *Leonardo*, Milan 1976.

C. de Tolnay, *Michelangelo. Sculptor, Painter, Architect*, Princeton 1981.

P. De Vecchi, *Raffaello. La pittura*, Florence 1981.

K. and G. Noehles, "Cranach Lucas il Vecchio," in *Enciclopedia Universale dell'Arte*, Novara 1981.

L. Silver, "Forest Primeval: Albrecht Altdorfer and the German Wilderness Landscape," in *Simiolus*, 1983, 1, pp. 4-43.

J. Rowlands, *Holbein. The Paintings of Hans Holbein the Younger. Complete Edition*, Oxford 1985.

A. Hayum, *The Isenheim Altarpiece. God's Medicine and the Painter's Vision*, Princeton 1989.

P.C. Marani, *Leonardo*, Florence 1989.

La Cappella Sistina. La volta restaurata. Il trionfo del colore, ed. by P. De Vecchi, Novara 1992. Eng. trans. *The Sistine Chapel: A Glorious Restoration*, New York 1994.

Le siècle de Titien. L'âge d'or de la peinture à Venise, exhibition catalogue ed. by M. Laclotte, Paris 1993.

S. Zuffi, *Giorgione*, Milan 1994.

M. Lucco, *Giorgione*, Milan 1995.

F. Mozzetti, *Tiziano: ritratto di Pietro Aretino*, Modena 1996.

Dürer and his Culture, ed. by D. Eichberger and C. Zika, Cambridge-New York 1998.

L'anima e il volto. Ritratto e fisiognomica da Leonardo a Bacon, ed. by F. Caroli, catalogue of the exhibition (Milan 1998-99), Milan 1998.

Michelangelo, Florence 1999.

El Greco: Identity and Transformation, ed. by J. Alvarez, Milan 1999.

Il Rinascimento a Venezia e la pittura del Nord ai tempi di Bellini, Dürer, Tiziano, catalogue of the exhibition (Venice 1999), ed. by B. Aikema, B.L. Brown and G. Nepi Sciré, Milan 1999.

M. Marini, *El Greco*, Florence 1999.

K. Oberhuber, *Raphael: the Paintings*, New York 1999.

T. Pignatti and F. Pedrocco, *Giorgione*, Milan 1999.

L. Silver, "Nature and Nature's God; Landscape and Cosmos of Albrecht Altdorfer," in *The Art Bulletin*, June 1999, 2, pp. 194-214.

F. Valcanover, *Tiziano*, Florence 1999.

Hans Holbein: Paintings, Prints and Reception, catalogue of the exhibition (Washington, 2001), ed. by M. Roskill and J.O. Hand, New Haven 2001.

J. North, *The Ambassadors' Secret*, London-New York, 2002

17TH CENTURY

S. Zamboni, *Frans Hals*, Milan 1964.

J. Bolten and H. Bolten-Rempt, *Rembrandt*, Milan 1976.

E. Larsen, *L'opera completa di Van Dyck*, Milan 1980, 2 vols.

Zurbarán, catalogue of the exhibition (New York-Paris 1987-88), ed. by J. Baticle, New York 1987.

E. Larsen, *The Paintings of Anthony van Dyck*, Düsseldorf 1988, 2 vols.

M. Jaffé, *Rubens. Catalogo completo*, Milan 1989.

J.M. Montias, *Vermeer and His Milieu*, Princeton 1989.

R. Zapperi, *Annibale Carracci: ritratto di artista da giovane*, Turin 1989.

C. Grimm, *Frans Hals. The Complete Work*, New York 1990.

Murillo in Focus, catalogue of the exhibition (Liverpool 1990-91), ed. by X. Brooke, Liverpool 1990.

Rubens, catalogue of the exhibition (Padua 1990), ed. by D. Bodart, [n.p.] 1990.

G. Bonsanti, *Caravaggio*, Florence 1991.

M. Marini, *Poussin*, Florence 1991.

L. J. Slatkes, *Rembrandt*, Florence 1992.

M. Gregori, *Caravaggio*, Milan 1994.

P. Rosenberg and L.A. Prat, *Nicolas Poussin. 1594-1665*, Paris 1994.

J. Thuillier, *Rubens' Life of Marie de Medici*, with an appendix by J. Foucart, New York 1970.

H. Wine, *Claude. The Poetic Landscape*, London 1994.

Johannes Vermeer, ed. by A.K. Wheelock Jr., Milan 1995.

J.P. Cuzin and P. Rosenberg, *Georges de La Tour*, Paris 1997.

M. Marini, *Velázquez*, Milan 1997.

M. Bona Castellotti, *Il paradosso di Caravaggio*, Milan 1998.

H. Langdon, *Caravaggio: a Life*, London 1998.

S. Alpers, *The Art of Describing: Dutch Art in the Seventeenth Century*, Chicago 1983.

C. Dempsey, *Annibale Carracci and the Beginnings of Baroque Style*, Fiesole (Florence) 2000.

La luce del vero. Caravaggio, La Tour, Rembrandt, Zurbarán, catalogue of the exhibition (Bergamo 2000), Cinisello Balsamo (Milan) 2000.

Murillo: Scenes of Childhood, catalogue of the exhibition (London-Munich 2001), ed. by X. Brooke and P. Cherry, London 2001.

Velázquez, catalogue of the exhibition (Rome 2001), ed. by F.V. Garín Llombart and S. Salort Pons, Milan 2001.

18TH CENTURY

F. Antal, *Hogarth and His Place in European Art*, New York-London 1962.

D. Panofsky, "Gilles or Pierrot," in *Gazette des Beaux-Arts*, 1952, 5, pp. 319-40.

G. Mandel, *L'opera completa di Hogarth*, Milan 1967.

J. G. Links, *Canaletto and His Patrons*, London 1977.

Thomas Gainsborough, catalogue of the exhibition (London 1980-81), ed. by J. Hayes, London, 1980.

P. Rosenberg, *Tout l'œuvre peint de Chardin*, Paris 1983. Italian trans. *L'opera completa di Chardin*, Milan 1983.

Watteau 1684-1721, catalogue of the exhibition (Washington 1984), Paris 1984.

Antoine Watteau (1684-1721). The Painter, His Age and His Legend, ed. by F. Moureau and M. Morgan Grasselli, Paris-Geneva 1987.

W.G. Constable, *Canaletto – Giovanni Antonio Canal*, Oxford 1989.

M. Gemin and F. Pedrocco, *Giambattista Tiepolo. I dipinti. Opera completa*, Venice 1993.

F. Pedrocco and T. Pignatti, *Tiepolo. Itinerari veneziani*, Venice 1996.

Giambattista Tiepolo nel terzo centenario della nascita, proceedings of the international congress of studies, Padua 1998.

F. Haskell, *Mecenati e pittori*, Turin 1998.

A. Pinelli, *Avanzare regredendo. Neoclassicismo e Primitivismo tra XVIII e XIX secolo*, Pisa 1999.

P. Rosenberg, *Chardin*, Paris 1999.

G. Cowart, "Watteau's Pilgrimage to Cythera and the Subversive Utopia of the Opera Ballet," in *The Art Bulletin*, September 2001, 3, pp. 461-78.

W. Vaughan, *Gainsborough*, London 2002.

19TH CENTURY

J. Renoir, *Renoir, My Father*, Milan 1962.

S. Orienti, *L'opera pittorica di Edouard Manet*, Milan 1967. Eng. trans. *The Complete Paintings of Manet*, New York-London 1985.

G. Boudaille, *Gustave Courbet*, Milan 1969.

R. and M. Wittkower, *Born Under Saturn: The Character and Conduct of Artists*, New York 1969.

S. Orienti, *L'opera completa di Cézanne*, Milan 1970. Eng. trans. *The Complete Paintings of Cézanne*, New York-London 1986.

J. Rewald, *History of Impressionism*, New York 1973.

H. Borsch-Supan, *L'opera completa di Friedrich*, Milan 1976.

David e Roma, Rome 1981.

L'opera completa di Géricault, introduction by J. Thuillier and apparatus criticus and philological appendices by P. Grunchec, Milan 1981.

J.M.W. Turner, catalogue of the exhibition (Paris 1983-84), Paris 1983.

Renoir, catalogue of the exhibition (London-Paris-Boston 1985-86), London 1985.

U. Eco and O. Calabrese, *Le figure del tempo*, ed. by L. Corrain, Milan 1987.

Vincent van Gogh. La vita e le opere attraverso i suoi scritti, ed. by B. Bernard, Novara 1987.

Courbet Reconsidered, catalogue of the exhibition (Brooklyn-Minneapolis 1988-89), ed. by S. Faunce and L. Nochlin, New Haven-London 1988.

Edgar Degas, ed. by R. Kendall, Novara 1988.

Manet. A Retrospective, ed. by T.A. Gronberg, New York 1988.

The Art of Paul Gauguin, catalogue of the exhibition, Washington 1988.

Vincent van Gogh, catalogue of the exhibition (Rome 1988), Milan-Rome 1988.

A. Zanni, *Ingres. Catalogo completo dei dipinti*, Florence 1990.

Seurat, catalogue of the exhibition (Paris 1991), Paris 1991.

I.F. Walther and R. Metzger, *Vincent van Gogh. Tutti i dipinti*, Cologne-Milan 1990, 2 vols.

Toulouse-Lautrec, catalogue of the exhibition (London-Paris 1991-92), ed. by J. Drew and J. Saillois, London and Paris 1991.

M. Vescovo, *Cézanne*, Florence 1993.

Ottani Cavina, *I paesaggi della ragione, la città neoclassica da David a Humbert de Superville*, Turin 1994.

Ingres, ed. by G. Vigne, Paris 1995.

Paul Gauguin e l'avanguardia russa, catalogue of the exhibition (Ferrara 1995), Florence 1995.

Corot. 1796-1875, Milan 1996.

F. Castellani, *Pierre-Auguste Renoir. La vita e le opere*, Milan 1996.

Goya, catalogue of the exhibition (Madrid 1996), ed. by J.J. Luna, Madrid 1996.

La Modernité – Collections du Musée d'Orsay, catalogue of the exhibition (Tokyo 1996), ed. by C. Mathieu, M. Bascou and A. Takahashi, Tokyo 1996.

Transports: Travel, Pleasure, and the Imaginative Geography. 1600-1830, ed. by C. Chard and H. Langdon, New Haven-London 1996.

K. Bowie, "Chemins de fer et paysage: Turner, Inness, Duchamp," in *Ligeia*, October 1996-June 1997, 19-20, pp. 36-42

G. Malacarne, *Le cacce del principe*, Modena 1998.

J. Ruskin, *Modern Painters*, London 1987.

Renoir dall'Italia alla Costa Azzurra 1881-1919, catalogue of the exhibition (Roma 1999), ed. by F. Verlinden and M. Vescovo, Milan 1999.

Rêve et Réalité – Collection du Musée d'Orsay, catalogue of the exhibition (Tokyo 1999), ed. by C. Mathieu, M. Bascou and A. Takahashi, Tokyo 1999.

S. Lee, *David*, London 1999.

A. De Paz, *Géricault: la febbre dell'arte e della vita*, Naples 2000.

B. Aikema, "Incroci transalpini," in *Opere e giorni*, ed. by K. Bergdolt and G. Bonsanti, Venice 2001.

E. Di Stefano, *Friedrich*, Florence 2001.

Monet – I luoghi della pittura, catalogue of the exhibition (Treviso 2001-02), ed. by M. Goldin, Conegliano 2001.